3-4-65 (65-11522)

# Harold Wilson

## THE AUTHENTIC PORTRAIT

by LESLIE SMITH

## Charles Scribner's Sons
NEW YORK

PICTURE ACKNOWLEDGMENTS

Black Star: 15 (Terence Le Goubin)
Family Collection: 5, 6, 7
Pictorial Parade: 1, 2, 3, 4, 10, 14 (all London *Daily Express*), 8 (The *Times*, London), 9 (Washington Bureau), 13 (Central Press Photos Ltd.)
Wide World: 11, 12

# Harold Wilson
## THE AUTHENTIC PORTRAIT

## AUTHOR'S FOREWORD

I first met Harold Wilson shortly after his resignation as President of the Board of Trade in 1951. He had agreed to join an independent committee appointed to study some of the economic aspects of what was commonly called "the East-West conflict." This committee, part expert and part amateur, worked unobtrusively and voluntarily. With no possibility of personal or political "kudos" resulting from his labours, and with many more pressing public duties on his hands, Harold Wilson regularly devoted his formidable knowledge of facts and theories to the committee's deliberations.

I was Secretary of the Committee. My admiration for his remarkable intellectual capacity soon widened into appreciation of other qualities less immediately obvious: generosity, sensitivity to others' feelings, and an unexpected sense of fun, for example. The normally accepted image of Harold Wilson is so at variance with the actual man, that I welcome this chance to describe him from close observation.

Since I like Harold Wilson, I suppose I cannot claim to be unbiased—though in this book I have not overlooked the failings and errors often attributed to him; and in one important respect I can certainly claim to be unprejudiced—I am not and have never been a member of the Labour Party.

In gathering the material for this book I have had all the help I wanted (and it was usually a great deal) not only from Harold Wilson himself, but also from his wife, his father, and his sister; from his secretary, Marcia Williams, and from previous secretaries. I am grateful to them for their willingness to provide

iii

me with everything I required, and to put at my disposal relevant letters and documents. I am equally grateful to Lord Attlee—and to the many other people who, whether friendly or unfriendly towards Harold Wilson, readily gave me useful information and opinions about him. I recorded most of my interviews, and in time acquired a large number of tapes which have provided valuable material.

What follows is not meant to be a customary biography. It is more a portrait—a study of the character and personality of the man, drawn in chronological outline, and covering many events which have previously remained quite unknown, or have been partly and erroneously dealt with by others without first-hand information.

In reconstructing some episodes I have introduced direct conversational "quotes." Where I have done so without the aid of verbatim records, I have relied on the recollections of people whose memories in other matters have proved verbally accurate.

# Contents

# INTRODUCTION

As Attlee and Gaitskell both discovered, the Leader of the modern Labour Party automatically becomes the target for the enmity of his rivals, as well as for the more straightforward antipathy of his political opponents. But the personal antagonism, distrust, and scorn directed against Harold Wilson from some very mixed quarters have had an intense quality about them—even more intense, perhaps, than that aroused, for example, by Lloyd George, Winston Churchill, or even Nye Bevan in their earlier days.

Why?

One reason, undoubtedly, is his seeming emotional remoteness, an almost icy detachment, believed by some to spring from an assiduous, if puzzling, resolve never to reveal passion—and by others to be the plain result of having no ordinary human feelings to display anyway.

Another lies in his intellectual prowess. Few would now be inclined to dispute the reality of this, and some would admit to fearing it—though others regard it as superficial "cleverness" rather than innate brilliance. Those who hold this view usually overlook his spectacuular rise to Cabinet rank as President of the Board of Trade at the age of thirty-one. It was, indeed, his resignation from that office which first released the flood of conflicting speculation about his motives and character: indulgence of conscience and principle to the point of splitting his party and imperilling the Government—or a carefully calculated move in a long-term scheme for personal advancement?

On balance, the image which usually emerges veers between that of a cunning politician whose self-interest has repeatedly been reinforced by good luck, and that of a superhuman intellectual who is emotionally sub-human. Whatever the image of this undoubtedly complex personality, the essential feature usually ignored is the complete "ordinariness" of his background and upbringing.

Nobody seems quite sure how to classify him. It is easy enough to recognise and label a political leader born to the "ruling classes" —or, for that matter, a horny-handed son of the soil who has risen to the top from the bottom rung of the social ladder. Both can provide, in their different ways, a valued source of sentimental satisfactions in our class-conscious society, whether of deferential adultation, or patronising indulgence. And both have trodden paths which are clearly-defined, orthodox channels to power in Britain. But Harold Wilson has emerged from a social grouping historically not associated with high office—from that amorphous and unromantic section of the community, the "lower middle-class".

It has never happened quite like this before, so there is no ready-made social label for him. Could some of the virulence of his critics be explained not so much by resistance to the notion of a highly disciplined professional politician at the helm, as by the half-realised fears created by someone who has audaciously disrupted the traditional pattern of power?

There is no escaping the fact that he sprang from a milieu of the most unpretentious kind; and that his origins not only produced indelible characteristics, but also profoundly affected all his aspirations.

# PART ONE

# The Early Years

### CHAPTER ONE

The First World War was barely half-way through when Harold Wilson was born. It happened to be a Saturday, and the weekly edition of the local paper—the *Huddersfield Examiner*—provided a useful mixture of local reports and national war news.

Many of the local items were characteristic of a town traditionally noted for its highly developed religious sense: temperance views, Band of Hope activities, Free Church news and so on. But for a local paper a surprising amount of space was devoted to the course of the war.

The German Slaughter of Innocents: over 400 Non-Combatants Killed in England. British Advance on the Tigris, and so on.

According to one report—

It was stated on Thursday that Colonel Winston Churchill has an extension of leave. So far as is known, however, the right hon. gentleman has not yet arrived at any decision as to his future course of action.

The workings of the Military Service Act were evident in several lengthy columns about Conscientious Objectors' Tribunal decisions locally. Reported in a separate column was Mr. Asquith's pledge to Mr. Snowden in the House of Commons that unmarried sons of widows might hope for exemption. And in the previous Thursday's Parliamentary debate, the Chancellor of the Exchequer "informed Mr. Byrne (who was asked whether he had considered the desirability of increasing the old-age pension to 7/6 per week) that he hoped to make a statement shortly on the question of old-age pensions."

Among the items of purely local interest were reports from the surrounding areas. Under the heading of "Milnsbridge" came the following:

Lecture:—A fairly good audience assembled at the Milnsbridge Baptist School on Tuesday evening, when a lecture was given by Madam A. L. Ward on the subject 'London in War Time.' Mr. H. Wilson presided. The lecture was given in Madam Ward's usual racy manner, and was followed with interest. The proceeds were for the soldiers' comforts funds.

It was to Milnsbridge, a town in the Colne Valley at that time one mile west of the Huddersfield boundary, that Herbert Wilson, his wife Ethel, and their three year old daughter Marjorie had moved from Manchester in 1912. Herbert, a works chemist, had secured a job with a Huddersfield firm at £2/10/0 per week —not a large sum, yet providing a reasonably comfortable living at a time when a ton of coal cost £1, meat was 9d. a pound, boots 10/6 per pair, a frock coat and waistcoat 30/-(15/- extra for the trousers), and cigarettes were 3d. for ten.

His salary, paid monthly by cheque, compared favourably with the weekly wages earned by local engineering workers, for example, who were paid according to time, and who, in a fifty-hour week, could earn an average maximum of 36/-. But Herbert's new job brought more than financial advancement. He was to be in charge of the explosives department of his firm, thus becoming a member of the administrative class.

Ethel and he hoped they would have another child, so they looked for a "family" house. They found one at 4, Warneford Road in Milnsbridge. It was a small terraced house, black with the smoke from the surrounding mills, and typical of row upon row of small dwellings in the lower middle-class sector of any industrial northern town: downstairs a sitting-room, dining-room, and scullery/kitchen; upstairs three bedrooms, and a bathroom/lavatory combined; outside, a tiny garden back and front. The rent was 12/- per week, with extra for rates and internal maintenance.

The household budgeting was supervised by Ethel. With careful management the family were able to enjoy an above-average standard of living. There were no extravagances, and few luxuries. Visits to the theatre or music-hall were rare, and entertaining was done only on a modest scale. Apart from a glass of wine at Christmas, there was no alcoholic drink in the house. The one regular "indulgence" was a good holiday. Every Whitsun and August holiday was spent at the attractive village of Old Byland, in the North Riding. Even this, however, required no excessive outlay, because the family stayed with cousins who owned a small inn and farm, and who expected no more than the bare cost of their hospitality.

Herbert and Ethel shared two dominant interests. One was a passionate adherence to radicalism. A forebear was John Edward Taylor, founder of the *Manchester Guardian*, which came second only to the Bible in its influence on succeeding generations of the family. Herbert's father had been an ardent political worker for the Liberals. When Herbert himself was ten, he was already distributing Liberal handbills. As a young man, he campaigned actively on behalf of Winston Churchill in the local by-election of 1908. As time went on, however, Herbert became more and more convinced that the really important thing was to be anti-Tory, and, with the growth of the Labour Party, his radicalism inclined increasingly towards socialism.

The other abiding interest shared by Herbert and Ethel was the Church. Both were deeply committed Congregationalists, who identified their faith with strict moral principles, and who regarded voluntary social work as the inescapable practical outcome of regular worship. One serious problem immediately facing them at Milnsbridge was the absence of any Congregational Church nearby. The nearest, geographically and denominationally, was the Baptist Church, which was supported by most religious people in the neighbourhood. Although unable to subscribe to all aspects of the Baptist faith, Herbert and Ethel thought

3

there was sufficient in common with their own to justify their attendance there. This view was shared by the minister, who warmly welcomed the newcomers to his congregation.

Nobody at the time could have foreseen the immense influence this arrangement was later to have on the development of a future political leader.

\*     \*     \*

When war broke out, Herbert's work assumed increasing importance as the demand for explosives grew more pressing. Output had to be increased, and this meant harder work all round. Even on Sunday mornings Herbert was at his office, and as a result his Sunday School teaching had to come to an end. Early in 1916 new plant was installed in the factory, and extensive alterations were required. The many complicated mathematical and chemical calculations were Herbert's responsibility, but he did not allow his concern with these to overshadow his joy over a family matter. Ethel was to have another baby.

As she got ready for the confinement at home, Herbert and she discreetly prepared their daughter for the arrival of a baby brother or sister. Herbert was proud of his family name. His married brother had two daughters, and his married sister two sons. So the birth of a son would provide the first hope of the name being continued. Otherwise they had no strong preference.

On the night of Friday, 15th March, 1916, Herbert was heavily engaged on some intricate calculations he had brought home from work. But the baby's birth was almost due, and as the evening wore on Ethel felt the first pangs of labour. Herbert stayed up most of the night, dividing his time between Ethel, fetching the doctor and midwife—and working on his calculations.

At 10.30 the following morning, a bitterly cold day, the baby was born. Mother and son were in excellent form. Marjorie had been whisked away before breakfast by a friendly neighbour who had promised to take her out for the day. When she was brought back, her delight over the arrival of a baby brother was enhanced by the fact that her seventh birthday was only one day

4

off. She adored small babies, and from the first moment he became not only her "birthday present" but *her* baby—to be loved and protected at all times. She looked forward to putting his name on the Cradle Roll in the Primary Department of the Sunday School.

Meanwhile, the Christening had to be arranged. There was never any doubt about who should perform the ceremony: the Rev. Robert Sutton, Minister of Lees Street Congregational Chapel in Openshaw, Manchester, who had married Ethel's parents, christened Ethel, and married Ethel and Herbert. Ethel's father had been Deacon and Treasurer of the Church, and both Ethel and Herbert had been Sunday School teachers there.

Before a congregation who knew the parents well, the baby was christened James Harold. The choice of names had presented no problem. Both Herbert and his father had James among their Christian names, while Ethel's brother in Australia, and a cousin killed at Gallipoli, had both been called Harold.

*    *    *

As the war progressed, prices and earnings rose sharply. By the time Harold was born, Herbert was earning £260 a year, and in addition was awarded an annual profit bonus of £100. By average local standards he continued to be fairly well-off, but the household, as always, was managed on a careful basis. Ethel, who took great pride in her family and home, ensured a comfortable standard of living without ever losing sight of thrift—or of charity to others.

In 1917, when Harold was exactly one year old, the family moved from Warneford Road to 40 Western Road. It as only a stone's throw away, and suffered from the usual coating of grime, but the new abode was considered "superior." Although terraced, a back-to-front covered passage divided each house. The garden was slightly larger, the outlook pleasanter, and the house itself a little bigger, with a large attic room which proved an ideal place for the children to play. Built of stone in 1914, the house cost £440 freehold. Herbert paid half from his own savings, and raised the remainder from a building society mortgage.

Eighteen months later, Herbert changed his job. He now became works chemist in charge of the dyes department in a different local firm at a commencing salary of £425 a year. He still regarded himself as lower middle-class, but always defiantly described himself as "working-class" to Tory friends. As the war ended, and the social aftermath became clear, he felt bitter about what he regarded as the betrayal of the aims and claims of Lloyd George and his colleagues.

He was greatly shocked by social injustice, especially the bad housing conditions ("homes fit for heroes") spreading unemployment and the constant attempts to cut down wages. In particular, he thought the railway workers and the miners were shabbily treated. He distrusted the influence and prominence of the "military class." By now, in fact, his remaining Liberal loyalties dwindled to nothing. Henceforth he was a full-blooded supporter of the Labour Party.

On a more personal level, he had always felt acutely the financial and social limitations he suffered through having had no university education. As one of five children in a family where money was short, a university education was to be out of the question—unless he won a scholarship. Although a brilliant mathematician, his attainments in other subjects were not up to scholarship standard. So his status in his own profession was permanently impaired.

There was constant friction between the "academic" chemists with degrees, who became public analysts, senior research workers or teachers, and the "technical college" chemists like himself, who were lucky if they secured a well-paid job in industry. The Institute of Chemistry, ordinarily open only to "degree" men, made the wartime concession of all owing applications for associate membership from those hitherto regarded as "unqualified." Herbert applied. After two years' consideration of his application, he was granted the highly-prized right to put the letters "A.I.C." (later A.R.I.C.) after his name.

Herbert was determined that his own children should fare better. He greatly valued education for its own sake, and he wanted them to have it at its best. He was also anxious that they should both do outstandingly well in whatever careers they might eventually choose.


## CHAPTER TWO

In a town of textile workers like Milnsbridge, Herbert Wilson's salary alone would have been enough to give the family a distinctive status in the community. But there was more than that behind the respect accorded to the family. After all, most of their immediate neighbours and friends were at least as well-off, yet even among them the Wilsons were regarded as "superior."

They were also regarded as slightly apart, being relative newcomers to the district: despite their reputation for hospitality and warmth, West Riding folk tend to be clannish; and the fact remained that the Wilsons had come from Manchester—a distance of less than thirty miles, but in another county—and far enough away to make them feel "comers-in," as strangers were locally described. The feeling of being newcomers faded only gradually as the years passed.

From the first, however, they had thrown themselves into the religious life of the neighbourhood, and into all the social activities of the Church. Herbert, as well as being a Sunday School teacher, became a Rover Leader, eventually District Commissioner for the Scouts, and also Secretary of the Church Amateur Operatic Society. Ethel was a founder and organiser of the Women's Guild, a Guide Captain, and a Sunday School teacher. Marjorie was a keen Guide; she too became a Guide Captain (and eventually District Commissioner). Religion within the family was taken seriously: regular attendance at Sunday School and Church, grace before meals, and avoidance of any boisterous or flippant activities on Sundays.

All this was in keeping with the patterns of much of the neighbourhood. What especially distinguished the Wilson family was their attachment to cultural pursuits, and their interest in educational affairs. When others would spend their spare money on outings to the music-hall, perhaps, or on purchasing a gramophone, Herbert spent his on buying more and more good books and, sooner than most, a wireless set: in those days radio, still very much a minority medium, concentrated strongly on culture.

He did, however, make one very big purchase which some considered extravagant at the time: in 1918 he bought a second-hand motor-cycle with sidecar for £50. But this was for the all-important purpose of family holidays. With Marjorie on the pillion seat, and Ethel carrying Harold on her knee in the sidecar, he transported them regularly to Old Byland, and occasionally to visit relatives in Manchester.

With prices steadily rising, the buy proved profitable, because after enjoying its use for over two years he resold it to its original owner for £60. With this money, and an additional £100 from his savings, he then bought a new model, which he kept until 1925.

The family was closely-knit and there was not much entertaining done. Quite often some church friends would come in for hymn-singing round the piano after the Sunday evening service. And sometimes a few close friends would be invited to tea at the week-end; on such occasions the conversation often turned into political discussion and argument. From the first Harold was a keen listener at these gatherings.

High among the family's attitudes was an absolute hatred of snobbery in any form. Although the Wilsons were regarded as a "cut above" most of the neighbourhood, and although they themselves were aware that their own background gave them some clear advantages, they regarded these as privileges. Snobbery was the one unforgivable social sin—the ultimate foe of all their religious and political convictions.

Another guiding influence, no less important in the formation of Harold's personality, was a striking family characteristic of individual self-containment. The very deep bonds of love uniting all four were never displayed in public, and seldom even in private. This was due partly, of course, to the traditional North Country distrust of sentiment and hatred of sentimentality. But this "Yorkshire grit," so carefully fostered in the West Riding, happened to match precisely—and therefore to reinforce—the individual temperaments of both Herbert and Ethel. Each was an exceptionally self-contained, self-sufficient person, disinclined to display feelings.

From an early age Harold understood that feelings were private experiences, to be kept strictly to oneself, and therefore best kept under careful control. It was not that they were in any way to be despised: but they became suspect if they were publicly exposed. So long as they remained quite personal, they could be assessed at their proper value. The same thing applied, of course, to anxieties. In fact, Harold had few serious worries as a young child. But when they did arise, he generally thought it right to sort them out without reference to anybody else. To have discussed them, he felt, would have seemed rather disgraceful—would have indicated an inability to cope on his own. (These characteristics are indelibly part of the grown man.)

At one stage in his early years at school, for example, he had a strict woman teacher who used the cane freely. Corporal punishment was a new experience which he found frightening. On the rare occasions when he misbehaved at home the only punishment he received was parental disapproval: in his tightly bound family this was a painful experience. But this teacher scared him—and filled him with a sense of injustice. He even used to contemplate jumping off his father's motor-cycle on the way to school and playing truant. Yet although he was only six at the time, he kept his fears to himself. In fact, his parents knew all along about her treatment of the little children in her care, and greatly disliked it. But they too kept their characteristic silence, believing it best to let Harold cope with the situation himself—which he did.

A year or two later he fell foul of another teacher. This time there was a much more personal angle to it, because the teacher in question (a man) had had a disagreement with Ethel about a Chapel matter. In discussing it afterwards with Herbert, he had reiterated his own point of view with greater emphasis, adding: "Not that I'd want to *criticise* your wife."

Herbert was so incensed by the mere suggestion that Ethel could possibly be open to criticism that for once he actually declared some of the great anger he felt. Subsequently the teacher did everything he could to make life difficult for Harold at school. Again, both parents knew at the time what was happening, and felt most uneasy about it; and again nothing was said to Harold. It was best that the lad should cope on his own.

Not surprisingly, two basic traits in Harold's personality were quickly and effectively developed. One was resourcefulness. The other, closely akin, was a rare degree of emotional endependence, often equated with shyness. If shyness means a natural disinclination to obtrude or reveal personal sentiment, then shy he certainly was—and is. But shyness is an incomplete description for this partly innate, partly cultivated mechanism which, in time, became a source of great strength: quite simply, an ability to separate subjective experience from objective judgment. He learned that both were to be respected. But at all times they were immediately to be recognised as distinct entities. Resourcefulness and detachment together created in the young Harold a formidable, almost forbidding, combination of self-sufficiency and apparent self-assurance.

On the rare occasions when he felt an imperative need to confide some hurt or anxiety, it was to his mother that he turned. He felt especially close to her, and he resembled her much more than his father. From her he inherited two marked constitutional features—low blood pressure, and a very slow pulse rate. His natural ability to relax completely and to sleep well has thus an hereditary as well as an emotional basis.

From his father he inherited a restless and insatiable curiosity, and an extraordinary power of memory: but from his mother he acquired the main basis of his personality. Temperamentally, Herbert was volatile while Ethel was unusually calm but intensely shy. She was respected and liked by everyone who knew her. She had great dignity, was unfailingly cheerful with friends and acquaintances, and always gave the impression of having no personal worries. She was never known to lose her temper, or even to seem ruffled.

Harold admired his mother's poise, tranquillity and patience. He too has never been known to lose his temper—except on one or two occasions in adult life when he has thought it expedient to be seen to do so. He also admired his mother's constant thoughtfulness for other people; not least of the many things Harold learned from her was a conviction that, however important beliefs and sentiments might be, real virtue ultimately resided in right action. She was a very practical person, and he noted that her devoted preoccupation with her own family and home never prevented her from unobtrusively helping other households in all kinds of practical ways—clothing and boots for children in need of them, for example, or cakes specially baked for invalids, or visits to friends or neighbours who were bereaved: a woman who gave practical expression to her strong Christian faith, and who was as incapable of ostenatation as she was of rancour. These were among the characteristics which in time became part of Harold too.

## CHAPTER THREE

When Harold was four he decided on his future career. He reached his decision one day while watching a local joiner at work. He was already a Meccano addict, and he was fascinated by the precision as well as the skill of the carpenter. He noted that the local craftsman in question was known as "Joiner and Undertaker." He concluded that the two occupations must be indivisible. So Harold told his parents that he was going to be an undertaker. When they pointed out to him the more melancholy aspects of the job he said he would employ an assistant to deal with that side of the business.

At this time Marjorie, now aged eleven, was awarded a County Minor Scholarship (the equivalent in those days of the 11-plus) to Huddersfield Girls' High School. She was the only one in her class at school that year to be given a place, and triumphantly announced at home: "I've won a scholarship." Harold burst into tears, crying: "I want a ship, too." He was told the kind of "ship" Marjorie had acquired, and the ambition to become an undertaker quietly vanished.

He was nearly due to start going to infant school. There was never any doubt about where he would attend. Herbert could by now just have afforded private school fees, but the thought never occurred to him. This was not because of the financial sacrifice, but because all fee-paying schools were to him "snob" schools and therefore intolerable.

Besides, he had complete faith in the merits of the state schools. His brother and two sisters had been state school teachers, and so had Ethel herself. So, at the age of 4½, Harold became a pupil at New Street Council School in Milnsbridge, in a class of about forty children, most of whom were expected eventually to follow their parents into the local textile mills.

It was apparent from the start that he was an outstanding pupil, bright at all subjects, and invariably top of the class. Two things in particular aided him in achieving this supremacy. One was his prodigious reading ability, and the other his intense interest in every subject. He thoroughly enjoyed school work, and astonished and delighted his teachers by his apparently effortless ability to learn and to remember everything.

A typical instance of his constant alertness arose one day when the teacher asked each pupil to write on the blackboard the longest word they knew. Harold, aged six, won the day with the word "committee." He spelt it correctly, too. He explained to his startled teacher that he knew the word well because he saw it every day on his exercise book—"West Riding Education Committee."

He played around with the other lads after school—especially at cricket and football—on a field near his home. But there was always homework to be done first. He mastered his homework very rapidly, to leave as much time as possible for playing. Often on the way home from school he would be calculating the answers to sums in his head, or composing a short essay, in readiness to put it on paper the moment he entered the house.

He was a reticent child, and often appeared to be aloof. Sometimes this made him unpopular. In general, however, he was admired and liked: admired for his superior brain, and because he read "quality" papers like the *Meccano Magazine* and the *Chil-*

*dren's Newspaper* as well as the usual run of popular comics, and liked because of his constant readiness to help other children.

Despite the reticence and seeming aloofness, he was never known to be priggish. Indeed, it was an understood thing among all the children of his acquaintance that Harold would always gladly help them out with any difficulty over their homework—even children older than himself. However private a person's *feelings* should remain, he had no doubt that brains were public property.

As well as being more serious-minded than most, he was also more punctilious in his manners. When most local boys would barge in and out of each other's houses, for example, Harold would ring the bell and wait courteously on the doorstep until he was invited inside. And he would remember to remove his cap on entering. Yet, side by side with this politeness, went a real pleasure in all the usual boyish pastimes; some of his playmates recall that after the "gang" had had their evening's play, it might well be Harold who emerged the grubbiest of the lot.

Although he greatly enjoyed playing soccer and cricket, he excelled at neither. He ardently followed the fate of Huddersfield Town and the fortunes of Yorkshire cricket, and read everything he could lay his hands on about the great sporting stars of the day. He also made a close study of the principles underlying championship play—the various bowling theories in cricket, for example. So he acquired a great deal of knowledge about sport which he passed on to others. But he was less proficient at putting this knowledge into practice than some of his friends. He was relatively slender in build, and seemed less robust. In fact, he suffered little more than all the usual round of children's infectious illnesses, although he had startled everyone, not least the doctor, by having measles diagnosed three different times—at the ages of two, four, and six.

At the age of seven, however, he was taken badly ill with appendicitis—quite a serious occurrence in those days. Herbert and Ethel thought it best that the operation should be performed in a private nursing home. There, as distinct from the ordinary hospital, it would be possible to visit him regularly every day—a

13

very desirable facility, they felt, for a young child, especially with Christmas only a fortnight ahead. With Herbert's salary now having reached £500 a year, and with some savings in the bank, it was a practical proposition.

While Herbert and Ethel were visiting him on the evening of the day after the operation, most other people were going to the polling booths: it was voting day in the General Election of 1923. Harold greeted his parents with two major concerns. Had they brought his copy of *Bubbles?* They had. And had they cast their votes for Philip Snowden, the Colne Valley Labour candidate? They had not. In that case, they must hasten to do so. He urged them to leave him in time to vote before the booths closed.

When Ethel arrived at the nursing home next day, the matron greeted her with some bewilderment. Harold had been pestering a nurse all morning to telephone the Returning Officer to find out the result of the voting. Only when she had done so, and had reported back to him that Snowden had, in fact, been returned, was he willing to co-operate in the various nursing routines.

It would be easy to exaggerate the significance of this episode. He was almost as interested in reading about Buffalo Bill in *Scouts of the Great Wild West,* which his teacher had sent him, as he was in following Snowden's success at the time. In reality he understood very little about the issues involved in the election, and regarded the contest in the same kind of light as he regarded a match played by Huddersfield Town.

He knew, however, that the election was regarded seriously by his parents, and his own interest faithfully reflected theirs. In fact, he took it so seriously that for years afterwards his parents did not dare to tell him that after leaving him that evening, thick fog had delayed their tram, and they had arrived at the booth too late to vote.

Harold was allowed home the day before Christmas. As he was hanging up his stocking, he told his mother how a boy had told him Santa Claus did not really exist. Ethel knew he was seeking her support to repudiate this shocking suggestion. But she told him the truth. It dismayed him. He left his stocking hanging, however, and next morning found it duly filled (as it continued to be each Christmas for years afterwards).

He found something else which gave him even greater delight: a complete model railway. His father had provided the rolling stock, and his uncle the rails. As a keen train-spotter he had longed for a model of his own. He played with it delightedly, added the *Hornby Magazine* to his regular literature and, with the help of a book called *Engineering for Boys* which his father had previously given him, tried to design a new locomotive. Recently he had been privately planning a literary career: to be Poet Laureate in fact. Now he changed his mind. When he grew up he would be a civil engineer.

Herbert's gift of half a railway set was generous in the circumstances. The bill for the nursing home, including the fees for the surgeon and anaesthetist came to £60, and used up a substantial slice of his savings. But he had expected all along that the arrangement would be costly. It had served its purpose well, however, so with one small exception he paid the bill with equanimity. The exception applied to one item among all those listed: 1/11d. for a bottle of medicine. This, he felt, was a niggardly inclusion, and he grudged and resented it permanently.

In those days appendicitis was usually followed by a long period of convalescence, and Harold did not return to school until well after Easter. He had plenty to occupy him—his model railway and, of course, books. Arthur Mee's *Children's Encyclopaedia* had been acquired for Marjorie's benefit, but Harold eagerly tackled it all. He was especially interested in all the sections dealing with history, and read them several times. Some months later, when Ethel and Marjorie were both attending summer Guide camps, Herbert took Harold on a week's motor-cycle tour, starting with a few days' typical sight-seeing in London.

After booking in at a "bed-and-breakfast" place in Russell Square, they had tea in the ABC café by Westminster Bridge, and afterwards looked through a pavement telescope at Big Ben and the House of Commons. It cost 3d. a time to have a look, and Harold had a shilling's worth. Later they listened to the Hyde Park orators, had a look at Buckingham Palace, and studied the entrance to No. 10 Downing Street, where Herbert photographed Harold.

During the coming days they visited the Wembley Exhibition

and went on conducted tours of the House of Commons, Westminster Abbey, the Tower, St. Paul's, and so on. Everywhere Harold was comparing what the official guides said with what he had read in the *Children's Encyclopaedia*, and sometimes—to their consternation—he found it necessary to correct them on matters of fact. The same applied to their return trip via Runnymede, Oxford, Rugby and Stratford-on-Avon.

It is impossible to be sure who enjoyed the holiday most— father or son. Some of it was new to Herbert himself; but all of it was new to Harold, and everything made a lasting impression on him.

Two years later Harold had a much more adventurous trip: his mother took him for six months to Australia, where he saw her brother—his uncle Harold*—take his seat as a member of the Legislative Council in Western Australia. This uncle suffered from bronchial trouble and had been advised to leave Manchester for a kindlier climate. At the age of twenty he had gone to Australia and got a job on the railway. As the years passed he had progressed and prospered, and he persuaded his mother and father and other members of the family to join him. By 1926, however, the elderly father had become very ill. Ethel feared she would never see him again. So, with some difficulty Herbert scraped together enough money for her to go and take Harold with her.

It was an exceptional experience for a ten-year-old boy in Milnsbridge, and the trip greatly widened his horizons. On his return he spoke extensively about it to as many audiences as he could find. His lecture, illustrated by carefully purchased souvenirs, lasted two hours. The teachers were anxious not to curtail it, but considered this too long a stretch for one session. So arrangements were made for the lecture to be given in two parts of one hour each, with an interval of a week between each part. In this manner it was delivered to each class in the school. His delivery and confidence impressed his fellow-pupils no less than his teachers.

He also wrote extensively about the trip, including a book on

* Later, as Sir Harold Seddon, President of the Legislative Council.

the subject, using a complete school exercise book for the purpose. In addition he wrote article after article, and was undeterred when, without exception, each contribution was returned with the apologies of the Editor of every journal he tried —*The Scout, Meccano Magazine*, and so on. One, entitled *My Visit to Mundaring Weir* is the only survivor of these precocious journalistic endeavours:

> Many years ago, when Kalgoorlie first became of note as a gold-mining centre the supply of water was very limited. As the population increased this became a serious question. As a consequence of this it was decided to obtain water from the River Helena over 300 miles away. To do this it was necessary to construct a dam across the river, 760 feet in length. This formed an artificial lake 8 miles long.
>
> A pipe from Mundaring (where the dam is) to Kalgoorlie was then laid. It was 30 inches in diameter and withstood a pressure of 400 pounds to the square inch. Eight pumping stations were constructed on the way, to pump the water along. It is a wonderful engineering feat.
>
> A few months ago I paid a visit to Mundaring Weir. When I arrived there I was awestruck with the terrific volume of water and the massive concrete dam that held it in check. Suspended high above the dam is a pathway over which anyone may walk. Just below here is the overflow which bounds over the top of the dam into the valley below. Here is pumping station No. 1. Of all the wonderful engineering works, the Mundaring Weir water scheme is one of the greatest.

His prolonged absence from school in no way checked his meteoric scholastic progress. By the age of eleven he was sharing a desk with a boy of fourteen. And in 1927 his name was inscribed on the Honours Board of the school as a pupil who was awarded the County Minor Scholarship entitling him to a place at Royds Hall (Grammar) School in Huddersfield.

He has always retained a vivid affection for his primary school at Milnsbridge, and a feeling of close kinship with some of the boys who were—and have remained—his friends. Few invitations have given him greater pleasure than the one he received in the autumn of 1960 to attend the diamond jubilee of the school. By this time he had become Chancellor of the Exchequer in the "Shadow Cabinet," and was greeted as the school's most distinguished old boy.

Addressing a gathering which included former fellow-pupils and old school friends, he said with unmistakable conviction:

"I sometimes look at some of my colleagues in the House of Commons and feel sorry that they had not the same educational advantages we had. Many M.P.'s have been through Eton and other colleges. If they came to New Street, Milnsbridge, they would see a 'right' school."

## CHAPTER FOUR

Of all the formative influences in his early years, none affected Harold Wilson more enduringly than the Scout Movement. Those whose judgment of him is based on partial glimpses of his personality seldom take this seriously. I have questioned him at length about it, and have met the Scout leaders of his early days, as well as a number of his boyhood fellow-Scouts. The only possible conclusion is that his experiences as a Scout had a decisive effect on the development of his character, and on the growth of his religious convictions. His political principles, too, owe a great deal to his interpretation and practical expression of the Scout Laws. Indeed without this particular background it is doubtful whether he would ever have entered politics at all.

The Group Scoutmaster was also the Minister of the Baptist Church, the Rev. W. H. Potter, who gave most of his time to work among the youth of the neighbourhood. He had seven children of his own, and his liking for young people was fully reciprocated by them. He received not only their affection, but also their loyalty. His constant exhortations to follow strictly Christian principles were widely respected by them—partly out

18

of genuine conviction, but at least as much because they knew that any transgression would grieve "Pa" Potter.

His influence on the religious and social life of the adult community was immense, and to Harold and his friends he was a greatly admired leader. He ran his Scout Group as a constituent branch of his church. Every meeting closed with a prayer: thanksgiving, intercession, forgiveness. Members of the Group were obliged to attend Sunday School, so even Scouts who came from "non-church" families were directly involved in the work of the church.

Mr. Potter had a completely open personal relationship with his Scouts, and was ready to discuss anything with them. At their own request, for example, he agreed to hold discussions on sex problems and moral behaviour—in those days usually considered an indecent subject, especially for young people. He never allowed politics to feature at Scout gatherings, but he saw to it that the boys knew about the social conditions of the times, and he constantly reminded them of their promise "to help other people at all times."

To be one of "Pa" Potter's boys in Milnsbridge was to be one of the "gang"; but it was a gang held in high regard throughout the district. A great attraction, of course, was camping. The notion of escaping for a few days to the countryside was marvellous for youngsters surrounded by the grimy drabness of Milnsbridge, and all the routine of foraging, cooking, nature study, cricket and rounders proved to be a real adventure. Mr. Potter organised his camps with untiring zeal: one summer he took groups of boys to camp on twenty-five different occasions. His Scout group was 150 strong—the biggest in Yorkshire.

It was always in the natural order of things that Harold should become a Scout—partly because of his family's close connections with the movement, partly because of his regular Church and Sunday School attendance, and partly because among his own circle of friends everybody belonged. Characteristically, however, he reached his decision quite independently. Shortly after his seventh birthday he had picked up a copy of *The Scout* but found it mostly beyond his comprehension—not surprisingly, since it was for much older boys. But a few months later he tried again. This time he found much of it both intelligible and exciting. He was impatient to become eight and therefore eligible for membership of the Wolf Cubs.

On Tuesday evenings, when the Cubs met, Harold felt particularly excluded. That was the evening when his father as a Rover Leader, Ethel as a Guide Captain, and Marjorie as a Guide were all out, engaged in activities very close to his own desires. Being too young to be left alone at home, he used to go along with his mother to the Guides.

Several weeks before his birthday he made a discovery which shocked him: his birthday was to fall on a Tuesday, and, as it happened, on that evening there was to be no Cub meeting because the headquarters were to be taken over for a Guide Social. He would not be able to join until a week later. The prospect of being *late* appalled him. In high dudgeon, he sought the help of two officials. One was the Cubmaster, who was already well known to him as his Sunday School teacher. The other was Mr. Potter. Together, these two decided that in the circumstances the age rule could be discreetly waived. So Harold became a Cub a week earlier than was strictly permissible. At the time it seemed to him no more than ordinary justice, applied not a day too soon.

It was through the Scout Movement that Harold began to appreciate the significance of Christianity. Although the Wilsons were a devout family, the fundamentals of religion were never discussed at home. They were taken for granted, and Marjorie and Harold automatically went to Church at 10.30 every Sunday morning, and to Sunday School in the afternoon, where Harold was a very alert pupil, always ready to ask a lot of questions—and to answer them. As a young child he was not greatly impressed by the morning sermon. He tried to listen, but found his mind wandering. This could later prove awkward, however, because when he got home his invalid grandfather, who sometimes lived with them, used to question him closely about the text and the contents of the sermon. So he resolved to concentrate his attention and methodically memorised the sermons for his grandfather's benefit.

The real significance began to dawn one "Scout Sunday"—a

day set aside periodically by Mr. Potter for the entire service to be conducted by the Scouts themselves; his own role was confined to pronouncing the blessing. On this occasion the preacher was a Rover who had never been in a pulpit before. He chose as his text: "He hath made of one blood all nations that dwell upon the earth."

He preached vividly, and to Harold his words came as a sudden revelation. Many of the phrases and prayers he had previously heard in church now assumed a dynamic meaning. He has always treasured the impact of the sermon preached by that Rover—not only as an important starting-point in his own faith, but also as a permanent point of reference during the years ahead.

Harold was regularly aroused by another experience—the camp fire ceremony, and its accompanying incantations. This ceremony, dating back to the old Red Indian days, was frequently held in his Group. In summer it took place out of doors round a real fire, but at other times it was held indoors round a mock fire made by an apprentice electrician belonging to the Group: he achieved a realistic effect with sticks, red paper, and a flickering light bulb. All the boys sat on their haunches and clustered round the fire. The leader walked over to it, intoning: "Brothers, I light the Council fire to burn." Everyone then chanted: "Burn, fire, burn." The leader would then say: "Let it burn up all hatred." "Burn, fire, burn," chanted the chorus. "Let it burn up all greed," the leader added, with the chorus again chanting its endorsement of "Burn, fire, burn." And so on, with injustice, blasphemy, greed, intolerance and all other evils consigned to the flames. The boys all enjoyed the ritual, and Harold vividly recalls how he was invariably fascinated by its dramatic symbolism.

He revelled in the free-and-easy informality of all the Group's recreation. However appropriate reticence might be everywhere else, at least in Scouting he felt free to enter into things with gusto. He was determined to be left out of nothing; the plays, no matter how small his part, had him as an eager participant. So did the band, in which he played the triangle, and later the side-drum.

In the debates he made his mark as a pungent and irrepressible speaker. And once, at the age of thirteen, he took part in an impromptu mock trial. He acted as defending counsel, and during an exchange with the prosecutor, he asked his opposite number—a boy older than himself—where he had been educated.

"At Oxford University," came the hopeful reply.

"Oh," pondered Harold, "You went to Emmanuel College, I suppose?"

"Yes, that's right," the prosecutor assured him.

"But that," retorted Harold, "is a *Cambridge* College."

Harold's client was found not guilty.

Harold was an ardent camping enthusiast. Although the camps were usually held in the surrounding countryside, Mr. Potter sometimes took them further afield. On one occasion he took a party to Holland, having first secured special travel reductions which enabled the boys to go for only £3/12/6 each. The voyage itself was a thrilling experience, though Harold and a number of others were seasick.

While under canvas in Holland the party were joined by a Norwegian Scout of eighteen who had set out to walk round the world. Unfortunately he could speak no English. This was exactly the kind of challenge to intrigue Harold. He knew a little French and a few phrases in Esperanto. Within two days he was able to communicate with the Norwegian, and to act as interpreter for all the others who wished to do so, including the adult guide.

This was typical of the determination and thoroughness he brought to bear on any situation. He was never satisfied until he had mastered a difficulty, and mastering it meant achieving real proficiency.

It was as a Scout that Harold first discovered a capacity for leadership and organisation: he excelled as a Patrol Leader, enjoyed exercising authority, and valued the feeling of responsibility. He also learned the practical meaning of team work, and the value of friendly rivalry within the team; from this developed his sense of fair play and loyalty.

On one occasion as a young Cub he attended a West Riding rally to greet Baden-Powell. In their enthusiasm, they all rushed the platform and nearly swamped their Chief Scout and his party, which included Col. Malcolm Stoddart Scott. Several years later, as a Senior Patrol Leader, Harold helped to wait at the annual dinner given by the Rovers for a distinguished guest—on this occasion Col. Stoddart Scott, the Assistant County Commissioner.

The next time they met was years later in the House of Commons, where they sat looking at each other from opposite sides of the House. In fact, one of the first things Harold Wilson did on becoming an M.P. was to identify himself with the Houses of Parliament branch of the Guild of Old Scouts, where party differences are suspended by other loyalties.

For years he was Chairman of a North London Scout Association. During this time as "Shadow Chancellor," he was regularly confronting Heathcoat-Amory as Chancellor. On at least one occasion the two ex-King's Scouts met privately to agree a joint financial measure to help the Movement they both loved.

After his election as Leader of the Opposition, the first engagement Harold Wilson fulfilled in his constituency was to open a new Guide and Scout Headquarters. And some weeks later he was chief guest at the Commissioners' Dinner in London. On that occasion he said:

> The need for the Scout Movement is as great as ever because, if there is one big problem greater than any other in our modern world, so far as young people are concerned it is the problem of their use of leisure and the problem of inculcating a sense of purpose among them. I think one of the dangers in a society (I am not making a political point here) where there is a greater and greater emphasis on materialism—we get it in the papers, we get it on television, we get it in advertising: each political party accuses the other of it, so I am impartial in saying that— in a world where there is a growing emphasis on materialism, there is a danger of a loss of individual, and above all of moral purpose, especially among young people. And that is why the values taught by the Scout Movement are not only as relevant but are even more relevant today, I think, than they were in the

past, when many of us were first going round in our shirts and shorts, lanyards, neckerchieves and all the rest of it. So many of our young people, perhaps because of the heat put upon them, because of the meretricious values that they are taught, face the problems of the world with perhaps even more bewilderment than we did when we were at that age.

I think it is important that the Scout Movement gives them some basic elemental truths which, once absorbed, are never forgotten throughout their whole lifetime.

Harold Wilson himself owes not only "some basic elemental truths" to Scouting; he owes also several of his closest friendships. He was more serious-minded than most of his Scouting contemporaries, and too emotionally withdrawn to be liked by all of them. Yet the friendships he did form proved close and lasting.

One was with Harold Ainley, who lived near him. In fact, the two Harolds first became friendly at the age of five, and as the years passed became inseparable playmates, although their backgrounds and upbringing were quite different. Ainley's father earned more than Harold's; he did not share the Wilson enthusiasm for educational pursuits; nor did he share the Wilson churchgoing interests. And sometimes he frequented pubs.

None of this affected relations between the two boys. Herbert and Ethel took a close interest in Harold's friendships, but felt no misgivings over the young Ainley's "non-church" background. In any case, his Cub and Scout membership obliged him to attend Sunday School, and this in itself would have scattered any doubts they might have had. What they most liked about him was his genuineness.

Intellectually and temperamentally the boys could hardly have been more different. Ainley, who was no scholar, admired his friend's brain and application; he relied on Harold's very willing tuition in semaphore signalling and the like to help him through his various Scouting tests. Harold admired Ainley's superiority in sport and, being himself so reserved, he enjoyed his friend's uninhibited speech and conduct.

Besides sports and Scouts, the two had many other interests in

24

common, including Meccano and model trains. They also shared a common hero: Sherlock Holmes.

On one occasion Harold had successfuly engaged in some private detective work of his own. A nearby resident, who was so proud of his apple crop that he intended to enter them in the local show, awoke one morning to find the tree denuded and the entire crop vanished. On his way to work he saw Harold going off to school, and sought his help. Harold, who was twelve at the time, accepted the assignment without demur. Within forty-eight hours he had recovered the missing apples.

Not long afterwards, the Ainley household was robbed. They were holidaying at Blackpool at the time. On their return they notified the police who, to the disappointment of both Harolds, failed to find the culprits. They decided to take matters into their own hands.

After much searching they unearthed a clue—a shred of a torn letter, with the fragment of an address just discernible. Invoking a great deal of imagination and what they fancied to be powers of deduction, they concluded that the guilty party was a shady-looking character who, it turned out, lived about a mile and a half away.

They shadowed him methodically, and their suspicions were strengthened when they discovered that he lived next door to a woman who was in the habit of scrounging from the Ainleys, and who might have told her neighbour of their absence on holiday. Despite their careful observation, however, they failed to unearth sufficient evidence to take positive action.

Although the boys had their secondary education at different schools, their friendship was so close that it survived this separation. They played in the evenings and at week-ends. The friendship continued until the age of sixteen, when the Wilsons moved away from the district. After that they saw very little of each other, and during the war years they lost touch altogether. But when Harold Wilson became an M.P. in 1945, one of the first congratulatory letters he opened came from his old friend.

Some months later he was in Huddersfield for a one-day visit on urgent Government business. As soon as his mission was completed, he excused himself from the official escorts and set out to look up Harold Ainley, who was by now a husband and father, living temporarily with in-laws.

Unfortunately he had mislaid the address, and they had no telephone. He rang through to his secretary in London: all she could do was share his impression that the in-law residence was somewhere in Manchester Road. So he went to the Library and consulted the voters' list until he found the number of the house.

Thus armed, he paid his call—only to find that Ainley had just gone out, but would be back later. He said he would return. Meanwhile, he slipped over to Milnsbridge and arrived unexpectedly at an evening social at the Baptist Church. Afterwards he went back to Manchester Road—and this time found his old friend at home.

The reunion was one of mutual delight, and Ainley naturally also felt flattered that a member of the Government had taken so much time and trouble for the sake of renewing an old friendship with him. It is one which has remained close ever since.

Harold Wilson relies greatly on the strength he derives from friendships of this kind, far removed from Westminster. He has also found the advice and comments he often gets from private friends to be of practical help, as the following letter from him (as President of the Board of Trade) to Harold Ainley reveals:

Board of Trade,
Millbank, S.W.1
21st May, 1948

My dear Harold,

Very many thanks indeed for your letter. It was very good of you to write and send me your congratulations and good wishes, but I do regret not having been able to write in reply earlier. You will be glad to know that both wife and baby are doing extremely well and in fact are coming home from hospital today.

About coupon reductions: I am glad you liked them. As a matter of fact when I was making the announcement it just struck me to wonder what you and your wife would think about them. I certainly agree with you that the concession about children's shoes was one which makes an enormous difference in any family with young children. It was, in fact, my own idea. There has been a lot of twitting of me for having done this just a few hours before my second child arrived, though my excuse is that he won't be requiring shoes yet awhile.

As you say, the best one can do won't satisfy some people and we have had this press agitation ever since. In fact, when I made the first round of concessions I had it in mind to do more, but I could not say so or else the public would have stayed out of the shops waiting for the new changes to come into effect. However, I shall have another fairly big bite of the cherry next Tuesday afternoon and I hope you will be as pleased with that one as you were with the first bite.

It was very good of you to write and particularly to tell me your views on things like this, because, believe me, it is a great help to me to get independent advice and views from friends as to how policies of this kind are affecting them.

I am glad to hear your son is better and that all your family are fit and well and enjoying this nice weather.

Looking forward to seeing you and Dorothy again soon.

With every good wish,
I remain,
Yours ever,
Harold.

Harold Ainley by now was working as a chemist's assistant. This continues to be his occupation. As the years have passed, he too has developed political interests. He stood successfully as a Labour candidate for Huddersfield Town Council. In a subsequent election he lost his seat.

In May, 1963, he stood again. Anxiously awaiting the outcome was his friend Harold Wilson—he sat in the House of Commons, watching the results come in on the ticker tape. At 2 a.m. the news came through: Harold Ainley had been returned. The Leader of the Opposition waited no longer. He left for home, well content.

*      *      *

Family, early friendships, Church, Scouts: all are indivisible parts of an essential whole; together they formed the basic pattern of Harold's social conscience, and the structure of his whole career. Every major decision he has taken has been closely, and often consciously, related to the experiences of his boyhood. He never misses an opportunity of renewing these inspirations of his early background, almost as if to fortify the very fabric for his life.

While President of the Board of Trade he went to Milnsbridge for the anniversary of the Baptist Church Sunday School. From the same pulpit he had preached in as a Scout nearly twenty years earlier, he preached again.

"In the crisis that faces us today," he said, "we must re-dedicate ourselves to the faiths and principles which brought together the founders of this Sunday School in Milnsbridge over a hundred years ago. Since that time the industrial age has laid a greater emphasis on material things in the lives of our people. Man has learned to control nature, but not to control himself. He has learned how to control the atom, but not to control the uses to which it could be put; he has learned to turn deserts into fertile lands, but not to distribute the products of his bounty to meet the needs of the world.

"Personal goodness of itself will be of little value unless we can all work together and realise in our activities as a community those same ideals which the Christian believes should dominate his personal life. The world will still not be saved even if each individual lives a good life, if nations follow policies which, to the individual, are abhorrent. No Christian believes in murder, yet we prepare for war. Every Christian must take his principles out of his own life and into the world. It is my belief that no Christian can ever be far from politics. The nation's life has always been closely associated with our national religion, and all our leading parties have a strong religious background.

"No one should be in a political party unless he believes that party does represent his own highest religious and moral ideals.

No Christian can accept the full responsibilities of being a Christian unless he plays his part in seeing that the political life of his township, and his country, follows as near as possible his own beliefs in what is right and what is wrong."

The brunt of this sermon at Milnsbridge in 1948 was simply an extended adult version of a theme Harold had expressed a long time earlier: he had written much of it in an essay on the duty of helping the underdog. It was based on the rather rhetorical keynote of Can England Stand Aside in This Hour of the World's Need? But he was awarded a Missionary Prize for it. At the time, he was only nine years old.

# PART TWO

# The Emerging Pattern

❦

## CHAPTER FIVE

When Harold Wilson was twelve there occurred an event which was to become an important milestone in his development, although at the time it seemed of no special significance.

It happened on holiday. Herbert had by now abandoned his motor-cycle and sidecar in favour of an Austin 7—an open model with a hood. Complete with speedometer, self-starter, and electric lighting, it had cost him £149 in cash two years earlier. Possession of a car enabled him to plan more enterprising holidays, and in the summer of 1928 he took Ethel and Harold on a tour of Scotland, including a night in Stirling.

As soon as they had found a suitable boarding house at their usual price of 6/6 per person for bed and breakfast, Herbert took them to see the statue of Campbell-Bannerman, who had represented Stirling in Parliament. Herbert had learned little history at school, but had studied it as closely as he could through his political interests. He had a deep admiration for Campbell-Bannerman. As a youth, he had heard him speak in Manchester in the Free Trade Hall during the Boer War. He was the first political leader Herbert had heard, and for many years afterwards he regarded him as an honest and straightforward politician. Now, standing by his statue, he was anxious to convey this admiration to his son.

He started by explaining a few of the outstanding facts of political history centred around Campbell-Bannerman. Bearing in mind Harold's youth, he decided to keep them simple. To his surprise, Harold wanted to know more and more. He gave him fuller details about Campbell-Bannerman's Liberal Leadership during the great landslide in the 1906 election. Question after question came from Harold. Herbert warmed to the subject. In dramatic tones he told of the heavy defeat of the Tories, describing them vividly as the class of privilege and greed.

He went on to tell of the rise of the Labour Party. Ethel meanwhile was also listening with interest to her husband recounting events of their younger days. But it was Harold who was spellbound. What, he wanted to know, was the difference between the ideals of these parties, and why had his father gone over from the Liberals to Labour?

Herbert could no longer cope with the question in the simple terms of good and bad, right and wrong, he had thought appropriate for a child. With greater detail he filled out the picture of the decline of Liberalism, the rising strength of the Labour party, and, as he saw it, the totally negative position of Toryism. He spoke above all of his hatred of the militarism he associated with the "ruling classes."

Harold was still not satisfied. How, he demanded, did all this apply to their own local affairs? Herbert explained that no Tory had ever represented the Colne Valley. He recalled how even Liberal supporters in the Valley were so radical that they had actually marched behind banners demanding the abolition of the House of Lords, and used to sing, "God Gave the Land to the People" in the Nonconformist chapels. As long ago as 1895 the Socialist Tom Mann had gained 1,500 votes in the Valley, and the whole country had been startled by the famous by-election in 1907 when Victor Grayson, the independent Socialist, had been returned. And so on, up to more recent times: to Philip Snowden, in fact, to the General Strike—and to the fears of rising unemployment.

Harold took it all in eagerly. He was silent as they walked away from the statue, much later in the evening than Herbert had expected.

Shortly afterwards Harold reached his decision. Henceforth, only one career lay open to him. Only through politics, he was convinced, could he put into practice everything he had learned about religion and about his Scout obligation "to help other

32

people at all times." Besides, a political career must obviously provide the most exciting life imaginable. Nobody could have listened to his father without feeling quite sure about that.

If there began to form within him at that moment in Stirling something like a missionary zeal, the crusade was to have a more permanent basis than the fervour of a schoolboy's ideals. The ideals were present, for sure, but they sprang from two fundamentals already emerging into consciousness, both ready to play their decisive parts in shaping the future.

One was an inner certainty of destiny, an absolute conviction about his future mission and his unique fitness to undertake it. This "calling"—it was no less—ran parallel to an equally potent basic force: a driving ambition for supremacy. At times in the years ahead those parallel fundamentals were to vie with each other for mastery.

Although from Stirling onwards Harold knew for sure where his future must lie, even an exceptionally precocious boy of twelve could hardly appreciate the labyrinthine complications of a political career. Sometimes he found it difficult to decide exactly which office he would choose. Occasionally the Foreign Secretaryship seemed the best, but usually his first choice was to be Chancellor of the Exchequer. In this he was also inspired by his hero-worship for Snowden.

When his class were set an essay on "Myself in 25 Years," Harold wrote his in the form of an interview between himself as Chancellor of the Exchequer and a reporter, discussing the Budget he planned to introduce. An important item was to be a tax on gramophone records—a reflection of Harold's resentment that, unlike so many others, his family possessed no gramophone.

Before writing his essay, he had asked his form mistress the number of the Chancellor's house in Downing Street.

"Why did you want to know?" she asked, after telling him.

"Because I will be there one day," came the reply.

"Are you sure number ten wouldn't suit you better?" she queried.

Harold ignored the gibe. "Number eleven will do me quite well," he said simply. As time went on, however, he began to wonder. Perhaps, after all, number ten *would* be the right target. His family had meanwhile explained to him some of the complex factors involved in a political career, pointing out that the highest offices were not attainable merely by setting out to achieve them. From then on, his statements of fact became statement of intention. When he and his closest friends were discussing their future careers, Harold's contribution was confined to the simple observation: "I should like to be Prime Minister."

His form mistress was a benevolent confidante, who heard his unfolding ambitions sympathetically, but who felt there was no special reason for believing them to be more than transient wishes. After all, she had heard other bright schoolboys make similar declarations about their vocational urges.

Exactly twenty years later she sent a light-hearted enquiry to the President of the Board of Trade about curtain material, stockings and clothing, and received a reply in similar vein:

Many thanks for your letter. I am advised that it would cause considerable administrative difficulties to initiate discriminatory supply arrangements in respect of teachers, and in order to avoid the necessity of your initiating the smash and grab tactics referred to I have thought it better to tackle the question on thorough lines. (You will observe that my ability to write good Whitehallese—on which you once commented some 20 years ago—is in no way dimmed.) So in the hope that you have not already bought your curtains I would invite your attention to the statement I shall be making in the House on Tuesday next. I hope it will also assist—even if only indirectly—with the stocking and dress problem to which you refer.

Well, when you have read the statement (which I would ask you to do in full and not merely the Press garbled version of it) I shall be very glad of your comments and advice on where I should go from here.

I have just been enjoying three or four days complete holiday in glorious weather—at home—and feel ready to start in on films, cotton, the "new look" and what have you, not to mention a few trips here there and everywhere. I look forward to seeing you in the not too distant future. Please let me know if you are coming up to London at any time.

Yours very sincerely,<br>Harold

## CHAPTER SIX

The information that Harold would like to be Prime Minister was invariably accepted by his close school friends at Royds Hall as an honest and unexceptionable aim. They neither expressed nor felt any surprise over the striking contrast with their own relatively limited ambitions. He was, after all, a patently honest boy, and if he stated this as his target, it must be authentic.

Besides, his scholastic ability was high. Why, therefore, should he not seek to be Prime Minister? Had he been less liked and respected, the assertion would certainly have been treated with the derision of an absurdly pretentious boast. But his self-assurance never appeared to his schoolmates in the guise of boastfulness or arrogance.

With the staff, however, the position was different. Although they all found him exceedingly bright and alert, several of them found his manner and outlook excessively precocious. He was quite unaware of this view, and never realised that his attitude to them, to his work, and to his professed future career, was sometimes interpreted as an attempt either to impress or to curry favour.

At times he seemed irrepressibly exhibitionist, even in small matters. On one occasion, for example, when he had received an attractive propelling pencil as a birthday present, he proudly took it to show his teacher. He was puzzled as well as crestfallen when one of his classmates advised him not to be babyish.

Again, his own interest in serious magazine articles led him to suppose that the teachers would be similarly fascinated—and, no doubt, impressed by the breadth of his outlook. With the geography teacher this did, in fact, prove to be so. Although a woman who was as sincerely anxious to learn as she was to teach, she was regarded by her class as a tedious mentor, and they enjoyed their periods with her best when she was so absorbed in some private study that she would instruct the class to occupy themselves with their own reading—a sure signal for geography textbooks and atlases to be replaced by comics.

Sometimes it was Harold who created this situation. Just when it seemed that all hope was lost, and the class were doomed to endure an uninterrupted period of dull listening, up would go Harold's hand. "Excuse me, but I've brought an article you might like to read about South Africa." It seldom failed to preoccupy her for the rest of the lesson.

Royds Hall had all the social and sporting facilities found in the best kind of pre-war grammar school for boys and girls, and Harold was determined to be involved in all of them, although by now he had developed the total reticence which was to become a lifelong characteristic.

Almost by way of protective compensation, however, he hurled himself with gusto into all the activities where extrovert energy was a desirable feature—and where any revelation of deep personal sentiment was irrelevant. Besides acting as a shield, this zeal had its own authenticity: it sprang partly from genuine interest and enthusiasm, and partly from a thrustful resolve to be left out of nothing. The net result was a display of exuberant showmanship over a wide field of activities.

Having for years unsuccessfully tried his hand at journalism, for example, he now enjoyed a ready market for his contributions in the school magazine *The Roydsian*. He valued his reputation as a wit, and the following article gives a fair flavour of his humour at the time. He was twelve when he wrote it:

Form 2C live in Room 8 under the father-like guidance of Mr. Wilkinson. We have a splendid (?) football team, although we have only won one match so far. Unfortunately we have one more subject in which to get a BC as we are now troubled with Latin.

Here are some questions:

(1) Which jazz band does X—— intend joining when he has completed his ukulele?

(2) Who is King Charles?

(3) Who so neatly evades every Latin test by taking up an absence slip?

(4) Who will need a boxer's training?

(5) What is exactly meant by Density?

(6) Is it because of our form room that the members of Form 2C are noted for their gas?

J. H. Wilson.

He became an indifferent goalkeeper for his form's soccer team. Once, having let six goals through, he was chased off the field by another member of the team (his pursuer, Willie Watson, in later years became an English football and cricket International). He was an equally indifferent member of the choir. He had a shrill treble voice, which the choir mistress tried to persuade him to mellow, commenting: "Oh Harold—you always have to put your little bit in—just like Cock Robin, don't you!"

Neither she nor anybody else realised that behind the piping shrillness lay a staunch effort to overcome the inadequacy he felt. His toughest ordeal had come at an evening service at the Baptist Church, when he had to sing a solo verse at the age of eleven.

Many years later he referred to this on one of the visits he paid to Milnsbridge while President of the Board of Trade. After listening to the solos sung by pupils of the Sunday School, he told them how he had once done the same, and added: "I can assure you, you will never again have to face anything so nerveracking as that. Not even making a maiden speech in the House of Commons filled me with so much awe as that Sunday solo."

Nevertheless he enjoyed his association with the school choir, not least because the choir mistress, who was also his form mistress, was a great favourite.

Just before his fourteenth birthday he contributed the following to *The Roydsian*:

*July 26th*
For the first time in history the RHS Choir turns up in full
force, to do justice to the *free* train trip and tea, on the occasion
of the annual choir picnic to Hope Bank Pleasure Grounds,
Honley. Unaccountable loss of water from the "lake" during
afternoon.—For solution ask the winners of the splashing bout.
Choir attempts descant while singing grace and fails miserably.
The tea, together with the roundabouts and swings, create dis-
turbance in the interior of choir boy.

*July 27th*
Rush to join Choir.

*December 18th*
Choir comes out of hibernation to find that many fourth form
"old contemptibles" have finally staggered out.

*January 15th*
Great event. Miss Whelan lets choir go home at 4.29 p.m.

*February 12th*
Choir is warned of approach of speech day. Boys are advised to
begin scrubbing the visible parts of their anatomy. Great
rejoicings shown by two first trebles who have just invested in
pair of long trousers. It is said two boys also say they had long
collars and "scrum caps."

*February 19th*
First layer of dirt begins to show signs of dispersing. Choir
practice last period, during which Miss Whelan and many first
trebles nearly collapse as a result of the afore-mentioned first
trebles singing "Hark, Hark, the Lark" without going flat. The
entire choir dances the hornpipe on hearing there will be no
after-school practice.

J. H. Wilson, 3B.

If his singing was unsuccessful, his acting ability was markedly
the opposite. He won high praise for his portrayal of Shylock in
his form's production of *The Merchant of Venice*, and in the

school production of *She Stoops to Conquer*, he stole the show. On the first night of this, he had appeared to be too restrained, and was urged to act more demonstratively in the subsequent performances. He took the advice to heart. On the following night some girls from a neighbouring school were among the audience, and they contributed a review for the next issue of *The Roydsian* which contained this paragraph:

> On Friday evening, 29th January, a party of us set out from Ellam to see the play *She Stoops to Conquer* presented by the pupils of Royds Hall School. The actors and actresses entered into their parts with true spirit, and made the parts of most interest most entertaining. Tony (H. Wilson) is worthy of first mention since he is the soul of the play. He took his part with gusto, in fact over-acting in places, for he diverted the attention of the audience from the other proceedings. He was very amusing in his relations with his mother and Miss Neville (Olga Gledhill).

Of all his social activities at school, the one which gave him most excitement was his membership of the Debating Society. This had a curiously inauspicious start. *The Roydsian* of October 1929 reported a debate on the motion "That in the opinion of this House a reform of men's dress would be a blessing to mankind":

> When the debate was thrown open, the secretary took advantage of the opportunity to meet the staff as equals in argument, and Wilson delivered a brilliant opening sentence that unfortunately got no further. The mists which gathered round the summing up did not altogether obscure our intelligence in voting, and the motion was carried by 66/46.

The explanation was all too simple. He had but one point to make. Having made it in a sentence, he sat down. Only after reflection did he recognise his error in not elaborating and labouring it, even if only to conceal the isolation of the single point. He never made the same mistake again. As time went on, he became the most effective debater in the school, and made a memorable impression on one occasion when the motion was: "That in the event of a state of war, one ought to do one's duty and go to fight for one's country." Harold, who was nearly sixteen at the time, opposed the motion. After a heated discussion, the motion was lost.

Despite his wholehearted participation in so many different activities, he seldom lost sight of work and learning as the primary reasons for being at school. Even his various leisure pursuits were assessed for their potential usefulness, and he discriminated between them accordingly. Although he joined the Scientific Society, for example, he played little part in its affairs: knowing he was not to have a scientific career, he considered its activities less valuable for the future. The Historical Society, in contrast, claimed much of his time: its potential usefulness was obvious.

Yet his record of outstanding scholastic progress at Milnsbridge Council School was not maintained at Royds Hall. The transition from primary to secondary school can have an unsettling effect and, like many another child before and since, Harold found that brilliant success at the one did not presuppose equal distinction at the other. He was now mingling with boys and girls with similarly distinguished records from other schools, and the atmosphere was more fiercely competitive than anything he had known before.

Besides, with so many new distractions there seemed to be less opportunity for actual study. He was also giving more time than ever to Scouting interests, and at home the acquisition of a half-sized billiard table, given by an uncle, was proving a novel temptation. As a result, he relaxed his highly disciplined routine for doing his homework, and his placing in class declined. Some of his school reports sharply reflected this adverse development by criticising an apparent lack of application and diligence.

In time, however, his guiding principle of "first things first" reasserted itself, and once again he had the highest marks—though seldom at Royds Hall with the same distinction and consistent regularity as at Milnsbridge. One or two of the teachers at Royds Hall did regard him as a boy likely to go far, but most of the staff considered him to have no more special promise than many another hard-working pupil with first-class brains.


## CHAPTER SEVEN

When he was fourteen, and due to enter on a crucial stage of school work, Harold Wilson suffered a setback which was almost fatal. He had gone camping for a few days in September near Honley, and on one expedition went to a nearby farm to buy milk to make custard. He drank some of it, and some days later fell ill. His condition progressively worsened; he had to be rushed to Meltham Isolation Hospital—a victim of typhoid fever. Eleven others were victims of the same local outbreak.

The mortality rate of typhoid in those days was very high. However serious it is now, at that time it was much more likely to result in death than it has been since the discovery of antibiotics. A milk-and-water diet used to be the main form of treatment, in the belief that the microbes themselves had to be starved out. The risk of the patient dying from malnutrition could be almost as great as the risk of death from the disease itself.

Throughout October Harold remained seriously ill, gradually making slight progress. His parents were allowed to visit him once a week only—for half-an-hour each Saturday afternoon. Marjorie, by now a student at Leeds University where she was well on the way to becoming a teacher, was not allowed to visit him at all. Being a contact and possible "carrier," she had to remain at home meanwhile. She wrote to her brother every day. It had to be a postcard, for fear of reinfecting him; so she used a mapping pen to crowd as much writing onto it as possible.

There was no telephone at home, and every morning and evening Herbert went to a call-box to get the latest news from the hospital. There was great anxiety at home until the end of October, when Herbert returned from his telephone call one evening, thankfully able to report that Harold was now considered to be out of danger.

Their confidence was premature. Almost immediately afterwards he had a relapse. Now the outlook suddenly became extremely grave. Six of the original twelve victims had by this time died; Herbert and Ethel needed no warning from the hospital that their son might at any moment become the seventh. The nightmare of anxiety the family suffered during the prolonged period of crisis nearly overwhelmed them. More than thirty years afterwards none of them could recall their anguish at this time without distress.

For nearly six weeks Harold remained in a critical condition. Herbert was so afraid of the news he might hear that he could hardly bring himself to make his 'phone call each morning and evening.

Each time a nurse greeted his urgent query with the same flat response: "Just a minute, Mr. Wilson."

Each time those words brought the same dread: that the next voice would be the matron's, summoned to tell him the worst.

But each time it was the nurse who returned to the 'phone, reading out a carefully worded summary of the latest position.

At last the news was really reassuring. Harold had safely recovered from the relapse, and with continued careful nursing in hospital should be well enough to return home in another month or so. Under the heading of "School Gossip," the Christmas issue of *The Roydsian* published the following:

J. H. Wilson (4A) has been absent during most of the term through a serious attack of typhoid fever. He is still at Meltham Isolation Hospital making slow progress towards recovery, but is not expected to return to school for some considerable time. He wishes to thank his many friends at the school who have written to him during his isolation.

Throughout his stay in hospital, Harold was unaware of the seriousness of his condition. The news of the death of six fellow-victims was naturally kept from him, and he had no inkling of how near to death he was himself. To him, the enforced isolation was a bore, and the rigorous diet a frustration, especially as his appetite returned. He appreciated the bunch of flowers which came regularly every week from the church, but for many years afterwards had a highly developed dislike of chrysanthemums.

He spent most of his time reading. He asked for all his large stock of old Meccano and Scouting magazines to be brought from the attic at home, and he re-read the lot. He also secured a copy of the Automobile Association Handbook, and opimistically planned camping and cycling holidays for the future in various parts of the country, paying special attention to the appropriately lavish meals he would eat in each place. In addition, he read some more of Dickens and Stevenson, two of his favourite authors, and for the umpteenth time re-read *Three Men In A Boat*. He also read Whitaker's Almanack from cover to cover.

The last week or two in hospital brought an improvement in his diet. The milk and water could be supplemented by light solids. Immediately a former neighbour and close friend of his mother, Mrs. Gledhill, baked a sponge cake and delivered it to the hospital.

The Gledhills eventually retired to Blackpool. Many years later, when Harold was a member of the Government, he visited Blackpool, and on a sudden impulse looked up the Gledhills' address in the directory. Arriving unexpectedly on their doorstep he greeted Mrs. Gledhill with the tribute: "I'll never forget that sponge cake you baked for me. It was the finest thing I've ever tasted."

When Harold came home on January 2nd, 1931, it was Grandpa Wilson who summed up the whole family's relief and thankfulness when he observed to his son:

"Herbert, that lad's been spared for something."

For nine weeks his sole diet had been milk and water. After the three full months in hospital his weight, at the age of nearly fifteen, had gone down to just over 4½ stone. He was ravenous; and throughout the remainder of his boyhood, he used his period of near-starvation as a jocular justification for any apparent tendency to gorge.

"Don't forget I had nine weeks on milk and water," he would reply every time his mother commented on an over-hearty appetite.

He was faced with several months' convalescence at home, but the prospect of missing a further term at a crucial stage of his schooling hardly worried him at all. He left confident that by working on his own at home he could keep abreast, if not ahead. This proved to be so, with one important exception: when he returned to school after Easter, he discovered that he was badly behind in mathematics. His maths. teacher F. S. Wilmut, immediately made an offer. He would give him extra tuition after school every day, provided Wilson undertook to co-operate fully. Harold instantly accepted the proposition.

The offer was a relatively unusual one. It was, after all, impossible for teachers to give individual tuition after school hours to every boy who had fallen behind through absence. But Wilmut regarded young Wilson as a boy of exceptional promise. He admired his speed of thinking and his power of assimilation.

He also admired what he took to be a remarkable power of imagination. This arose in a curious way. Wilmut, besides teaching mathematics, edited *The Roydsian*. He had been impressed by Harold's contributions—especially his first, made shortly after he went to Royds Hall at the age of eleven:

### A Visit To An Australian Gold Mine

Few of my readers will have had the opportunity of inspecting an Australian gold mine, so the following may be of interest to some of them.

A few months ago, on a visit to Australia, I had the opportunity of visiting the Kalgoorlie Perseverance Gold Mine. When I arrived there I found about a dozen mines in Kalgoorlie and the neighbouring town of Boulder. The stretch of land where they are situated is known as the "golden mile."

First of all I visited the engine room where are the massive engines that work the Pit Head Gear. There were many interesting dials, one of which showed at which "station" the "cage" was.

I did not go down the mine, but contented myself with seeing the very interesting process of extracting the gold from the ore.

The first part of the process is the crushing up of the ore.

44

The stones are put through a sort of revolving drum, known as the "crusher." They are then about two inches long, so they are put in a "mill" where they are crushed, by means of heavy balls, to powder finer than flour. This powder is scattered about everywhere, and I got some on my boots and clothes, making me look very dirty indeed. After being put through a furnace the powder is taken to some huge vats, containing water and cyanide, when, after 18 hours continuous stirring, the gold takes a liquid form. The mud at the bottom is put through a filter press to remove all traces of gold. It is then put on trucks and carried to a "dump" or mound. Each mine has at least one of these "dumps."

The liquid gold is passed through some zinc shavings and then roasted in a furnace, from whence it comes out in solid gold.

It is very rare that gold is found in nuggets in Kalgoorlie, but it may be mentioned that a man who had made his fortune in Kalgoorlie when re-visiting it, picked up a large nugget which was worth many pounds.

J. H. Wilson, 1C

Wilmut noted the precocious phraseology, and marvelled over the highly imaginative contents. It never occurred to him that Harold had actually been to Australia—the idea of a young child from a Milnsbridge Council School having gone on such a trip would have been almost inconceivable. Years later he was much amused when, by chance, he discovered his misjudgment.

Wilmut came from a background of great poverty. His father, who had been to school for only one year in his life, was a cobbler in Bristol who brought up his family of nine sons and one daughter in a house built over a coal mine. Both parents often went without food themselves for the sake of their children. Of the ten, only five survived to adulthood.

At the time, Harold knew nothing of his teacher's early hardship and struggles—of how he had become a student teacher at the age of fifteen or how, when he was forty, the Headmaster of the school in Southampton where he taught had sacked him in front of his class because he had sympathised with the teachers' strike for better pay.

What Harold did recognise was Wilmut's dedication to his profession. And from his willingness to provide free extra tuition he learned a great deal about devotion to scholarship for its own sake—much more than Wilmut could ever have guessed at the time from his young pupil's characteristic reticence.

Fourteen years later the following letter reached the newly-elected M.P. for Ormskirk:

July 29, 1945                                           Huddersfield

Dear Harold Wilson,

The old schoolmaster hastens to write to you to offer you his sincerest congratulations upon your own personal brilliant victory!

It may be—it probably is—that with the passing of the years my memories of you are clearer than yours of me. But your achievements, subsequent to leaving Royds (in 1932 or 3?) have been no great surprise to me.

I most sincerely express the hope that this, your first political triumph, will be but a precursor of great triumphs to come. I am equally sincere in the hope that, whatever distinctions the future may bring you, you may never forget that the cause is greater than any individual adherent to the cause—which was what Ramsay M. forgot in his passing triumph.

I worked very hard for Mallalieu—speaking most nights in the three weeks that preceded the election. He tells me that he hopes to get into touch with you at Westminster. "Curly" is a fine fellow—and very sincere!

What exactly does the *News Chronicle* refer to when it mentions your "statistical digest of the coal industry?" Is it anything I can purchase from the publishers? I have read "Britain's Coal" with great interest.

Do you remember my son Jack (Bonzo!). He is a maths master at a school in Coventry. Edgar (now a staff sgt in R.E.M.E.) is, in civil life, manager of an optical department of the co-op at Mansfield.

I have been in retirement since Xmas 1942—but it is a very busy retirement.

Again, sincere congratulations!

Yours very sincerely,<br>F. S. Wilmut

P.S. Isn't it J. H. Wilson?

Were you in the school that morning in March 1931 when I brought A. V. Alexander to speak to the school? He was a boy in the first class I went into when I commenced to learn to teach. Do you remember that he said that perhaps in the Hall there was a future Cabinet Minister? Think it over! ! !

Back came the reply:

15th August, 1945

Dear Mr. Wilmut,

I do thank you most sincerely for your kind letter of congratulations and good wishes on my Election for Ormskirk. It was very nice indeed of you to write.

The idea that I had forgotten you or your connection with the movement is most fantastic. In fact when I ran into Miss Caruth for the first time 18 months ago I was asking her about you and she told me about everything at Royds and about your having left. I well remember too how after I had missed two terms in the Fourth Form with Typhoid you took me in hand after hours, coaching me in the work I had missed and pulling me up to third place. I remember also the time you brought my now very exalted colleague Alexander to the school.

Of course I know Mallalieu very well and he told me how much you had put in during his Campaign.

I well remember Jack and Edgar and have heard of Harold's (formerly my House Captain) work at Caterham. I wondered if he had left there as I see someone of his name as Secretary of the Fabian Society at Stratford.

Again all my thanks and very best wishes,

Yours very sincerely,<br>Harold Wilson

Yet another fourteen years later Wilmut happened to be staying in Mansfield at the time of a miners' rally. Although he was now in his late seventies, he joined the crowds lining the streets to watch the procession go by. To his great surprise, he saw at the head of it the former pupil who had eventually become President of the Board of Trade and who was now "Shadow Chancellor" of the Exchequer.

As the procession drew abreast, Harold spotted his old teacher standing on the kerb. Immediately he left his place at the head of the procession, and walked over to him. They had a chat about old times, and again exchanged recollections of Alexander's visit to Huddersfield.

Wilmut was greatly delighted by this evidence of affectionate loyalty from their old association. He was also again impressed by the accuracy and length of his former pupil's memory, and pleased by the impact Alexander's speech had obviously made nearly thirty years earlier.

A. V. Alexander (later Lord Alexander of Hillsborough) had been brought up by his mother, an impoverished widow. He had risen from the elementary council school where Wilmut was first a student teacher to become First Lord of the Admiralty. The pupils of Royds Hall gave him a rousing reception. "What a warm-hearted lot you have here," he commented afterwards to the Headmaster.

At the time Harold was fifteen, and was beginning to devote more and more well-informed attention to political issues. When the 1931 election was held he was in the fifth form, with more time allocated for private study during school hours. With a group of several others he held intense discussions about current issues—sometimes to the joint detriment of their proficiency in the standard subjects they were supposed to be studying.

He and several others were especially incensed by a Ministry of Education circular the following year concerning fees for schools. Hearing that the local M.P., E. L. Mallalieu, was to address a meeting to explain why the Liberals had pulled out of the National Government, Harold organised a delegation of schoolmates to be present. The guest speaker was Dingle Foot, then Liberal M.P. for Dundee, who fascinated his listeners by his observations on the financial crisis.

Afterwards questions were invited. Greatly excited, Harold and his friends sent up their question about the Ministry of Education circular. Neither Member of Parliament knew how to answer. It was left to their Headmaster, who was also present observing the proceedings with quizzical interest, to provide the kind of comment the boys had come to hear.

The growing awareness of contemporary issues, and their relation to basic ideals, was a constantly developing process. It was accelerated by the decision of Snowden to join Ramsay MacDonald's National Government. Locally this was greeted as a stark betrayal in the midst of a general disaster.

Snowden had had a devoutly loyal following all over his constituency. Now a wave of anger and grief surged throughout the Valley, as groups of lifelong radicals in the mills, in the streets, and in the shops stood commiserating with each other. Some men unashamedly wept when they first heard the news.

Harold's grandfather was one of them.


## CHAPTER EIGHT

Some of Harold Wilson's decisive political ambitions were maturing against a background of great anxiety in the family: there was continuous distress over a situation which was kept private within the family circle.

Even Harold himself was only just allowed to share the secret. Shortly after he came home from Meltham Isolation Hospital he awoke one morning and heard his parents whispering in bed:

"Shall we tell him?"

Later that day, the news was broken to him: his father had lost his job.

The blow had fallen a month earlier, at exactly the same time as the news came of Harold's recovery from the relapse. His employer, who had a reputation for autocratic decisions of the kind, had suddenly dismissed him with a month's salary, making some casual mention of "new arrangements" and "redundancy." Now the month was up, and at the age of forty-eight Herbert was suddenly without any income. The prospects were bleak. Openings for works chemists were far from numerous, especially when their experience lay chiefly in explosives and dyestuffs.

Harold was still too dazed after his long and serious illness to appreciate the significance of the situation. He instinctively understood one thing immediately, however: the need to keep the information entirely to himself. Not a whisper came from Harold to anyone—even Harold Ainley knew nothing of the disaster threatening his closest friend's family. In remaining silent, Harold was automatically reflecting the disciplined self-containment of his upbringing: this was exclusively a family matter, and must remain so.

There were additional reasons for the family remaining reticent about its breadwinner's misfortune—so reticent that for many months not even the Minister, Mr. Potter, knew anything of the difficulties surrounding this very active churchgoing household. Herbert was proud, and there was still in many lower middle-class circles the idea that to be out of work was a disgrace —the same kind of "disgrace" associated with a middle-class man who had failed in business.

Besides, large numbers of others were unemployed at the time. Although the West Riding suffered less unemployment than many other areas, there were some pockets of great hardship. Herbert did at least have something in the bank. For him to mention his difficulties might have seemed like grumbling about a situation which was far worse for many others.

The situation could certainly have been worse. His savings amounted to the equivalent of some months' ordinary salary. With provident management, he thought they could be stretched out for quite a lot longer if necessary. In the event, he was able to supplement them by occasional consultancy fees, and he also got casual work as an invigilator at the local county minor exams. But these few meagre earnings over many months added up to very little.

Harold first noticed the results of his father's position in small practical ways. Although his parents took good care to ensure that he had, as always, plenty of good food and enjoyable holidays, some economies had to be introduced right away. Worn-out clothing was more sparsely replaced, for example, and extras like the 4/6d. he wanted for a new sheath knife for Scouting were no longer available.

None of this disturbed him much. What did dismay him was the effect the enforced idleness had on his father. Nothing, of course, was said. But as time went on, Harold increasingly noticed his father's declining morale and ebbing self-confidence. He began to appreciate more deeply the things he had often heard and read about the suffering of people who could find no work, and who felt unwanted and useless.

The discovery affected him much more than he realised at the time. Often in the years ahead he used the plight of his father at this time as a point of reference in discussing the causes and effects of unemployment. Characteristically, he felt impelled later to distinguish between the lingering subjective distress over his own father's predicament, and his rational analysis of its implications.

This process of differentiation led him to regard this situation —and many other situations in the future—as intellectually outrageous rather than as emotionally shocking. Everyone directly or indirectly involved in unemployemnt found the situation personally distressing. Such personal feeling was (and is) just as inescapable to Harold as to everyone else. But to him the subjective was merely the initial reaction, the necessary starting-point. It was important, he believed, to proceed quickly to the next stage: an objective analysis of cause and effect—to appreciate, in fact, that his father and every other able and willing person denied the chance to contribute to the community was both the victim and the symptom of a disordered society.

This cultivated mechanism of jumping from the subjective to the objective has become very rapid with the passing years, and is now a faculty in its own right. It has certainly led to more misconstruction of Harold Wilson's motives and personality than any other characteristic he possesses. Time and again observers have deduced from it the absence of personal feeling or caring, understandably failing to recognise that to Wilson his personal feelings, no matter how strong, are almost irrelevant compared with the source of their inspiration. Thus it can seem that someone in difficulty or trouble, for example, who seeks his aid (and he never fails to try to help) becomes to him not so much a person in distress as a symptom of a problem to be solved—and, equally, as a challenge to his knowledge and ingenuity.

Herbert was unemployed for sixteen months. Then he found a job in Cheshire. Arrangements were made for the family to move to a house in the Wirral, and for Harold to be transferred to the grammar school there.

The family's relief over Herbert's new job was marred only by their concern lest Harold, now sixteen, would find the upheaval disturbing at an important stage of his schooling. Several of the Royds Hall teachers, however, thought he could benefit from the fresh incentives of a different school. They were sure he ought to secure a university education, but were afraid he might fail unless he worked harder.

By now, Harold's resolve to make his career in politics had become fixed, and was much more in tune with reality. He knew now that he could enter politics only through a carefully chosen pathway—perhaps through the civil service or foreign service; he had heard about them and various other careers at school. He was also seriously considering journalism as a possible route to Parliament. In any event, he was very keen to go to university, and had his sights trained firmly on Oxford.

Whatever his interim career might be, he realised that his hopes of eventually reaching the highest political ranks must depend on his first becoming an M.P. The day the family moved house in November 1932 found him thinking out the speech he would make at his adoption meeting as the Labour candidate for Huddersfield. His mother had asked him to buy some firelighters, and on his way to the store his imagination jumped quickly from the adoption meeting to the maiden speech he would make in the House.

It was all part of a dream world, and he was determined meanwhile not to have his parents or any other adults destroy it with the anxiety—or the ridicule—he instinctively knew he might incur. His father, for example, had become more than ever concerned with security since his own experience of unemployment, and would deprecate a political career with its inherent insecurity.

So he kept his day dreams strictly private nowadays—they were more exciting like that, anyway. And excitement was a big element in his plans. It seemed to him that a political career would enable him to lead the most adventurous life possible. But he also had constantly in mind his urge to help the community—the social conscience permanently implicit in his Scout promise "to help other people at all times."

Wirral Grammar School had opened only a year earlier. Apart from the Headmaster, all the staff were under thirty. They were dedicated to the task of making the new school a success. They took their latest pupil's abilities very seriously, and as time went on predicted great success for him.

Harold entered the first sixth form the school had had, and was the only one in it. This gave him the solid advantage of individual tuition—much of it in the school library. He was obliged to study Latin, and came under the influence of the classics master who was an accomplished athlete and great music lover; he was also an ardent socialist and Christian. He introduced Harold to serious newspapers, took him to Gilbert and Sullivan operas, took him to hear Norman Angell speaking in Birkenhead—and constantly argued about politics and religion.

Harold's character and thinking were influenced also by his other teachers—by his history master, for example, who was also his form master. He was studying for a London University M.A. and shared with his ever-interested pupil many of the advanced books he required for his own purposes. Like all the staff, he had a dynamic approach to his work, and never tired of challenging the assumptions his sixth form pupil had previously taken for granted. Although all the staff were Christians, Harold found the whole range of his religious and political thinking seriously questioned for the first time.

The circumstances could not have been more favourable for

serious scholarship, and Harold took every advantage of them. At the same time, he became even more gregarious than he had been at Royds Hall. He joined every society and club connected with the school. Where none existed, he created it himself—a debating society, for example. He took part in school plays, joined the school Scouts and became a Troop Leader, and took a very active part in athletics.

Running was the only form of sport at which he excelled. He had won occasional races in Huddersfield, but after the typhoid illness had had to abandon all sport for a while. Now he took up sprinting seriously, and put in a lot of hard training.

His build was right—very thin, long legs, and a natural long stride. He was also light (even at the age of 21 he still weighed less than 9½ stone). After winning a silver medal in his first cross-country run, he joined the Wirral Athletic Club, and captained their team in the Liverpool district championships. The team finished third and received a bronze medal from Sir Fred Marquis (later Lord Woolton).

Being the senior pupil, Harold became School Captain at the age of seventeen—the first to hold the office. The powers of leadership he demonstrated gained him the respect of the boys as well as the staff. He enjoyed testing his ability to exercise authority. At one stage he was concerned about what he regarded as unwholesome tendencies among some boys in the fifth form. With the approval of the Headmaster, he organised lunch-time soccer matches, believing the mischief resulted simply from idleness. The smuttiness evaporated, and if Harold's puritanical instincts were thus satisfied, so too was his mounting enthusiasm for organising others.

He figured prominently at the annual prizegiving—not only on account of the awards he himself received. The local press commented:

A novel feature was introduced by the report of the school captain, J. H. Wilson. The activities of the school, he said, were so rich and varied that no boy could fail to find a subject in which to interest himself. The house system had become a necessary part of school life and four houses were organised at the Wirral School. The house spirit was growing and there was keen rivalry between them. The system, however, meant much more than mere rivalry, for each house organised games for the benefit of its members. Among other activities, organised by the school throughout the year, was the summer camp in which 50 boys took part, and a successful Scout troop comprising 45 boys.

None of these activities ever induced him to relax his intense concentration on the main current objective: Oxford University. To everyone's delight, he was awarded a History Exhibition for Jesus College worth £60 a year. To everyone's disappointment, however, he did not gain a high enough mark in his final school exams to win a county major scholarship; this, he believed, was due to a poor effort in the English section—he regarded English as his weakest subject.

Without further substantial financial help, Oxford would be unattainable. Herbert and Ethel were determined that Harold should get to Oxford—however great the cost and the sacrifice. They would have reduced themselves to penury rather than see the golden opportunity lost.

The Headmaster sought a special county grant, but the Director of Education resisted. He argued that Harold was too young, and should try again in another year. The Headmaster persisted, however, and eventually it was agreed to award a county grant. From these two sources, he was only £50 short of his requirements.

Herbert gladly undertook to provide the balance. He had never looked forward so enthusiastically to parting with so much money.

## CHAPTER NINE

The principles of "first things first" which governed Harold's approach to life did not oblige him to ignore the attractions of the opposite sex, although his reticence usually inhibited him more than most of his schoolmates. He often discussed girl friends with his confidants, and was always willing to act as a go-between with messages, or help along a promising affair in some other manner. But when it came to his own interests, he seldom got round to declaring them directly to the girl of his fancy.

At Royds Hall, for example, he was at one stage especially attracted to a girl of the same age: she had an air of remoteness and detachment about her which fascinated him. This particular passion lasted for several years, and his closest associates knew all about it. Sometimes he felt unsure about how best to handle the situation, and occasionally sought senior counsel—from his sister, for example, or even from one of his teachers.

He was delighted when the apple of his eye joined the school Rambling Club (which he himself founded with the Headmaster's consent) but he had the utmost difficulty in bringing himself to declare to her even a fraction of the feelings he bore for her.

The most he felt able to do was to walk home from school with her closest girl friend. In that way, he felt, he was somehow brought nearer to his beloved.

As time went on, more and more people knew how Harold felt about this girl, and he was never short of advice about how to proceed. Not surprisingly, the girl herself knew clearly how he felt—but not as a result of anything Harold said to her himself.

With the move to Cheshire, his ardour cooled, and in time he lost touch with her altogether. His Wirral school had boys only, and his preoccupation with school affairs left small scope for meeting girls.

In the early summer of 1934, when his final school exams were nearly over, he decided one evening to go out for a stroll. He had been cramming Marlowe's *Dr. Faustus*, and felt so congested with verse that the need for a sharp relief suddenly overcame his concentration.

He wandered through nearby sports grounds and stood watching a game of tennis. The players looked about his own age, and he envied them their freedom. How pleasant, he thought, to be able to be carefree like them; how pleasant to spend evenings on the tennis courts, instead of swotting for exams.

He began to observe the players. His attention kept returning to one in particular—an exceptionally graceful and pretty girl. He felt captivated by her attractions. He heartily wished he could play tennis well.

In fact, he was an indifferent player. But by the end of that week he had joined the club. He quickly sought out the girl he had seen on the court. She immediately recognised the rather untidy boy who had been staring at her a few days earlier. Her name was Gladys Mary Baldwin, and Harold found her even more charming to meet than he believed possible. One thing only disconcerted him—her first name. But he discovered that she herself disliked it too, and much preferred to be known by her second name.

He soon discovered many other things about Mary—that she too was eighteen, that she worked as a secretary at nearby Port Sunlight, that she attended morning service at the same Church as Harold (who went in the evenings) and that her father was a Congregational Minister in Penrith. He walked back with her from the tennis club to her digs, and persuaded her to attend the evening service at church next day.

He walked home with her from church, too. He found her company increasingly congenial, and within a few days his mind was made up: this was the girl he was going to marry. He admired everything about her—her appearance, her personality, her background, and her independence in leaving home and earning her own living. He knew it would be years before he could afford to marry anyone, but there was no vestige of doubt in his mind that this was the girl who would one day be his wife.

Mary realised how seriously Harold was interested in her, and she liked him very much. She enjoyed his attentions, too, but they amused her as much as they pleased her. She was, after all, already supporting herself, and she felt much more mature and grown-up than boys of her own age. It was difficult to take seriously professions of lifelong love from a schoolboy, and a rather dishevelled-looking one at that.

She soon recognised, however, that this was no ordinary boy. He was exceptionally clever, and was held in very high regard at his school. She also found in him personal qualities none too common among other boys of her acquaintance: he was very affectionate, kind and gentle in his relations with her and with his own family, and unusually considerate.

She admired his powers of argument, and his ability to remain relaxed, no matter how heated the other participants in a discussion might become. It seemed impossible to rile him, and this slightly worried Mary at first; he was almost unnaturally even-tempered. But she began to realise that this personal detachment was a family characteristic.

The moment she met Harold's parents she understood him better. She also saw how happy they were as a family. Her own family always showed their affections very openly. By contrast, however, she found the Wilsons singularly self-contained and undemonstrative. Knowing the deep devotion between Harold and Marjorie, for example, she could not at first understand the casualness with which they greeted each other after an absence— a nod and a peck, it seemed, compared with the hearty kiss and warm embrace always accompanying her own family's greetings to each other. But she began to understand that the Wilsons made a point of keeping their personal feelings entirely private, and that the love binding them all very closely together depended not at all on any outward display of affections.

She felt more and more at home with her ambitious schoolboy friend, perhaps because in so many respects they were as dissimilar in interests and temperament as the artist and the intellectual. He was the rational, and she the romantic. She felt as ingenuous as he was purposive. He was gregarious, and she enjoyed solitude. Her delight was to read and write poetry, and his to argue politics.

He would often confide to her his plans for the future. He explained he would first have to get a good degree at Oxford, then find a secure job, and when he was about thirty, perhaps, he would be in a position to start on his main objective—a political career. She knew very little about politics—just enough to realise that his views accorded with her own family's traditional Nonconformist radical outlook.

She thought that in social status, as well as political outlook, their families were very similar. In the village where she spent her early childhood the social hierarchy was clearly defined: at

58

the pinnacle came the squire in the manor house, next the yeomen farmers, then the Church of England vicar—and finally the "chapel" folk with their minister, her father. Compared with an Anglican parson, a Congregational minister was of lowly status. Her father's occupation had determined the family's ranking: lower middle-class, just like the Wilsons.

Harold and she met as often as they could in the coming weeks, but agreed to say nothing meanwhile to their respective parents about their developing friendship. Herbert and Ethel, however, needed no telling. They quickly guessed how much Mary meant to Harold: there was no other explanation for his unwontedly long absences from home in the evenings. In any case, he never concealed where he had been. They encouraged him to bring Mary home after chapel on Sunday evenings, and the more they saw of her, the more they liked her.

Sometimes they felt a little anxious when they contemplated Harold's leaving home and going to Oxford. They never seriously doubted his family loyalty or his ability to adhere staunchly to the principles of his upbringing, but the fact remained that—apart from a few days at a time on camping holidays—he had never really been away from home on his own. Shortly he was going to be removed from the discipline of school, from the environment and influence of his home, and from the church and scouting activities of his boyhood. He would have more freedom than he had ever experienced, and the sophisticated atmosphere of Oxford University was known to produce new temptations. So they privately welcomed his friendship with Mary. They hoped it would flourish, and provide a valuable sheet anchor at home.

Mary's landlady took a kindly interest in her young lodger's activities. She too knew of the friendship with Harold, but was troubled when she discovered that Mary's parents knew nothing about it. She wrote privately to them, saying she thought they should know that their daughter was confining her attentions to one boy, and spending a great deal of time in his company.

Mr. and Mrs. Baldwin appreciated that their daughter was nearly grown-up, and were anxious to respect her sense of independence. They decided it would be wise, however, to find out for themselves exactly what was happening, and immediately made discreet arrangements for doing so without revealing their purpose.

The next letter Mary received from home contained the news that her father was shortly coming to preach locally, and that her mother would be coming with him. Mary, of course, attended the service, accompanied by Harold. Afterwards she introduced him to her parents. He was very shy, but they took to him immediately. In fact, they liked everything about him, and they were very impressed by his scholastic attainments.

Any incipient fears raised by the landlady's letter were stilled. Mr. and Mrs. Baldwin returned to their home in the Lake District greatly pleased by their daughter's choice of boy friend, and determined to say nothing to her about the original reason for their visit.

The weeks were passing, and soon Harold would be going up to Oxford. There could be no question of an engagement for a very long time. But in their circle there existed the valuable convention of the "regular" boy and girl friend. According to this, if a boy and girl were "going steady" it was taken to imply that neither would go out with anybody else of the opposite sex. The convention had to be strictly observed—any flouting of it would end the relationship.

There were going to be very long separations once Harold was in Oxford, and it might have seemed rash for two eighteen-year-olds to exclude themselves from any other associations during all the many months ahead. But when Harold went up to Oxford in October of 1934 there was no doubt about it: Mary and he had firmly agreed that they were going steady.


## CHAPTER TEN

Pre-war Oxford University had a multitude of excitements, and lacked the intense pressure towards success in exams which became such a marked feature of post-war university life. Many undergraduates had no money problems, and blatantly enjoyed their freedom to approach their studies and exams as lightly as they chose.

The so-called "smart set" shocked Harold. Many of them, he thought, were public school snobs, irresponsibly squandering their parents' resources, and occupying places which could have been better filled by boys who would have prized the supreme opportunities provided by the university. He felt outraged by their drinking habits, and horrified by all the waste of money.

He came across some of them at lectures. His own College life was much more to his own liking, with a solid tradition for hard work and good exam results. The majority of his contemporaries at Jesus came from social backgrounds similar to his own; he shared his rooms with the son of a Welsh plumber.

He spent his first week finding out about the routine and personalities of College life. It fascinated him, and he was exceedingly proud to be there. Yet within days he felt homesick. Everything was so new and different from all his past experience. He found the two weekly letters from Mary, and every scrap of news from home, a welcome reassurance; and already he began to feel glad about the visit his parents had promised to pay each term, bringing Mary with them.

As he observed the behaviour of some of his contemporaries, he thought he could see all too clearly the pitfalls of adolescent liberty. He decided to protect himself, and at the same time consolidate his own ambitions, by an almost fanatical application to work—to the exclusion of nearly everything else—and by a rigid attitude of thrift to the money at his disposal.

He carried frugality to such extremes that he arranged for his mother to send him a joint every week-end: he thought the charge of tenpence for a plate of beef from the College kitchen was too high. He also grudged the College laundry charges, so sent his weekly washing home. The joint and the clean washing were regularly despatched to him in the same parcel.

His attitude to study was no less puritanical. The feeling of privilege made him determined to justify his presence by outstanding academic achievements. He was conscious of his father's sacrifice in helping out, and he was anxious not to let his tutors feel he might in any way lack diligence. But above all, he kept reminding himself of the large numbers of other very able boys who were not enjoying his good fortune in being at Oxford.

As a token of his planned zeal, he made an arrangement with a like-minded undergraduate called Eric Sharpe, who had rooms below his in College. Sharpe (who eventually entered the Baptist ministry) was also a scholarship boy who came from the north of England, and who had the same kind of home background. They each bought a large Boots diary, and at the end of every day recorded the precise way in which every hour had been spent. The aim was to devote a minimum of eight hours daily to work. Next day they exchanged diaries and "marked" each other. A day on which over eight hours had been spent on work was encircled in red, and if ten were exceeded, a red and blue circle was the award.

The marking was done with a pencil which they had jointly purchased, and which could write in both red and blue: the blue appealed to Harold's journalistic ambitions—he had always understood that editors "blue-pencilled" censorable material, and fancied some practice in handling the appropriate implement. The one who had worked longest retained the pencil as a trophy for the duration of his supremacy. This competitive agreement provided a useful "pace-setting" incentive to both. The pencil was in Wilson's possession much more frequently than Sharpe's. On one occasion, however, Sharpe regained it with a handsome total of over eleven hours. Harold retaliated with a marathon effort of over twelve hours, and never had to part with it again.

By his second term, Harold had made an important alteration in his curriculum. He had gone to Jesus on a History Exhibition, but decided he would be wiser to change to Philosophy, Politics, and Economics. The College had to grant special permission for this change to be made.

He was meanwhile intent on securing as many official distinctions as possible. He entered for the Cecil Peace Prize, submitting an essay on the private manufacture of armaments. His entry was written more in the form of a declamatory sermon than a serious study, and brought him no success.

It was his only failure. In his second year he won the Gladstone Memorial Prize with an 18,000 word essay, supplemented by 400 footnotes, on 'The State and the Railways 1823-63.' The prize was awarded on Honorary Degree Day, when the successful entrant—clad in white tie and tails—had to read a page from his winning essay in the presence of Honorary Degree recipients: in Harold's case, Anthony Eden. Proud witnesses of this were Herbert and Ethel, who paid a special visit for the occasion.

In the course of his researches, sometimes conducted at Hawarden, Wilson had discovered that gladstone once devised a scheme for nationalising the railways. He also noted with interest that Gladstone had once been President of the Board of Trade. He developed a strong admiration for him.

He spent his next summer vacation preparing to enter for the Webb Medley Junior Economic Scholarship. This was awarded on the results of an exam, at the beginning of the October term. He did very badly in economic theory, well in economic history, and extremely well in economic organisation, which he based on his knowledge of the Colne Valley Co-op Movement. G. D. H. Cole later told his tutor that the brilliance of this section decided the examiners to award him the scholarship. It increased his resources by £100 a year, and this made him quite independent of his father. He opened his first bank account.

Cole warned Harold's tutor that his pupil's relative weakness in economic theory might jeopardise his chance of a good Honours Degree in his Finals. His doubts were soundly based. To Harold, economic theory seemed (and always has seemed) quite unreal—a mixture of absurdity and dishonesty. He neither understood nor believed in it. To him, economics must lie in practical reality or be meaningless. So he concentrated on the organisational aspects. *British Industries and their Organisation*, and *British Trade and Industry; Past and Present* were books he knew almost by heart. He made no attempt to study Marx because he thought it would be a pointless waste of time. This became a permanent conviction, although he has since read a little *about* Marx.

He was, of course, prejudiced against materialist thinking by his whole background and upbringing. This led to a strong antipathy to the outlook he found in the Labour Club. He had joined this with the highest hopes, but instead of finding the kind of radicalism he already knew, he believed their policy was largely Communist-dominated; worse still, that the Marxists in question were from public schools. He found the combination anathema. Later, he felt his attitude might have been intolerant and unfair. But at the time he rejected any notion that they could be either right or sincere, and left the Club.

Towards the end of his second year he joined the Liberal Club. He had first carefully enquired about its membership and outlook, and felt satisfied that its aims were genuinely progressive—almost semi-socialist, in fact. With the intention of converting it wholly to socialism he actively participated in its affairs, and even became an officer of the Club. But as time went on, he realised his original hopes were futile; so he ceased to take any further part in its affairs.

He allowed himself only one relaxation—athletics. During his first year he kept up his training, and in his second year ran four times for Oxford University before giving it up altogether. He made a brief appearance in the College Dramatic Society in a sketch, written by himself, which had a College background.

Otherwise, everything he did was related to his work, and to his resolve to get a good degree. He helped to found the College Debating Society, and became its first secretary. Lord Sankey came as guest of honour to its inaugural dinner, and the society was thus named the "Sankey Society." In his third year he became President of the Henry Vaughan Society; this had mainly a literary function, but he gave a lecture called: "The Last Depression—and the Next."

He also became President of the Meyricke Society, which was semi-philosophical. To the latter, he read a paper on the Two Nations—not the rich and the poor, but the north and the south. He felt he had a missionary responsibility to inform the ignorant south about where all the work was done. He was also President of the University Political and Economic Society.

There was one conspicuous gap in his undergraduate career. Although he joined the Union, he played virtually no part in its affairs. In retrospect, this seems an astonishing omission. He was, after all, already an experienced and skilled debater, and he had great confidence in his intellectual powers. But the thought of taking part in a Union debate made him acutely nervous. He feared, above all, that a supercilious *Isis* reviewer would tear his maiden speech to shreds (and perhaps also his north country accent). This would have wounded him and, he feared, might have driven him to the conclusion that he was less able than he liked to believe.

Yet he felt he must make at least one appearance. So he chose an end-of-term debate and made a brief contribution. Thus he ensured the impossibility of an unfavourable *Isis* review, because there was no issue published during the vacation.

Although derisory criticism of his speech had been his chief fear, he also regarded the Union politicians as "clever-clever" types with whom he had nothing in common. He has always retained this impression, and has consistently declined the many invitations he has received to speak at the Union since he became politically eminent.

Throughout his three years at Oxford he never missed Sunday worship. Sometimes he attended College Chapel services; at other times he went to the Congregational services at Mansfield College Chapel. Occasionally he was accompanied by a friend—his circle of close friends was limited to a few who, although serious-minded like himself, could not devote the relentless application to study he himself maintained. Sometimes they thought he led an over-regulated life, as if he feared that any minute departure from his highly disciplined routine would knock him completely out of gear.

The qualities his friends found most attractive in him were openness and sincerity. They found him exceptionally reserved, however, in matters of personal sentiment. All feelings of anger or hurt or even of affection were rigorously kept hidden.

Knowing his formidable intellectual abilities, and being un-aware of his private political ambitions, his friends assumed he would choose an academic career. He was content to let them believe this; in any case, there came to be some substance in it. As the time drew near for his Finals, he felt confidently hopeful of securing a good degree, and the idea of pursuing an academic career appealed to him more than other possible interim occupations, though he still occasionally toyed with the idea of journalism. But he never lost sight of his ultimate goal. Even during the closing stages of his intensive cramming he indulged in his favourite imaginings.

He had bought a gramophone for 39/6: and enjoyed the relaxation of playing it for a while each day after lunch. The music not only soothed—often it proved an inspiring background to daydreams of being adopted as Labour candidate for Huddersfield or for Colne Valley—to daydreams of eventually becoming Britain's Foreign Secretary, and so on.

There was the immediate future, however, to be planned. Before he sat his Finals, he applied for two university posts. One was a Lectureship at St. Andrews University, and the other a Lectureship at Christ Church College in Oxford. He was able to support his applications with outstanding testimonials from his tutors:

"From the outset," wrote one, "Mr. Wilson showed great promise. He is a man of considerable intellectual ability, a hard worker and well fitted to undertake research in economic subjects."

After listing his various awards, he continued:

"In Economic History and Political and Constitutional History he has displayed a great facility for dealing with the more difficult problems involved, critical insight and a clear grasp of general issues. He is, far and away, the ablest man I have taught so far, and, in my opinion, he will if given the chance, make his mark in whatever field of study he makes his own."

Another wrote:

"Since the Trinity Term 1936 J. H. Wilson has read his economics for Modern Greats with me. I find him a very pleasant

66

and entertaining person to know and to work with. There can be no doubt about his ability. On the economic history and institutions side of that school his work is extremely good: his economic theory is not so outstanding . . . He has shown many signs of being able to deal originally with material; plenty of common sense: he knows his own mind on a question; and his industry can only compel admiration. I have never felt more prepared to write for a man . . ."

Harold knew his parents would share his pride in these remarkable tributes. He wrote out copies and sent them home, closing his accompanying letter with the words:

"I am enclosing copies of the testimonials—which *please preserve* carefully, as I may want them.

> Love,
> Harold"

He faced the Finals with some understandable apprehension. All the zealous preparation of years was now to be put to the test, and the outcome was crucial for his whole future. His hopes for eight of the nine exam papers were reasonably high, his main fears being centred on the paper on his pet aversion—economic theory. When he came to do the paper on this particular subject, he experienced something like despair. Indeed, he nearly tore the paper up halfway through. He plodded on, however, and hoped for the best.

The day after his last exam he looked forward to some relaxation in the six weeks which were to elapse before the last stage of all—the oral examinations. But three letters reached him, all containing bad news. One was to say his Christ Church application had been rejected, and another that his St. Andrews application had likewise been unsuccessful. Both disappointed him, since they impeded his hopes for an academic career. But the third letter distressed and shocked him much more.

This came from Marjorie. It was to tell him that, once again, their father had lost his job. This news came as a cruel blow; the

67

prospects for an unemployed man of 54 with Herbert's specialised experience were extremely bleak. Harold decided he must
instantly find himself a job which would enable him to help
support his father and mother.

It was the last day of term, and he urgently sought out one of
his tutors, who happened to be the Oxford correspondent of the
*Manchester Guardian*. Armed with an introduction to the Editor,
Harold was offered a probationary job as a leader-writer on that
paper, starting after his oral exams.

This was a great relief. Now he knew for sure he would be in a
position to help his parents, and at the same time doing a job he
believed attractive and useful. There was a curious irony in the
prospect, however; each time he had casually mentioned his interest in journalism, his father had vigorously opposed it on the
grounds of its insecurity. Now, it seemed, a job in journalism was
to be the very means of providing security for the family as well
as himself.

Meanwhile, Harold still had some time before his orals. He had
acquired a portable typewriter with money he received from an
uncle for his twenty-first birthday. Using two fingers, he typed
applications for work for his father to firms all over the country.
Not one brought any hope of employment. Once again, he noted
with dismay the sense of humiliation his father was suffering in
silence.

Harold also felt he must do something to prepare himself for
his coming orals. He thought he had perhaps been rather vague in
one paper about Canning's views on Parliamentary reform, so he
went to the Liverpool Public Library and meticulously refreshed
his memory.

When he came before the examiners, the Chairman greeted
him with the observation: "Mr. Wilson, I've been asked by my
fellow-examiners to congratulate you on the uniform excellence
of your papers."

Harold was completely taken aback by the unusually fulsome
compliment. He felt almost tongue-tied with embarrassment, but
managed to convey a halting "thank-you." One examiner, he

heard afterwards, whispered to another: "Damned good thing this man's First doesn't depend on his orals."

Suddenly he found his tongue again. They were asking him to elaborate on Canning and Parliamentary reform. There was no holding him back after that.

Later, he was able to 'phone home with very important news. He had secured the top First Class Honours Degree of his year, and the best First award in Oxford for a long time.

Meanwhile there was another important development. He had been awarded the Webb Medley Senior Research Scholarship. This was worth £300 a year for two years, and would enable him to remain at Oxford—to pursue an academic career, in fact. Best of all, it involved working with Sir William Beveridge on problems of unemployment.

The Editor of the *Manchester Guardian* advised him to accept the Scholarship, and assured him a journalistic job would await him two years hence if he still wanted it. By that time, he pointed out, Harold would have become a real specialist in certain sociological matters, and would be employed accordingly.

Harold accepted the University post with delight. He had secured in his Finals seventeen alpha marks out of a possible total of eighteen: the one "miss" was a beta-double-plus.

He also discovered that for economic theory he had gained an alpha-plus.

# PART THREE

# The Temporary Bridge

## CHAPTER ELEVEN

All the family came to Oxford to see Harold receive his degree. Mary came with them. She had always so far been accompanied by one or both of Harold's parents on her visits to Oxford. Now, however, the days of chaperoning were at an end; though still not formally engaged, Harold and she had come of age. Henceforth she could come on her own whenever it was possible.

She had grown very fond of Oxford. Her delight over Harold's success was based partly on the assurance it evidently brought of an academic career. She enjoyed contemplating future married life in the gentle surroundings of Oxford—in a setting where intense political aspirations seemed remote.

Only one aspect slightly disconcerted her. When she attended College functions she felt an awkwardness at the sherry party which seemed inevitably to feature as a part of any proceedings. Temperance had formed an integral part of her upbringing. As time went on, however, she came to appreciate that a sherry party could be a useful and pleasant social occasion, and her embarrassment subsided.

For a young bachelor in 1937, £300 a year was a good income. After one term, Wilson was appointed to a part-time lectureship at New College, and thus became a don at the age of 21. This brought him an additional £125 a year plus dining rights in College. From this relatively affluent position he felt confident of being able to help his parents and at the same time save towards his own future.

His teaching duties were concerned mainly with economic history and organisation. He found these rather unsatisfying, and was thankful that they were part-time only. He felt he was not naturally a good teacher. For one thing, he easily grew impatient; for another he never quite knew how best to use the hour.

Some of his pupils were older than him. As a 21-year-old don responsible for teaching several as old as twenty-five, he tried to bridge the gap (and camouflage his self-consciousness) by growing a moustache.

By registering for the degree of Doctor of Philosophy on "Aspects of the Demand for Labour in Great Britain" he was able to do any relevant research to suit the interests of Beveridge and himself. Compared with his teaching, he found this aspect of his work constructive and rewarding.

Beveridge had been puzzled by certain features of unemployment: some prosperous areas, for example, had a high unfilled vacancy figure, and he wondered whether the problem of unemployment was one of transferring labour from, say, the north to the south.

Harold's first two terms were concerned with investigating unfilled vacancies at employment exchanges in prosperous areas where the unemployment rate was only about 2%. He spent a lot of time in the exchanges at Luton, Bedford, Swindon, Reading, Banbury, Northampton and Oxford. He meticulously examined all the unfilled-vacancy records from "behind the counter." By checking every unfilled vacancy to see how long it had remained unfilled, and why it had remained so, he came into close touch with the human situation as well as the statistics. He also learned for the first time how the clerical officer grade of the Civil Service functioned. In later years this knowledge was to prove useful.

He drew up a full interpretative report. This showed that there was something artificial about the unemployment figures. When there was a boom, the unfilled-vacancies figure certainly increased. This did not necessarily mean, however, that a large unsatisfied demand for labour existed. Many jobs might remain on the books of the exchanges even if they were filled at the works gates. But if the actual figures were apt to be misleading, the trends were certainly significant. His findings were accepted by Beveridge, who later incorporated them in his book on unemployment.

By his third term Wilson, at Beveridge's wish, had turned his attention to cyclical variations in unemployment. By taking the full unemployment figures for every one of a hundred different industries over a period of nine years, Beveridge had discovered regular seasonal variations in certain industries. He also discovered a key turning-point: the British unemployment rate always seemed to move first in the export industries—both a recovery and worsening occurred initially in those. Furthermore, the changes seemed always to occur at the same time of year—the autumn.

This encouraged Beveridge to revert to the theory of sunspots —to believe that the conjunction of export industries with autumnal fluctuations must have some connection with harvests. Wilson treated this as a suspect hunch, and hotly disputed it. Later, when Beveridge had to stay in hospital for many weeks with a serious infection, Wilson was left to conduct his own researches.

He devised a complete correlation of all the principal exports and imports in terms of prices and quantities. This demonstrated that the slump occurred because of a connection between the fluctuating ability of other countries—due to a slump in raw materials or food prices—to purchase goods of ours, such as cotton or machinery, and their fairly constant sales to us of food and raw materials. Once again, Beveridge accepted this as a viable theory.

In the summer of 1938, while events abroad were moving towards the crisis which had its outcome in Munich, Harold and Mary became officially engaged. There was no question of an early marriage, however. Harold was still building up his savings, and there was no sign yet of work for his father, so substantial financial help to his parents remained a regular commitment. Even when Herbert did find a job at the end of 1938 Harold had to continue helping for a while: for some months his father's starting salary as works chemist at a small factory in Cornwall manufacturing blasting powder was only £3 a week and was insufficient for the basic needs of Ethel and himself.

Meanwhile, Harold did allow himself one luxury: he bought a car. An elderly Austin 7 model named Eustace, it did good service. He used it for occasional journeys home from Oxford to Cheshire, and for driving Mary around on her trips to Oxford. Once he even motored her as far afield as Sussex to visit her old school.

Eustace had cost £11. The following year he was sold for £3 15/0 and replaced by a superior seven-year-old Wolseley which cost £25.

Just after the Munich crisis Wilson was appointed a Fellow of University College, and took up residence there in rooms next to John Maud (who eventually, as Sir John Maud, became Master of the College). The new appointment obliged him to relinquish the Webb Medley Scholarship and the New College part-time Lectureship, but he became even better off financially. The fellowship was worth £400 a year plus free rooms and food in College. In addition, Jesus College started sending him pupils for tutorials, and paid a capitation fee of 15/ - an hour.

With this new appointment, Wilson found himself in demand for the discussion group which Beveridge, as Master of the College attended these, Rhodes Scholars among them. Two of the latter eventually became leading members of the U. S. Administration. Wilson sometimes read a paper as well as helping with the discussion.

He also attended G. D. H. Cole's influential discussion groups on politics. Cole, who was a University Reader, was finding it difficult to cope with the increasing number of economists requiring teaching, and Harold's Fellowship was awarded partly to enable Cole to secure his assistance. Politically, Wilson was increasingly influenced by Cole's outlook. He co-operated with him not only academically, but also with some writing for the Fabian Society. The Fabians and the Student Christian Movement were the only two extra-mural organisations to win Wilson's serious attention at this time.

There was, in fact, little scope for anything but work. Beveridge saw to that, and Wilson was his most willing accomplice. He had thought himself unusually industrious in his undergraduate days, but now, he felt, he was beginning to understand what hard work really meant. From before breakfast until late at night

74

every day he applied himself unremittingly to the highly complicated statistical problems of unemployment, slumps, booms, poverty, and prosperity. He even spent his summer vacations at
Beveridge's country cottage in Wiltshire where they worked
with still more intense application than during term.

Towards the end of the summer in 1939 he took time off to go
north to Dundee. There, at the exceptionally young age of 23, he
read a paper on unemployment and industrial problems to the
annual meeting of the British Association.

In the middle of his lecture a note was brought in to the
chairman. It contained a grim item of news. Hitler had invaded
Poland.

## CHAPTER TWELVE

Harold sped south, but made an important stop en route at the
home of his future in-laws. Mary had just given up her job and
had gone to live at home—the intention being she should spend
six months with her parents, learning more about housework,
before getting married the following spring.

Now, however, war was imminent and inevitable. Nobody
knew what would happen, but it was widely expected that all
young men would immediately be called up. The bloodshed of
another possible Flanders, and the slaughter of likely mass bombing at home, filled the imaginings of many a household.

To a young engaged couple, the future seemed cruelly uncertain. No one could foretell the long separations there might have
to be, let alone the delay imposed by harsh circumstances on
plans for marriage and setting up home.

There seemed only one sensible thing to do: to ensure that
meanwhile they were together as much as possible, and not unnecessarily separated by great distances. This must mean Mary
returning to Oxford with Harold.

The prospect upset her parents, who had been looking forward
to having her at home for a while. But they recognised the di-

lemma of the situation, and sympathised with its victims. Mary went back with Harold to Oxford.

She found digs over a café in the old part of Oxford, and got a job right away with the Potato Marketing Board. Harold immediately registered with the Joint Recruiting Board and expected his call-up papers to follow at any time. Meanwhile he became a temporary employee of the Potato Control Section of the Ministry of Food. Everything was in flux, and chaos from mass bombing was anticipated: emergency plans had to be made for the distribution of food in such an event.

A month passed with no bombing and no chaos. Harold returned to College—by now a rather depleted and disorganised College—and resumed his teaching and research for the remainder of the term, still expecting to be called up at any time, and making plans with Mary for an early wedding.

They chose a day they hoped would be particularly auspicious: the first of January, 1940—a Monday, as it happened, and therefore the start of the week, as well as the first day of the month, the year, and the decade.

The wedding took place in Mansfield College Chapel. Mary's father assisted at the ceremony, and her brother gave her away. Many of the fifty guests were University friends. The organist, a family friend, refused to play "Here Comes the Bride," insisting on "Gaudeamus Igitur" instead. He compromised, however, with Mendelssohn's "Wedding March" coming out of the church.

It was a day of thick fog, and the bride and bridegroom were suffering from heavy colds. After the reception they thankfully escaped to the small hotel in the Cotswolds which they had chosen as their honeymoon retreat. There they spent their days walking in the snow, and nursing their colds before a large log fire.

After a week a telegram arrived. It was from Beveridge. Honeymoons were all very well, he implied, but there was urgent University work waiting to be completed. Harold and Mary returned to Oxford.

A few weeks later he was invited to an interview in London in connection with a possible job at the Ministry of Supply. The

Director of Statistics there confronted him with what was clearly intended to be a test question: had he seen the article in that week's *Economist* about mobilisation of the war's economy?

Wilson assured him he had.

"In that case," continued the Director, "imagine you worked in my Department, and that the Minister called for a brief on this question. How would you provide a concise and easily intelligible summary to suit the purpose—using that article as your basis?"

Wilson gave his answer so fluently and rapidly that the Director looked bewildered.

After a pause, Wilson smilingly added: "I must confess that I myself wrote that article in the *Economist*."

Far from feeling in any way cheated, the Director was doubly impressed. He immediately engaged Harold, and Mary and he moved from Oxford to London. After occupying temporary rooms in Earl's Court and Pimlico, they moved to a rented flat in Twickenham by the river.

The day after he started work at the Ministry of Supply, Wilson had a 'phone call from John Maud, by now holding a senior position at the Ministry of Food. He invited Wilson to join him. The work sounded more interesting, and the position in question was on a higher grade. Wilson readily assented.

He heard no more about it. Two months later he lunched with Maud, and asked him what had gone wrong.

"Oh," said Maud, "it was blocked by the Ministry of Supply people: they said you didn't want to move."

The war-time control over employment was rigidly applied within the Civil Service. Nevertheless Wilson was astonished. Nobody at the Ministry had consulted him, and this obviously unfair method of retaining his services angered him. In any case, his present job was turning out to be disappointing, and he was even more anxious now for a change.

One evening he was invited out to dinner by three members of the Cabinet Secretariat. Two of them had met him at the British Association, and the third had heard of him through Beveridge. They explained they were building up their staff, and he accepted their invitation to join it.

77

He was meanwhile appointed Joint Secretary of the Anglo-French Co-ordinating Committee. France was by this time beginning to collapse. Weekly reports—and soon daily reports—were required on available supply routes as port after port was knocked out.

After the collapse of France, he was employed on manpower statistics. The Cabinet established a Committee to calculate the whole requirements of manpower in detail. Beveridge, who had been brought in as a part-time adviser on manpower problems to the Ministry of Labour, was appointed Chairman of this committee, and Wilson became its joint secretary. Five months later Beveridge was appointed an Under-Secretary at the Ministry of Labour and invited Wilson to join him there. He did so, and left the Cabinet Secretariat having meanwhile acquired experience of its machinery which was to be of great value in the future.

At the Ministry of Labour he was made Head of the Manpower, Statistics, and Intelligence Branch. Several months later, the Cabinet appointed a Committee to investigate the many rumours (and some direct public accusations) of foolish wastage of skilled men in the Services. Beveridge was made chairman, and Wilson joint secretary. Together they travelled round all the main service establishments, and conferred regularly with the leading Service representatives on their committee. Their eventual findings highly commended the Admiralty, mainly exonerated the Air Ministry, and severely criticised the Army.

By this time the German bomber raids on London had abated. For a while Mary had gone to stay with Herbert and Ethel in Cornwall, and afterwards had evacuated to Oxford, where she had a room in the house of the chemistry don at Jesus College. Harold's department in the Cabinet Secretariat had a hideout in Oxford ready for continuous use if London became impossible. He was able to work there for long week-ends, and during the week worked in the London Cabinet Offices, sleeping in a deep shelter at night.

Now, however, Mary had rejoined Harold. They rented another flat in Richmond, and Mary devoted herself once more to keeping a comfortable home for her hard-working husband. This she has always regarded as her real responsibility, rather than attempting to enter into the daily happenings of his high-powered professional responsibilities. Work and home have always been preserved as distinct spheres.

In the summer of 1941 the threat of a coal crisis was beginning to loom. Coal was the responsibility of the Mines Department—a semi-autonomous Department nominally under the Board of Trade, where Sir Andrew Duncan had just become President with the express injunction from the Cabinet to keep a special watch on coal. The Department urgently needed strengthening on its statistical side, and senior officials approached Harold to invite him to head this branch.

By now his work at the Ministry of Labour was becoming less interesting, and Beveridge was beginning to withdraw. This new opportunity seemed challenging, and at the same time offered promotion. He transferred in August 1941, and found himself working alongside John Fulton, whom he already knew well as a distinguished Oxford don (and who, in 1959, became Vice-Chancellor of the University of Sussex).

Sir Andrew Duncan had the difficult task of running the Mines Department from outside. He held a weekly meeting of senior officials, and relied on Fulton and Wilson as his constant eyes and ears from within. This was Wilson's first experience of working directly with a Minister. He formed a very high regard for Duncan, and admired his controlling grip. He began to appreciate the importance of Ministerial authority and ability. He could see that under a man of Duncan's capacity the most able senior officials automatically and steadily gave of their best, while the less able produced far better results than under a less effective Minister.

His own first main task was to build up rapidly a statistical machine where virtually none had existed. The quality and speed of statistics were so drastically improved that it was soon possible to collate the exact and comprehensive coal output figures for the previous week each Monday afternoon by 3 o'clock.

His next main task was to investigate the manpower problem. He unearthed causes of the loss and wastage of men, and this led to changes in recruitment, release of men from the services, and eventually the "Bevin Boy" scheme of working in the mines as a form of national service.

According to the mine owners, the coal crisis was due to absenteeism and to a fall in output per shift. The figures certainly showed that absenteeism had increased, but on investigating them closely Wilson discovered that this increase had dated precisely from the time when the working week had been increased from five to six days. This had led not only to more absence, but also to an increased *proportion* of absenteeism.

The number of shifts worked per man, however, had actually gone up. The fall in production was not (as mine owners had been arguing) due to lack of effort, but was due to the loss of men from the coal face. The fall of France, and the loss of manpower to the Services, had seriously depleted the mines. Each pit required a minimum number of men to be engaged on essential tasks such as haulage, safety, and winding, so the coal face itself always had to yield its workers first. By collating and analysing all the figures, Wilson discovered that although the *percentage* of shifts worked at the coal face had decreased, the *output* per shift had actually gone up.

Duncan accepted these findings with great interest. At last, he felt, he had a conclusive answer to give to the mine owners who kept complaining about indifference and laziness on the part of the miners. Lord Aberconway was one. At Duncan's request, Wilson spent all Boxing Day of 1941 collating and analysing the figures for each of Aberconway's pits. The following day Duncan met Aberconway and confronted him with the inescapable facts.

In the spring of 1942 Dalton became President of the Board of Trade, and was made Chairman of the Coal Production Council, which Wilson had been servicing with figures for some time, and to which he submitted a full-length paper on the problem of absenteeism and of output per shift. This, in effect the first definitive study, was called "Absenteeism and Productivity." It was the first occasion when the word "Productivity" had appeared in an official document. It was later picked up by the Ministry of Production, and shortly became common currency.

The next crisis arose over wages. Dalton agreed with Ernest Bevin, Minister of Labour, to appoint the highest-level possible Board of Enquiry, under the chairmanship of Lord Greene, to investigate the whole problem. Two secretaries were appointed. One of them was Wilson, chosen by Dalton at the suggestion of his Personal Assistant—Hugh Gaitskell.

Wilson had foreseen a serious problem arising over wages, and on his own initiative had been collecting wage slips from mines all over the country. He already had a comprehensive view of the wages position, and was well equipped to commence the formidable task of learning in a few days the entire wages ascertainment system in order to brief Lord Greene on it.

Action was urgently required to avert a serious crisis. The miners were asking for an extra 4/- per shift, and for the reestablishment of a national minimum wage, which had been abandoned in 1926.

Wilson, who was responsible to Greene as Chairman, was also responsible to his Ministry: he had to represent the Ministry view to Greene, and Greene's view to the Ministry. He felt as if he were playing both ends off against the middle—in the last resort, he pursued the policy which he himself thought best either way.

Greene took him out to lunch to find his views, and started off by saying:

"I understand there's no scientific basis for assessing the appropriate increase in miners' wages. They've asked for four bob— they don't really expect four bob, do they?"

"No," replied Wilson, "of course they don't."

"Well," said Greene, "suppose we give them two bob?"

"I suggest you don't," said Wilson. "It would look as if you'd simply halved their demand. Then they'd wish they'd asked for eight bob so as to get four. Since there's no scientifically correct figure, rather give them 2/3d. or 1/9d. than two bob. But much better to be generous. Why not give them a good boost, and make it half-a-crown?"

"Right," said Greene, "we'll do that." "By the way," he added, "they're not expecting that we'll concede the national minimum, are they?"

"No," said Wilson, "they're not."

"So we can leave that one safely," commented Greene.

"With respect, Lord Greene, I suggest you give it," countered Wilson, "because this was what 1926 was about. This would show the miners that the nation is behind them."

Greene looked troubled. "But what figure could it be?" he asked. "If it's too high, it will simply create fresh problems of differentials."

Wilson explained he had been gathering a representative selection of pay slips, and had worked out figures for a national minimum—78/- for surface workers, and 83/- for underground workers. He pointed out that these were low figures—only 1½% the industry earned less—so they would cause no problems of differentials.

Greene accepted them.

Then Wilson, remembering he was a Civil Servant, added:

"I think I should point out that a national minimum could lead to strains and stresses between different districts, and would certainly mean that in peace time the system of levies and subsidies under the Coal Charges Order would have to be continued—or else replaced by some system unifying the finances of the whole industry."

"I have no doubt whatsoever what it means," replied Greene. "It means the nationalisation of the whole coal mining industry—but I'm not afraid of that!"

The report was duly completed and signed.

Fulton and Wilson, meanwhile, drafted the setting up of a Coal Board and planned the whole regional organisation to take over operational control of the mines.

While the Greene Board had been sitting, the Ministry of Fuel and Power was created. Dalton ceased to be the Minister responsible for mines, and Gwilym Lloyd George (later Lord Tenby) was appointed Minister. Wilson, armed with the Greene report, went to meet Lloyd George in his West End hotel, and, for the first time, met Ernest Bevin.

Lloyd George began to rely more and more on Wilson—for help with his speeches and, above all, for facts and figures. The statistics on wages and distribution became the most detailed and exhaustive ever secured: the source, destination, grade, type and transport used for virtually every ton of coal was known and charted. He appointed Wilson Director of Economics and Statistics at a salary of £1,150 a year and with a staff of 350, and moved his office across the road to be nearer his own. He issued instructions that there must be no intermediate interference from senior Civil Servants: Wilson was to report direct to him.

In 1943 Wilson became involved in the plans for the Second Front. He joined a number of secret War Office committees concerned with the prospective supply requirements of particular areas—first Italy, then France. It was necessary to formulate as precise assumptions as possible about the speed of the invasion, and about how much coal would have to be moved in.

In the winter of 1943 there emerged the special problem of building up the coal stocks of all the consuming points on the south coast. This was complicated by the secret plans to create a decoy—the large number of ships kept in Dover harbour, for example, to encourage the Germans to believe that the invasion would come from that side.

During this time many disagreements arose with the Americans about the amount of coal required, and who should be responsible for providing it. A Joint Committee had been set up: the Combined Production Resources Board and Combined Raw Materials Board. Wilson became Secretary of the British Committee of this comprehensive machinery which, not surprisingly, was invariably referred to by its initials only.

At one stage the British and American figures got so seriously out of gear that Wilson was despatched to Washington to try to sort everything out. It was his first visit to America. He spent two weeks conferring individually with representatives of all the many relevant departments and finally reached a satisfactory agreement.

Just as he was about to fly back to London, yet another American department suddenly claimed that their authority was required before the agreement could finally be concluded. They withheld the authority—and repudiated the terms already agreed.

Wilson cancelled his return flight, and insisted on calling a combined meeting to be attended by everybody concerned—including the official responsible for the repudiation. When the latter entered the room, Wilson immediately recognised him as a former Rhodes Scholar who had been one of his own pupils at Oxford. They left the meeting together, and a short while later returned with the news that the agreement had been amicably and satisfactorily concluded.

Early in 1944 preparations for the Second Front were becoming more intense. There was now so much knowledge available about the coal industry that the security authorities were consulted, and raised no objection to most of the information becoming publicly available. Only a few items had to be excluded.

A Parliamentary Debate was due shortly, and the Digest was going to make its appearance in time for this. At the last minute, however, the premises where it was due to be printed were bombed. The whole type had to be re-set. With a team of assistants, Wilson rushed to alternative printing works in Harrow. They stayed up all night proof-reading until 9 a.m., when despatch riders collected the first batch and distributed them to the mining M.P.s and other interested parties—in time for the Debate.

The publication of the Digest delighted Wilson. Not only did it make available to the public for the first time the essential story about coal, but it also contained a mass of information required by him for a future purpose of his own—the writing of a book about the coal industry. He had already started work on it, but was not intending to complete it while still in the Civil Service.

Months later, when he had returned to Oxford, he realised that the Digest lacked certain basic information about the industry which he himself knew, but which had still not been made public. He was anxious to incorporate it in his book, but could not do so without committing a serious infringement of the Official Secrets Act.

Yet he was convinced that by now the need for security no longer applied to this particular information. The problem, however, was how to get the information published officially so as to be free to use it himself—without going through the lengthy processes of privately seeking permission from the security authorities and other official channels.

He approached an M.P. friend and asked him to put down a question for the Minister in the House, worded in such a way as to extract the information he wanted to use. The friend agreed, and suggested Wilson should draft the question himself. This he did.

He knew exactly what would happen afterwards—the question would be passed to Ministry officials who would prepare the appropriate answer for the Minister to give in the House.

He called in at his old office in the Ministry, and found several of his former assistants puzzling over a Parliamentary question which had just reached them.

"You might be able to unravel it," they said, handing it to him.

Casually he glanced at it, silently noting how clumsily he had worded the draft for his friend. Then he proceeded to explain what he thought the M.P.'s question must mean. Finally, he offered to suggest the wording for the Parliamentary answer.

His offer was accepted verbatim.

Thus he secured the publication of the information, and was able to incorporate it is his book, published shortly afterwards. Called *New Deal For Coal*, it helped to provide the basis for the Labour Government's subsequent nationalisation of the mines.


## CHAPTER THIRTEEN

There were few white feathers distributed during the Second World War. Cowardice was not automatically ascribed to a man who happened not to be wearing uniform. Compared with World War I there was a far wider public appreciation of the need to retain key civilians in vital posts.

In common with most other dons temporarily drafted into the Civil Service, Wilson suffered no qualms about not being in the fighting forces. Occasionally, unpleasant suggestions appeared in the press about "bureaucrats" avoiding military service. Each time these reached appreciable proportions, Churchill dismissed them completely, emphasising the supreme importance of the work being done by civilians in key positions. Wilson was fully content with such an authoritative verdict, and has remained so. Far from feeling any regrets over not being in the services, he felt proud of the work he was doing.

Besides, there were occasions when civilians, especially in London, were exposed to just as great dangers as the men in the forces. Wilson himself had two very close escapes. Once, while at the Ministry of Labour, a bomb destroyed much of the premises, including the room next to the one where he was sleeping at the time. On another occasion a direct hit on Board of Trade premises destroyed part of the neighbouring Ministry of Fuel building where he was firewatching.

Such experiences left him unperturbed. He was concerned, however, about Mary's safety and welfare. For years she was an A.R.P. shelter warden in Richmond, regularly conducting tours of inspection at midnight, donning her tin hat and rushing to unlock the shelter and usher people in to safety.

Her first child, Robin, was born in December 1943. Like many others, she found the suspense caused by "buzz-bombs" more nerve-racking than previous types of bombing. To the mother of a small baby, the effects could be terrifying. Mary found the strain increasing; it was difficult to relax enough even to read a book. Often she sat by the window, trying to occupy her mind with a jig-saw puzzle—ready to climb protectively over her baby in his cot the instant she heard another bomb approaching.

Harold urged her to evacuate, and she took Robin to Duxford in Cambridgeshire where her parents had by now gone to live. Harold joined her there as often as the slow train journey allowed. The return journey meant leaving Duxford at 6 o'clock in the morning in order to reach Liverpool Street Station by 9 o'clock: he passed the time working on his forthcoming book. On alternate nights he slept at the Ministry.

In a practical sense, fatherhood meant less to Harold than to many husbands. He was proud to have a child, but the mechanics of babyhood—the attention and practical caring—remained exclusively Mary's responsibility. When Robin became old enough to be recognised as a distinct personality with a mind of his own, fatherhood became much more meaningful.

The feverish nature of his Civil Service responsibilities allowed Wilson few opportunities for relaxation. Whenever possible he enjoyed some respite in Cornwall with his parents. He was there during the Whit week holiday of 1943 when a letter arrived from Dr. W. A. Robson of London University. Before the war, they had collaborated on a book for the Fabians under the editorship of Michael Stewart.

Now he was writing to ask whether Wilson would be willing to be nominated for the Fabian Society Executive Committee. The ordinary election processes had been suspended for the duration of the war, and the committee consisted partly of members co-opted in this way. Wilson unhesitatingly accepted the invitation, much to his father's satisfaction.

At this stage of the war, he was much too occupied with the work on hand to give any serious thought to the exact course of his future career. He knew, of course, that his College expected him to return, and that all kinds of rich academic plums might lie within his future reach. He also knew, as time went on, that if he chose to remain permanently in the Civil Service he had only to say so: he was assured of a welcome and a senior starting rank on the established staff.

In some ways this appealed to him. He felt he would be gaining additional valuable experience for his own ultimate usee. He had now observed at first hand the varying effectiveness of several quite different senior Ministers, and knew that for good government the real authority and power emanated not from the Ministry but always from the Minister. He was still only in his twenties. If he remained in the Civil Service and had a strong Minister over him, he believed it would develop his own capacity. And eventually, he hoped, he would become a strong Minister himself—perhaps in another twenty or thirty years.

Sometimes direct suggestions came from altogether different quarters. Sir Andrew Duncan, for example, told him of the rich rewards which he could be sure of having if he cared to join the

Iron and Steel Federation. Mining and other industrialists also approached him from time to time about the very lucrative openings they would be glad to provide to secure his experience and skill. He never gave a moment's thought to any of them.

In December 1943 he got in touch with Beveridge, who was still Master of the College, from which he was on leave of absence, and asked for a meeting. He was anxious to confer with him about an important development concerning his post-war plans, and they met for lunch.

Wilson explained that he had been asked to allow his name to go on the Transport House list of potential Parliamentary candidates to be circulated to constituency parties. The proposed nomination came from John Parker, General Secretary of the Fabian Society, and Tom Smith, a miner who was Parliamentary Secretary to the Ministry of Fuel and Power. Transport House was still in its wartime low gear, but a gradual start was being made in building up lists of possible candidates in readiness for a General Election at an unknown future date.

Although at a much later stage Beveridge stood successfully as a Liberal candidate, he was at this time toying with the idea of becoming Labour candidate for London University, and was in touch with Herbert Morrison about it. He knew enough at first hand about Wilson's abilities to recognise the validity of his aspirations, and he gave him his unqualified approval.

By late spring of 1944 Wilson began to receive letters about possible nominations for a number of constituencies. He first accepted nomination for Peterborough, and attended a selection conference there. The choice fell on a local man who was subsequently disendorsed by the National Executive.

Wilson, who had been runner-up, was then invited to meet the selection committee again to be formally confirmed as their choice. By this time, however, he was on the short list of candidates for Elland, Sowerby Bridge, Darlington, and Grimsby—all held by the Conservatives, but all possible Labour wins in a future election. He was also on the short list for Ormskirk, which had been won at a by-election in 1939 by Stephen King-Hall as an Independent National.

The selection conferences for Darlington and Ormskirk turned out to be on the same day, and this faced him with a difficult choice. His first inclination was to opt for Darlington, but he received a strong request from Ormskirk to go there—coupled with a broad hint that if he did so his chances of being selected would be especially favourable. He consulted Transport House, and learned that there was already a favourite candidate on the Darlington short list. He decided to go to Ormskirk.

The night before he went, officials from the Edmonton Labour Party came to see him. This was already a safe Labour seat, but there were local quarrels and they wanted to secure a new candidate from outside. Could they possibly persuade him?

It was tempting, because he knew it would guarantee him a seat, and one with the great advantage of being conveniently near Westminster. But he explained his commitment for the following day, mentioning also that the day after that he was due to attend a selection conference in Grimsby.

The Ormskirk selection committee chose him and he accepted. He sent a telegram withdrawing from Grimsby, but received yet another deputation from Edmonton, asking him to delay formal acceptance of Ormskirk and attend a selection meeting at Edmonton: it would be a mere formality, because he was certain to be chosen officially.

It was too late. He had accepted Ormskirk, and that was where he was to fight his first campaign.

The constituency, which was in a mainly agricultural area, was very scattered, comprising 37,000 voters within the Liverpool boundary, and stretching as far as the coast south of Southport and almost to the boundaries of Preston. It was clearly going to require a lot of attention. In any case, a Civil Service rule prevented staff from becoming candidates. He therefore resigned from the Ministry.

On his last day in the Civil Service, a friendly reference appeared in the Peterborough column of the *Daily Telegraph*. Mentioning his departure to become a Labour candidate, it said that friends predicted an outstanding political career for him, and saw

89

in him a future President of the Board of Trade—or Chancellor of the Exchequer.

On returning to University College, he found it far from full. He did, however, have some pupils. He was appointed Domestic Bursar, and thus became responsible for the catering finances of the College. He also completed his book on coal, prepared a report on the finances of nationalisation for the Railway Clerks' Association (which became the basis of their subsequent case for nationalisation) and lectured for the Admiralty, at their Black-heath centre, to officers who had returned from the Far East and were out of touch with current affairs.

This latter commitment made it desirable to retain the Rich-mond flat, where Mary and Robin were again living. But in Easter of 1945 they all resumed full residence in Oxford, and nobody could have been more pleased than Mary.

Throughout the war, she had looked forward longingly to the time when a return to the Oxford way of life would be possible. Now she felt she could count on its quiet seclusion for several years at least. True, Harold was standing for Parliament, but she found it difficult to take his chances very seriously. Everyone seemed to expect that the General Election, when it came, would result in a Conservative victory, and presumably this meant that Harold would continue with his academic career in Oxford. He might, of course, stand again at the next General Election some years hence, but she felt exceedingly content and secure where she was at present—and for the foreseeable future.

As the time for the election drew near, Wilson devoted more and more attention to nursing his constituency. He was regarded by his local supporters—and opponents—as an indifferent public speaker, but adroit and convincing when it came to answering questions.

He had two opponents—a Conservative, and King-Hall who was fighting to retain the seat. He already knew King-Hall, and had an affectionate personal regard for him. This was a reciprocal attitude, and one which has persisted and strengthened with the passing years.

The campaign proper was conducted vigorously by all three

candidates, but it was a clean fight throughout, with a friendly atmosphere surrounding it.

After the polling there was a gap of three weeks before the results were to be declared, to allow time for the service votes to be collected and counted. Wilson returned to Oxford, with one resolve firmly in his mind. If his hopes of having won the seat proved ill-founded, he would hope to fight a by-election at the first opportunity, wherever it might be.

He returned to Ormskirk for the count. His father went too. Herbert had been with him throughout the campaign, and was anxious to know the result at the first possible moment.

King-Hall secured 11,000 votes, the Conservative candidate 23,000, and to the triumphant J. H. Wilson went 30,000.

Mary knew how much the news meant to Harold. She knew, too, that her dreams of a future in Oxford must remain dreams. Her happiness was balanced by a feeling of dismay.

PART FOUR

*Government*

❦

## CHAPTER FOURTEEN

One of the first duties facing all newly-elected Labour M.P.s in the summer of 1945 was to attend a meeting in the Beaver Hall to elect a Leader. There was a move afoot to oust Attlee. Harold Laski and one or two others favoured Ernest Bevin for the position, but when the Beaver Hall assembly was held, Attlee's position as Leader was formally endorsed.

Wilson was due to attend a constituency celebration immediately afterwards. As it was the Saturday of Bank Holiday weekend, when the trains were sure to be crowded, he had decided to drive north as soon as the meeting was over. He had borrowed an Austin 10, and when he discovered four other Lancashire M.P.s equally anxious to visit their constituencies—and dismayed by the prospect of train travel—he packed them all into his car and drove off.

On the journey the car blew a gasket. They stopped at a garage, and arranged to hire a car, on payment of a £5 deposit, for the remainder of the journey. After proceeding some distance in the hired car, Wilson suddenly discovered to his horror that the brakes failed to work. Short of abandoning it altogether, which he decided was out of the question, he was obliged to face an uncomfortable choice. If he drove back to the garage, he would have miles of the same kind of extremely risky driving as if he went on. He decided to go on.

The journey was a nightmare. In those days the roads were far less congested than they afterwards became. Even so, the peril was real. He had to be prepared to crash into low gear well in advance of every potential need to brake. One M.P., George

Tomlinson, was not delivered to his destination until 2 a.m. Having safely delivered all his other passengers, Wilson reached his own destination at 4 a.m.

The following week came the Parliamentary swearing-in. The senior members of the Cabinet had by this time been announced, but many of the junior appointments had still to be made. Wilson had no expectations. He was very pleased, however, when he was approached by someone in the House, who said he had a great honour to convey to him: Emanuel Shinwell, who had been appointed Minister of Fuel and Power, wanted him to be his Parliamentary Private Secretary. To be a P.P.S. would provide valuable experience of Parliament, and the honorary position was usually regarded as a useful stepping-stone to eventual Governmental responsibility. He felt, too, that his inside knowledge of the Ministry of Fuel and Power would be valuable to Shinwell. He said he would gladly accept the invitation.

Meanwhile Dalton, who was appointed Chancellor of the Exchequer held a dinner for "young victors." He was keen to find the views of youthful newcomers to the House, and to discover potential talent. One of the main topics at the dinner was whether anyone who had become an M.P. for the first time should be regarded as eligible for government office. Wilson expressed his opinion vigorously. He was emphatically opposed to any such idea.

"None of us knows anything about how to handle Parliament," he said. "It would be quite wrong to put a newcomer in such a position."

Then he added decisively: "But I'd make one exception—on sheer merit: Hugh Gaitskell."

His former fellow-civil servant was not present at the dinner. As a "young victor" he had, of course, been invited, but was unable to attend owing to a bad heart illness.

The following week-end Wilson was back in Oxford. He was intending to make no plans at present for moving house. His father had now left the job in Cornwall, and was temporarily employed in London at the Ministry of Supply. He and Ethel were occupying the Richmond flat. Harold decided he would stay with them during the week, and spend his week-ends in Oxford. There was a shortage of economists, and he had undertaken to do teaching duties on Saturdays and Sundays at University College. The arrangements would have the advantage of enabling Mary to remain with Robin in Oxford.

When he returned from a shopping expedition on the Saturday morning the College porter told him he had been searching everywhere for him. "The Prime Minister was wanting to speak to you on the telephone."

Wilson was surprised—and anxious lest he had missed an important opportunity. He hurried to a telephone and got through to the Cabinet offices. As soon as he mentioned his name the voice at the other end said: "Oh yes—the Prime Minister has been trying to contact you."

In a moment Attlee's voice came over. He went straight to the point.

"I want you to be Parliamentary Secretary at the Ministry of Works. This is a planning job. George Tomlinson will be your Minister, and he's quite happy about your appointment."

Wilson was too astonished—and too delighted—to do anything more than mutter something about feeling greatly honoured. This, of course, meant becoming a junior member of the Government, and must take precedence over the position of P.P.S. to Shinwell he had expected to hold.

Attlee had been keen to appoint some young newcomers to junior ministries. He already knew of Gaitskell, and would have given him an appointment had he not been ill at the time. He had heard of Wilson partly from Hugh Dalton, and partly from Lord Hyndley, who had been Controller General at the Ministry of Fuel and Power; he had told Attlee about the brilliant young man who resigned from the Ministry to become a Labour candidate.

Attlee believed that this exceptionally able planner should prove a useful complement to the warm-hearted, if rather unmethodical, George Tomlinson. When he made the suggestion to Tomlinson he asked whether he knew Wilson.

"Ay, ah know him all reet," came the reply. "Apart from the fact he tried to kill me in a motor car, ah've nowt against him."

Attlee's concept proved exactly right. The partnership was happy on personal grounds and fruitful in its results. Tomlinson, who was as cautious as he was benevolent, relied on the planning skill of his subordinate, and valued his enthusiastic—if sometimes rather brash—determination to go full steam ahead with a massive production of bricks and building of houses. He quickly agreed that his Parliamentary Secretary should be responsible for the day-to-day executive control.

Oddly enough, Wilson's initial delight over his important new position was suddenly mixed with slight regrets. He had begun to enjoy again the relative freedom and relaxation of his Oxford life, and had vaguely expected his work as an M.P. to be part-time. Now he was faced with the prospect of returning to the daily grind of non-stop office routine and committee meetings.

The vastness of the challenge soon gripped him, and all qualms evaporated. He recalled his boyhood dreams of ministerial responsibility. He recalled his more recent excitement when, as a civil servant, he had once or twice had the responsibility of meeting and actually briefing a Parliamentary Secretary. Now, he was in this position himself. It was an important job. He was going to do it well and he was going to make sure that he was exercising his full authority. The success of the Ministry would be judged by the number of bricks produced—by the number of houses built.

He discovered to his regret that, on the initiative of the Permanent Secretary, some of the senior temporary civil servants had had their appointments terminated—Sir Hugh Beaver, for example, who had been Director General and Controller General, and Sir Frederick Pile, who had been brought in by Duncan Sandys.

He asked the Permanent Secretary to account for the shortcomings in the temporary housing programme: what had gone wrong, he wondered, with all the "pre-fab" plans? He took Wilson to the statistical chart room and showed him the programme. One basic part, he explained, was four months behind schedule. But this, he said, was of small importance, because the kitchen and bathroom units were six months behind schedule. And he added that the whole question was irrelevant anyway, because the Ministry of Health were ten months behind schedule in pro-viding the necessary housing sites.

Wilson received the information coldly.

After a moment he said quietly: "Right. Now we're going to get everything on schedule."

The Permanent Secretary heard the statement with an indul-gent smile and went on leave.

Wilson was meanwhile determined to investigate as quickly and as thoroughly as possible all the factors causing the delays. He called a series of meetings with the various officials con-cerned. Three weeks later the Permanent Secretary returned from his holiday. On his first day back he sought an interview.

He appeared agitated. "Parliamentary Secretary—a rather seri-ous thing has happened, and I feel I ought to speak to you quite frankly about it. I gather that when I was away you had a meet-ing in your room?"

"I had a great many meetings," replied Wilson.

"Well," he continued. "I gather there were people of different ranks round the table?"

"There might easily have been," said Wilson. "I simply told my secretary to get hold of all the people concerned with the problems, so that we could get on quickly with things."

The Permanent Secretary seemed shocked. "You must know this is completely contrary to Civil Service discipline?"

Wilson replied that he had never heard of any such regulations, and that he himself had attended innumerable meetings with people of different ranks round the table, called by ministers or by others.

The P.S. eyed him sternly. "Look—I must speak frankly to you. After all, I'm twice your age, you know."

This, in fact, was precisely true. At the time, Wilson was 29, and the P.S. was 58.

"I really must explain," he continued, "that this sort of thing simply isn't done."

Wilson's retort came sharply. "Look here," he said, "you'd better get this clear. I've served in more Government depart-ments than you. And this was how the war was won."

The P.S. was unrepentant. "Your attitude is going to cause a

97

lot of difficulty," he complained. "We've had enough trouble here already with Ministers trying to run the department—like Duncan Sandys, for instance. As I see it, a Minister should answer in the House of Commons for the department, but leave the decisions to the civil servants."

The Parliamentary Secretary left him in no doubt that this view was wholly unacceptable, and the interview ended on a note of deep antagonism.

Wilson had been attending meetings on housing presided over by Aneurin Bevan, Minister of Health. He had also been studying all the figures and trends. From these he could see that a serious crisis in building materials was developing, and he warned Tomlinson accordingly. He told him that there appeared to be no progress at all.

He also told him that he had heard of a brilliant administrator called F. W. ("Bomber") Smith, who had been put in charge of bomb production during the war at the Ministry of Aircraft Production. Lord Beaverbrook, the Minister, had thought very highly of him. Now he was doing relatively unimportant work, and Wilson urged Tomlinson to arrange to transfer him to a senior post.

Tomlinson listened sympathetically to his Junior Minister—and with equal sympathy to the Permanent Secretary. He decided to take no action meanwhile.

Shortly there came a minor crisis over one building commodity. There was trouble over it, and some public criticism. Attlee sent for Tomlinson and expressed his annoyance. Tomlinson decided to take action: "Bomber" Smith was appointed Director General of building materials production, and Wilson was asked to supervise that side of the work.

The Permanent Secretary was furious. He came to Wilson's room brandishing a copy of the office notice promulgating Smith's appointment, and announced that he was going to put another senior civil servant alongside Smith. Everything emanating from Smith for the Minister or senior officials, he said, would come through this other man.

Wilson strongly disapproved of this arrangement. The P.S.

was adamant. "I am in charge of the office arrangements," he said, "and this is what I am going to do."

"In that case," declared Wilson, "I must tell you that I shall answer no question in Parliament, make no speeches in Parliament, and take no briefs for any Cabinet committee unless my advice comes directly from the man actually doing the job."

The atmosphere became acrimonious and tense. The P.S. knew by now that, whatever Wilson said, he meant. He knew he was being out-manoeuvred, and he accepted Wilson's dictum with a very bad grace.

For his part, Wilson regarded the episode as pointing to one inescapable conclusion: the P.S. must go.

A month after "Bomber" Smith had taken up his new appointment, he reported that the anticipated crisis in brick production was unavoidable. It might be possible to minimise it, he said, and with luck it could be overcome quickly. But nothing could avert it.

When it did eventually occur there was an outcry and something of a scandal. Cartoons about the shortage of bricks appeared, and there was general public disquiet.

Attlee was most dissatisfied. He had heard from Dalton that young Wilson was highly critical of the Permanent Secretary. He sent Tomlinson and expressed strong annoyance over the situation, and cross-examined him about the department. "Are you satisfied with the way things are being run?" he asked.

The Minister thought everything was in order.

"What about the Permanent Secretary?" Attlee persisted. "I've been thinking perhaps we ought to move him. There's a good man who's at present Deputy Secretary at the Ministry of Supply —Oliver Franks. You could have him."

Tomlinson said he would prefer to stick to the present one, and Attlee pursued it no further.

Two weeks later, however, there was more trouble. Attlee again summoned Tomlinson. Again he asked him about his Permanent Secretary.

"I'm quite happy with him," he said. "But Harold isn't. Perhaps you'd better talk to him."

It was quite exceptional for a Minister to advise the Prime Minister to consult his junior on such a matter, but wholly in keeping with George Tomlinson's unassuming and magnanimous outlook.

Attlee followed the suggestion. In response to a formal note from him, Wilson went round equipped, as instructed, with all the plans and figures for building materials production. He spread them out before Attlee, who studied them carefully.

"They seem all right," he commented. "Why haven't they been carried out?"

"They have, mainly," Wilson replied, "but we've had some difficulties."

"What's wrong?" snapped Attlee.

Out of loyalty to his Minister, Wilson said he thought the Prime Minister should consult Tomlinson.

"I have already done so," retorted Attlee, "and he suggested I should send for you because your view is different from his."

"In that case," said Wilson. "I can speak frankly. That department will never be any good until you get rid of the Permanent Secretary."

"Exactly as I thought," Attlee said, pulling out a sheet of paper. He wrote on it a simple minute to the Chancellor of the Exchequer. "Please find another job for the Permanent Secretary, Ministry of Works." This was satisfactorily arranged.

Wilson was by now an authoritative and effective administrator, but he showed little Parliamentary flair. His maiden speech in the House, for example, in reply to an adjournment debate criticising amenities for Members, was heard by few and made an impact on none. It took place at a time of family sadness—his father-in-law was dying—but he gave a great deal of thought to it in advance, all to little avail. His later efforts in debate were slightly more successful, but nobody who knew him doubted that his primary métier was in administration.

In fact, he regarded himself as a kind of glorified civil servant, pursuing an extended version of his war-time duties, but with the addition of actual ministerial responsibility. Even his remuneration, at £1,500 a year, was roughly the same as he had latterly been receiving before returning to Oxford.

Had it not been for his weekend teaching duties, he might have seen even less of Mary and Robin than he did. He worked with intense application during the week in London, and enjoyed the week-end retreat to his old College. Mary was happy that their home remained in Oxford. But it was a most unusual arrangement for a junior minister to continue with a part-time University appointment, and it came to an end in December, 1945.

They decided, however, to delay moving house from Oxford for as long as possible. Harold's parents continued to occupy the Richmond flat, and he continued staying with them during the week. If a bed had to be found for another guest, Harold vacated his room and slept on a camp bed in the lounge.

On one occasion the guest, who had been a childhood admirer of Harold, asked him for his autograph. She secured the following above his signature:

> *England arise, the long, long night is over*
> *Faint in the east, behold the dawn appear.*
> *Out of your evil dream of toil and sorrow,*
> *Arise, oh England, for the day is here.*

<table>
<tr><td></td><td>Harold Wilson</td></tr>
<tr><td>House of Commons</td><td>13 December, 1945</td></tr>
</table>

If Wilson at this stage was a highly effective technocrat rather than a maturing politician, he never forgot his idealism, nor his ambitions, and was more than pleased when suggestions began to reach him of important possibilities ahead. He was much too absorbed in his administrative responsibilities to follow the various political shades within the party, but the more he saw of Aneurin Bevan at the housing committees, the more he admired him personally. He considered him an exceptionally able Minister: his civil servants greatly respected him and always gave of their best, partly because he gave them a feeling of importance. Bevan, for his part, formed an increasingly high opinion of his young colleague's ability and intellect.

Early in May 1946 Wilson was summoned by the Chief Whip. The Parliamentary Secretary to the Ministry of Fuel had resigned, he said, and Wilson was to succeed him. The prospect of returning as a minister to his old department delighted him. He was due to go in a few days to a housing committee meeting in Portsmouth, and wondered whether he should now cancel it. The Whip said he should keep the engagement—the change of office might not be confirmed until after that, anyway.

The night before his Portsmouth trip the Chief Whip told him a different arrangement was now going to be made, and it would be announced the following day. On his way back from Portsmouth next evening he read the announcement. The new Parliamentary Secretary to the Ministry of Fuel was Hugh Gaitskell. Attlee, he later learned, had decided to appoint someone of outstanding promise who was likely to remain throughout the three major nationalisation bills for coal, gas, and electricity. This could take two or three years, and he had already decided that Wilson would be due for advancement long before that: it would therefore be futile to impede his progress by transferring him to another office with the same rank.

In September of 1946 there was talk of some Cabinet changes. Dalton told Wilson privately that he was to be promoted to Minister of Transport. His friends, including Dalton and Bevan, had reported to Attlee on the continuing excellence of his work. Attlee, however, changed his mind. Wilson, he decided, still lacked the Parliamentary experience necessary to handle the vast programme of nationalisation envisaged for transport.

This was a disappointment. He would have enjoyed being Minister of Transport, and he would have welcomed the promotion. Still, he knew now that he was regarded favourably in circles where it mattered, and that his advancement could only be a question of time.

Shortly after this, Attlee suddenly summoned Tomlinson, much to the latter's consternation. The urgency of the call seemed to imply trouble of some kind. Knowing of the Minister's anxiety, Wilson delayed his departure that evening until Tomlinson came back.

"What's it all about, George?" he asked, as soon as he returned. "Is it anything serious?"

"Ay, it's about thee," replied the Minister, adding: "It's nothing serious though. It's very good."

## CHAPTER FIFTEEN

Tomlinson could see that Wilson was unable to restrain his curiosity. Smiling, he said: "Well, it's in confidence, really. But I'll tell thee as long as when Prime Minister sends for thee it comes as a surprise—tha knows *nowt* about it, see?"

He then explained that Attlee wanted him to release his Parliamentary Secretary for three months to enable him to lead a delegation to a food conference in Washington. Wilson knew instantly what this meant: at the Copenhagen conference of F.A.O., Boyd Orr had urged the creation of a working commission in Washington. Subsequently, he had pleaded with Attlee to send a Minister rather than a senior civil servant to head the British delegation. Clearly Attlee was making arrangements to invite him, and the prospect thrilled him.

He received his summons to Attlee very soon afterwards, and was greeted with a terse query: "F.A.O.—d'you know what that stands for?"

"Yes I do," replied Wilson.

"What d'you know about it?" asked Attlee.

Wilson gave a brief but comprehensive account of its U.N. origins and purposes, and emerged from Attlee's room a moment later with his appointment formally confirmed.

There was no change in his status. He continued to be Parliamentary Secretary, Ministry of Works, but was seconded for the duration of the Washington consultations. He looked forward eagerly to gaining more experience of overseas negotiations—and this, indeed, was part of Attlee's intention. He also welcomed the opportunity of trying to further the work of F.A.O.—its concept accorded wholly with the beliefs of his upbringing and ideals. And its practical aim of devoting hundreds of millions of dollars to buying up food surpluses to send to hungry nations could, he hoped, be aided by his economic experience.

In the event, the British delegation proved a disappointment to Boyd Orr. Signs of Britains coming dollar crisis were just beginning to appear, and the delegation felt unable to commit themselves to the contribution which was hoped. Under Wilson's guidance they tried to invent alternative ideas to give reality to their moral support: multilateral commodity agreements, for example, were devised.

From his personal standpoint, Wilson's three months in the United States were of value. He saw a great deal of the American system at work, and became especially familiar with their agricultural methods. He also made many useful personal contacts with diplomatic officials, journalists, and business executives.

Besides his leadership of the British delegation to the F.A.O. consultations, he was searching for timber. The housing programme at home was seriously threatened by the lack of it. If no more supplies could be found, housing would undoubtedly have to be cut. At this time, the purchase of timber was confined to Government buying, and Wilson spent a lot of time investigating potential American sources. He discovered that plentiful supplies existed. The officials at home, however, especially those at the Board of Trade, were denying this, and were planning to send a purchasing mission to Canada only.

Wilson came home for Christmas. His three months were up. The F.A.O. consultations were not completed, however, and he would have to return for another three or four weeks after Christmas. Meanwhile, he was determined to pursue the timber question vigorously.

He found Bevan very worried about the shortage, and inclined to believe the Board of Trade assurances that none was available in the States. Wilson insisted that this was untrue. He had lunch with Attlee at Chequers. After reporting on the F.A.O. developments, he went on to talk of the timber problem, and its possible solution through American supplies. Attlee urged him to take it up with Sir Stafford Cripps, President of the Board of Trade.

This he did.

But wherever he turned, and whatever he said, he always seemed to find the official view prevailing—no supplies of timber existed in America. The purchasing commission were shortly to set out for Canada, but they would certainly not be going on to the U.S.A.

As a Junior Minister, his persistence could not officially go beyond certain limits. He was determined, however, to prove his point—and to ensure that the necessary timber was secured.

He devised an ingenious scheme. "Bomber" Smith, he argued, ought to be a member of the purchasing mission. After all, as a senior Ministry of Works official he was directly concerned with the use of timber. Should he not, therefore, be actively involved?

This was agreed. He immediately had a private talk with Smith, and told him the position frankly. He also put him in touch with an important contact—Tom Meyer; the son of Montague Meyer, head of one of Britain's largest timber firms. Tom was at present on a tour of Canada and the U.S.A. partly to recuperate after the years he had spent as a prisoner of war. The Meyers were personal friends of Ernest Bevin and George Tomlinson, and Wilson knew Meyer would do everything possible to help.

Smith proved to be such an efficient member of the purchasing mission that the others soon gladly allowed him to take charge of the practical arrangements, including the travel and shipping. They went to Canada, and secured as much timber as they could. Smith suggested they should proceed to the States. This, however, the others flatly opposed. It was pointless, they said, because none was available there.

Smith proceeded to re-arrange the travel plans. Suddenly they all found themselves with so much time on their hands before they could start the journey home that it seemed pointless *not* to proceed to the States. They did so, and after an "accidental" meeting between Smith and Tom Meyer, an ample supply of timber was secured. This involved expenditure of precious dollars, of course, and in the months ahead the full significance of that became clearer. But meanwhile the continuation of the housing programme was assured.

For his final weeks in Washington Harold took Mary with him, while Robin was left behind in the care of his grandparents at the Richmond flat. This was Mary's first visit to America. They returned on the *Queen Elizabeth* at the end of January in 1947.

Back in London the situation was gloomy. The fuel crisis was just beginning, and the Government's popularity was at a low ebb.

The day of the Parliamentary debate on the F.A.O. report was the day on which Ellen Wilkinson died. There followed much speculation about her successor. It was generally expected that George Tomlinson would succeed her as Minister of Education, and this proved to be so. It was also expected that Wilson himself would succeed Tomlinson as Minister of Works. Instead, Attlee appointed Charles Key, who had been Bevan's Parliamentary Secretary for two years. Bevan wanted to strengthen his Ministry's links with Works, and Key, who had been very close to him, was regarded as the most suitable man.

Wilson would have liked to become Minister of Works, and was disappointed not to be chosen. But he was still only thirty, and there was plenty to do in his present job.

He had always spent a great deal of time going all over the country attending meetings of representatives of both sides of the building industry. A whole network of consultative machinery of this kind had been set up on a regional basis. He liked to attend all the meetings in every region, and to see for himself the exact nature of the difficulties involved.

Now he threw himself into the problems of the development areas. The factory building programme was going seriously wrong, and he wanted to discover why. He represented his Ministry on a Government Committee presided over by Dalton as Chancellor, and got himself appointed to investigate the development areas throughout England. The weather was very bad, and almost every factory site he visited seemed to be buried in deep snow.

He completed his tour and submitted to Dalton's committeee a report sharply criticising Board of Trade inefficiency. It amounted to a very serious indictment, and was therefore referred to the Board of Trade for comment—and any appropriate action.

Shortly afterwards Key and Wilson were together summoned by the Prime Minister. Wilson had a strong suspicion that the purpose of the occasion would be to deliver a rebuke in connection with his attack on the Board of Trade. He knew how particular Attlee could be when it came to formalities; presumably it was arguable whether a Junior Minister should feel entitled to make such a strongly-worded criticism of somebody else's department. He concluded that he was going to be officially reprimanded, and deduced that Key had been summoned simultaneously so as to share the reprimand. As Wilson's Minister, he could no doubt be held responsible for his subordinate's conduct.

Wilson had often heard of the sharpness of an Attlee rebuke. He had once experienced it himself, when there had been some misunderstanding over the Cabinet's policy towards homeless "squatters" taking possession on unoccupied property.

That had been a relatively minor display of annoyance, but it was quite unpleasant enough. Now he anticipated a major one.

## CHAPTER SIXTEEN

Attlee had his usual air of crisp formality, but gave no indication of anger. Amicably he beckoned them both to sit down. Looking at Key, he said: "I'm making some ministerial changes. Hilary Marquand is to become Paymaster General to do long-term planning. I want the Parliamentary Secretary to succeed him as Sec-retary for Overseas Trade."

Turning towards Wilson, he continued: "There's a big conference over in Geneva in a month's time, so you'd better get yourself briefed."

That was all. The interview was over.

Wilson was relieved that the purpose of the meeting had

proved to be so different from his expectations. His relief was exceeded only by his delight over his new responsibilities. His salary would remain the same, so there was no material advantage; but in status it amounted to real promotion. He would now be of ministerial rank, in charge of a vital Board of Trade department, with Cripps as his head.

Cripps immediately invited him to dinner and explained his co-ordinating methods. "Well, my boy," he said with a benign smile, "I hold two morning meetings every week with my senior officials. They start at 9.30 and I look forward to your presence at the next one."

Wilson was there punctually. He noticed the agenda contained a very controversial item: discussion of the extremely critical report on factory building which he himself had submitted a few days earlier to Dalton's committee. He imagined this would create an inauspicious prelude to his new responsibilities, but was determined not to allow such misgivings to deflect him. The departmental official responsible was present; and did his best to defend himself. But there was no mistaking the newcomer's determination to make his ministerial authority decisive.

The overseas trading position was at this time running into acute difficulties. Dollars were beginning to run out and the convertibility crisis was about to break. The Geneva conference, which was concerned with international trade agreements, was demanding a lot of Wilson's attention.

Meanwhile, the international political situation was also deteriorating. Ernest Bevin, the Foreign Secretary, was in Moscow attending the Council of Foreign Ministers. The discussions were not proceeding hopefully. Towards their conclusion Bevin, who was anxious to avoid a total rupture, saw Stalin and raised the question of a trade agreement. This, he thought, could help to keep at least some doors open. Montague Meyer had mentioned the timber shortage, so he raised this with Stalin.

Stalin said there was not much timber available, but he thought there might be some wheat for export to Britain. Bevin seized on this, and suggested sending a responsible Minister to Moscow to negotiate. Stalin readily assented and immediately afterwards

Wilson found himself en route to Moscow for his first visit to the U.S.S.R., at the head of a small team of civil servants.

They were accommodated in Moscow's National Hotel. Material conditions after the devastation of the war were still extremely bad: a severe drought the previous year had caused an acute food shortage, so on the physical level the delegates were very uncomfortable. In addition, there was an atmosphere of suspicion surrounding all foreigners, especially from the West, and not all the stories of hidden microphones and secret police snooping were unfounded.

A further discomfort was caused by the practical working arrangements. Stalin, who was in complete command, had the habit of working very late. All his senior officials had to do likewise. Ten o'clock at night was quite a usual time for a private meeting between a British and Soviet official and it was common for the actual negotiations to start at midnight and continue until three or four o'clock in the morning.

Mikoyan, Deputy Premier and Minister of Foreign Trade, headed the Russian team. Wilson quickly recognised the justification for his reputation as the toughest and most astute trade negotiator in the world.

He was amicably disposed, however, and seemed keen to establish pleasant working relations. On one occasion he threw a luncheon party for the British team of twelve, including the two women secretaries. The Russian hosts also numbered twelve—and included two women secretaries.

One high Soviet official referred incredulously to Wilson's reported youthfulness. Wilson assured him there was no mistake. His Government as a whole, he added, included many young men: "I'll pick a football team of British Ministers, and you pick one of Soviet Ministers, and we'll play you at the Dynamo Stadium in Moscow and knock hell out of you."

The lunch, which began at 1.30, ended at 7.35 with Wilson's secretary striking up "Auld Lang Syne." Many toasts had been drunk. But the Russians, ever practical, had a hospital ward upstairs with a doctor and two nurses. The beds available totalled the ominous number of twelve. Fortunately not all were needed

—in the course of the proceedings two of the British disappeared upstairs, and three of the Russians.

The object of the team's visit, besides its diplomatic motive, was to make a reconnaissance to discover genine trading prospects. Mikoyan was direct and practical, listing precisely the Russian goods which were available, and the goods he would like to purchase from Britain.

There was, however, one basic difficulty. The Russians still owed us a substantial war debt for civil supplies—electric power installations, for example. They were not in a position to pay this off quickly. Before starting serious negotiations, they said, they would like an agreement to reduce their down payment from 50% to 25%, and an agreement to spread the repayment of the balance over twelve years instead of the shorter period we had stipulated.

Having completed this initial reconnaissance, and having established good official and personal relations, Wilson brought his team back after three weeks, feeling fairly confident that some agreements might be reached in the future.

At home, the economic situation was causing a great deal of anxiety, rationing and continuing shortages generally were leading to much discontent; the effects of the fuel crisis were still not forgotten; everything added up to a severe reduction in the Government's popularity.

Morale within the Government was also at a low ebb. Dalton was among those who favoured a change in the leadership. Bevan also thought Attlee should be replaced. He concluded, however, it would be impossible to choose a successor from the present front rank: he believed unity could never be achieved if only the established figures were considered as prospective candidates. Somebody entirely new must be found—somebody who would bring a fresh approach, who was youthful and who had an unblemished record.

Bevan quite seriously canvassed Wilson's name among various senior colleagues. Those he approached rejected the suggestion as quite preposterous. To appoint a relatively unknown newcomer, however brilliant and capable, as leader of the Government seemed completely idiotic to all of them—as it did also to Wilson himself, when he later heard of it.

Bevan was sometimes capable of remarkably erratic judgment, and this hitherto unrevealed episode was undoubtedly a case in point. At other times he could reveal extraordinary foresight, and a small element of this may also have entered the scheme. But at least his timing was hopelessly at fault, and the idea was mercifully buried before it destroyed both him and his junior colleague.

In June Cripps urged Wilson to return to Moscow. Another timber shortage was developing and looked like endangering the housing programme. Equally serious was the shortage of grain for the feeding programme. Bread rationing was still on, and the Government had embarked on a big agricultural expansion programme depending on grain which had so far not been secured. Tom Williams, Minister of Agriculture, was extremely worried about the situation.

Wilson felt reluctant to return so soon. For one thing, he was becoming increasingly concerned with the Geneva conference on tariffs and trade, and disagreements with the Americans about aspects of this had some alarming implications. For diplomatic as well as trade reasons, however, an agreement with Russia could clearly produce important results. So early in June of 1947 he set off, this time taking a larger team: he was accompanied by an expert in each of the commodities to be discussed—timber, canned, salmon, wheat, engineering, and so on: the potential interests were comprehensive and included even hair from the tails of Siberian ponies for use in the manufacture of artists' paint brushes.

Negotiations began directly with Mikoyan and with subsidiary Soviet experts dealing with the specialist items. Wilson made some concessions over the Russian payment of the civil debt, though not to the limit sought by Mikoyan. Nevertheless, it provided a helpful start.

The minimum British grain requirement was 700,000 tons and Wilson's instruction from the Cabinet was to break off negotiations if he was unable to secure at least that amount. Mikoyan, of course, was unaware of this. He began by saying they could offer a maximum of 500,000 tons of grain. Wilson immediately said he wanted two million tons—not half a million. After several further meetings, Mikoyan was still adamant that half a million tons must be the limit. Wilson said there was clearly no hope of reaching a satisfactory agreement and he proposed, therefore, to conclude discussions and take his team home.

To indicate he meant this seriously, he went blatantly through all the motions of preparing to leave—even to the point of his team retrieving their washing from the hotel laundry; he also telegraphed for his aircraft—deliberately not using a coded message.

Some hours before his departure was due early on the Sunday morning, there was no sign of any relaxation. Discussions had never been resumed and he began to think he was going to have to use the aircraft after all. Suddenly he received a message, delivered at 10 o'clock on the Saturday night. It came from Mikoyan, and invited him to a meeting at midnight.

Mikoyan began by reminding Wilson that Stalin himself had to authorise all grain shipments; he was glad to say that Stalin had now authorised the release of 1,250,000 tons.

Although this was just about twice the basic minimum, Wilson contained his delight, saying simply that this seemed a step in the right direction and would justify the continuation of the talks. He would therefore postpone his departure, but would reserve the right to persist in his demand for two million tons—adding that he might, however, be prepared to settle eventually for a little less, perhaps 1,500,000 tons.

In fact, he regarded this as a major step forward, not least because it indicated a strong Soviet desire to reach agreement. For several weeks intense and complicated negotiations proceeded on every conceivable aspect of the price and delivery of the goods mutually sought. Wilson had learned some Russian phonetically and this made a good impression on Mikoyan and his team.

As a leader, Wilson was in complete command of his team. His total absorption in the intricacies of negotiating was offset by his habit, if things had not been going well, of retreating with some of his team to his hotel bedroom and singing songs, the favourite, not without its own significance, being "Poor Old Joe."

At times the atmosphere during the negotiations became tense. Wilson would then suggest a break in the formal meetings. The two respective large teams of officials would disperse, and Mikoyan and he would have a private meeting with only interpreters present.

Once when Russian confidence seemed at a low ebb, Wilson conceded the priniciple of arbitration in Moscow for their supplies, alongside arbitration in London for ours. Mikoyan was almost in tears with thankfulness for this recognition of the independence of the Russian arbitration courts.

On another occasion a much more serious crisis of confidence arose. A technical adviser on the British team impeded progress by introducing unacceptable conditions about shipping payments. Wilson had noted with misgiving this particular official's attitude during negotiations, and decided it looked unpleasantly like an attempt to sabotage agreement. He immediately sent him home.

Mikoyan had by now lost confidence in the British team's sincerity. Wilson met him privately and, as a gesture of trust, even left behind his own interpreter and relied solely on Mikoyan's. He told Mikoyan exactly what had happened and that he had dismissed the official concerned. He also withdrew entirely the obstacle about shipping payments. The effect of all this on Mikoyan was unmistakable. With confidence restored and personal relations strengthened, negotiations resumed on a much better basis.

Mikoyan often displayed a great sense of humour. He enjoyed "playing to the gallery" of his own team—and Wilson showed the same pleasure in relation to the British team. On one occasion Mikoyan observed "When an Armenian is dealing with a Yorkshireman, what chance is there of an agreement?" For years afterwards this comment was often quoted with a chuckle by Attlee in reference to Wilson's shrewdness and toughness.

Sometimes it was necessary for one side or the other to play for time. Either leader might be waiting for higher instructions, for example, or for information about the Chicago wheat prices. Wilson had arranged for this important information to be supplied to him quickly and regularly via the American Embassy. Mikoyan also required this information, but never received it quite so quickly. When one or other was not quite ready to make the next move, they would often enjoy discussing quite irrelevant topics—a potential exchange of ballet companies, for example, or a films deal.

Mikoyan was always stimulated by argument, especially of an ideological kind. Wilson used to tease him by quoting Marx. Mikoyan knew his Marx fairly well, but not quite well enough to be sure whether Wilson was inventing the quotations—which he invariably was.

There were, of course, some periods of great tedium. At the time, Wilson was a fairly heavy cigarette smoker. He felt he needed a more relaxing pastime, and resolved to take up a pipe as an aid to any future negotiations with Mikoyan.

Eventually progress was made. The timber agreement, for example, was completed and initialled, ready for signature in conjunction with the main contract. But several problems remained unresolved, especially the price of wheat and other grains. Five weeks had now elapsed, and material conditions for the British team were very bad—the heat was almost insufferable, and the food of grim quality and sometimes non-existent; sometimes breakfast was obtainable at the hotel only after a threat to telephone a complaint to Mikoyan himself.

Wilson felt they were nearing the "make or break" point. He sent for his aircraft. It was a charter 'plane costing £500 a day, but the contract under discussion was worth £40 million. As he put it to his team: "The presence of the 'plane may help to concentrate discussion."

Meanwhile, his instructions from the Cabinet were stiffening. The Canadians were objecting strongly to any possibility of a higher price being paid for Russian wheat than for theirs. In addition, Soviet diplomacy was becoming more intransigent, and Bevin was anxious that nothing should be done in trading which could imply weakness in other directions. There could, therefore, be no further concessions over the question of the down-payment.

It was over this point that deadlock was reached. Agreement on all the other main points, including grain prices, had been concluded in principle. Wilson had believed that Mikoyan would yield on the down-payment question, but he remained adamant. The point was reached when it seemed really futile to continue and after an acrimonious exchange, discussions were finally broken off one day at 2 a.m.

The 'plane, which had now been standing by for a week, took off with the British team aboard. At London Airport it shot through a hedge, skimmed over a ditch, and crashed into a field. Several delegates were quite badly hurt. Wilson, who was himself in much pain from badly bruised ribs, helped to get them out.

The accident was headlined in next morning's papers. Wilson went to report early to Cripps, and was greeted with a bland smile, "Well, my boy—surprising what some people will do for publicity!"

Cripps agreed that although the talks had broken down, nothing should be said to imperil possible future negotiations. He was anxious to keep the door open, and made a moderate statement in the House, offering no criticism of the Russians.

Wilson, feeling unusually tired, and in pain with his rib injuries, went to Oxford for the week-end. There was little time to relax, however, because the British dollar problem was becoming acute, and a serious crisis was developing in Geneva over the trade talks.

He flew again to Geneva and found the discussion there still centring on non-discrimination. He delivered a tough speech: it was all very well, he said, to be talking about a blueprint for the ultimate future—whenever that might be. But meanwhile Britain faced a crisis in her economy, and must do everything to save herself. She would therefore discriminate ruthlessly—would discriminate particularly in favour of the Commonwealth. The Commonwealth, he said, was going to be more closely linked together.

Suddenly he was urgently recalled to London. Cripps was ill.

In the middle of the convertibility crisis, Wilson found himself in charge of the whole department. He also found himself saddled with conducting an enquiry into the Bank of England. Dalton, who was being criticised for not having foreseen the financial crisis, blamed the Bank, and an enquiry was ordered by the Cabinet. In addition to this, bilateral negotiations had now to be intensified with many different countries.

Cripps returned in September. Wilson felt exhausted and decided to take a week off. He drove Mary and Robin to Cornwall.

## CHAPTER SEVENTEEN

Cornwall had become a favourite retreat. Harold knew it well— he had frequently visited his parents during the years they lived there. And for a long time Marjorie had been Headmistress of a nearby Infants' School, so the family link with the county was preserved. Whenever possible, he took Mary and Robin either to visit her, or to stay at a small cottage at Mullion Cove lent by friends.

He always found real solace in Cornwall. He had a favourite solitary walk there, and often it seemed to throw up solutions to awkward problems. For years this particular walk remained such a source of inspiration that he would sometimes defer an especially difficult political problem for final contemplation on it. If there was a solution, it was certain to occur to him there. Conversely—as occasionally happened—if no solution occurred there, he felt that none could exist.

Mary was also very fond of Cornwall, and was especially glad to have this particular holiday. What with Harold's latest Russian trip, and his various visits to Geneva, they had seen very little of each other for months. Even when not abroad, his working day was never less than fifteen hours. Not surprisingly, she had seen him for one week-end only throughout the summer. Although her devotion to Oxford remained constant, they both agreed they would soon have to move house to London.

Fishing was one of Harold's favourite pastimes at Mullion Cove. He enjoyed accompanying the local fishermen, especially when lobsters were the target. He spent some time steering a small boat for fishermen setting lobster pots.

He was sitting contentedly on a lobster pot one day when an urgent summons to the telephone was brought to him—a call, he was told, from Sir Stafford Cripps. In fact, it was the President's senior private secretary. The Prime Minister, he said, wanted to see him at Chequers on Sunday.

For a moment Wilson felt irked. "Listen—this is the first break I've had all year. I came here for a week only. Can't I have even five days without being recalled?"

The secretary was sympathetic. But the fact remained—the Prime Minister wanted to see him and lunch at Chequers on Sunday had been arranged.

Wilson quickly realised the occasion must be important and regained his equanimity. He asked the secretary to book him a sleeper from St. Austell on Saturday night, and a return sleeper from Paddington to St. Austell on Sunday night.

"I will gladly do so," came the reply. "But I think you will not require the return sleeper."

Wilson reckoned that changes in the Government must be in the offing, and that he was going to be involved in them. He arranged to have supper on the Saturday evening with Marjorie at her St. Austell bungalow before his overnight journey. They both spent the evening making various guesses, and narrowed it down to three possibilities. Marjorie wanted to know, first thing on waking the following Monday morning, what new office her brother was to hold. Harold arranged to leave a symbolic message on her breakfast table on his way back to Mullion Cove. A lump of coal would mean he was to be Minister of Fuel and Power, a strip of metal Minister of Supply, and a slice of bread Minister of Food.

On his arrival at Paddington on the Sunday morning he telephoned his parents at their Richmond flat and told them of his summons to Chequers. They too speculated about the future and looked forward to hearing all about it later in the day.

He was received cordially by Attlee, who proceeded to show him round Chequers. Lunch followed.

After lunch the Prime Minister took him aside and with a characteristic air of crisp authority indicated that he now wanted to talk business.

"I'm making some changes," he confided. "The economic situation is very disturbing. It needs better control. So Stafford is going to become Minister for Economic Affairs—a new position which will give him an over-all, co-ordinating and supervisory responsibility. I want you to succeed him as President of the Board of Trade."

Wilson was utterly flabbergasted. None of the guessing games had ever led him to imagine this. His astonishment very nearly overwhelmed him and he only just managed to say all the right things.

His amazement was rapidly replaced by a feeling he had never before experienced. For the first time in his life, he felt inadequate. It was not that he doubted at all his ability to administer the department: true, it was a vast empire, consisting of one-tenth of the entire administrative civil service and having probably the widest scope of any ministry—but he had no qualms about his competence on that score. Nor did he doubt for a moment in America and Russia and Geneva had reinforced his self-confidence as a negotiator.

No—it was in the realm of higher political initiative and leadership that he felt inexperienced and immature. Visions of Cripps in action kept shooting through his mind: the morning meeting, and some problem—to do with meat, maybe? Cripps knew how to handle it—"send for the Argentine Ambassador," he would say. Or a problem of exports? Cripps knew exactly what to do —"Right. We'll immediately call a top-level conference of exporting manufacturers." No matter what the problem, Cripps knew exactly what to do—and invariably introduced a touch of diplomatic panache which Wilson knew he had yet to acquire.

His rise had been rapid, and he had certainly had to develop and show qualities of initiative and leadership in various spheres —scouting, school captain, President of one or two Oxford societies, senior civil servant, University don: all that was true, he mused, yet these were all within a fairly routine framework—where the main "rules" were more or less pre-ordained. He knew well how to follow "rules"—or, for that matter, how to circumvent them. But he had not yet been a ruler himself, and this was exactly what he now had to become. He had always much admired Cripps, and thought him a great man. But now he suddenly seemed even greater. Cripps, the man he was to succeed, was an elder statesman. Wilson, in comparison, felt he was still a glorified civil servant.

These were the thoughts flashing through his mind as he muttered to Attlee his thanks, his sense of honour . . .

Attlee had nothing more to say, beyond wishing him well. They shook hands. Wilson bade farewell to Mrs. Attlee, and was driven to his parents' flat.

He had plenty to occupy his mind on the journey. He realised from the seniority of his new position that the appointment must have been made with the full assent of all the contemporary giants of the party—obviously Attlee and Cripps themselves, but also Ernest Bevin, Herbert Morrison, and Dalton. Aneurin Bevan, he felt sure, must also have been consulted. He later learned that Bevan had not only been consulted—but had insisted that Wilson was the only realistic choice. He gained some reassurance from the thought that six such very different people at the heart of the Government's affairs had all placed this confidence and trust in him.

The information about his appointment had to remain confidential for another forty-eight hours, but it was impossible to restrain his parents' curiosity.

"Can we try to find out by the 'twenty questions' method?" they pleaded.

Herbert asked: "Is it a change?" Harold nodded.

"Is it promotion?" Again, a nod.

"Are you to be in the Cabinet?" Another nod.

Ethel had a turn: "Are you to be President?"

Her shrewdness took Harold by surprise, and they knew the answer. For once they were unable to conceal their pride, and congratulations flowed thick and fast. Herbert's knowledge of political history came to the fore: his astonishment was as complete as Harold's had been. He was quick to appreciate that, at thirty-one, his Harold became the youngest-ever President of the Board of Trade, and one of the youngest-ever members of the Cabinet. But to Herbert the Board of Trade was associated with political giants—with Lloyd George and Winston Churchill, for example; he had always thought of it as one of the biggest jobs in the Government, a position often held prior to the Premiership itself. It was not easy to see his young son quite in the same great mould yet. Harold had a feeling that his father's unmistakable pride might have been privately mixed with a slight feeling that his rise had been excessively meteoric.

Meanwhile, there was an immediate practical family problem to be solved. There could now be no question of returning to Mullion Cove, yet the car was there, and Mary and Robin had somehow to be transported back to Oxford. Herbert took the car key, used Harold's night sleeper back to Cornwall, and did all that was necessary.

When Marjorie awoke next morning, no secret message lay on her breakfast table. She soon knew why. And when the news reached the fishermen of Mullion Cove, one of them said with a grin: "He may be all right as a Minister, but he's sometimes a bloody awful helmsman."

\*     \*     \*

He went to see Cripps first thing on the following morning, and was greeted with the usual benign smile.

"Well, my boy," he said. "You've seen Clem. Let me say I'm very glad indeed—and happy for you."

As the supreme economic co-ordinator, Cripps would continue to have a supervisory responsibility. There was to be no question, however, of the new President having a reduced status. Cripps made it clear that while he was not going to interfere with his youthful successor's interpretation of the Presidency, he would always be glad to give benevolent help and support. He discussed

1. Harold Wilson, with his elder sister—taken in 1918.

Harold Wilson at No. 10 Downing Street in 1924 when he was eight and one-half. A photo by his father.

3. *Harold Wilson in 1926—*
   *playing a part in* H.M.S. *Pinafore.*

4. *At Oxford in 1936 after reading*
   *the Gladstone Prize Essay.*

5. *Harold Wilson's parents, Herbert and Ethel.*

6. *January 1st 1940 wedding of Harold Wilson and Gladys Mary Baldwin.*

7.  The family at home in Hampstead Garden suburb, 1952.

8.  Wilson, with wife Gladys and son Giles at home after being elected leader of Labour Party in 1963.

the mechanics of the handover, mentioning several outstanding matters which required special attention.

Wilson wanted to raise an immediate query. What, he wondered, did Cripps think of so-and-so? (mentioning the name of a senior official he had often seen at the morning meetings, and whose ability he seriously doubted).

"If you've decided to get rid of him, you must do so at once," Cripps said. "I've never had time to get round to it myself, but you're probably right."

Wilson went along to his Overseas Trade office, and started to make arrangements to transfer his personal papers to his new office. He had a visit from Sir John Woods, the Permanent Secretary, who knew by now of the confidential Government changes. He congratulated Wilson on his new appointment, adding:

"I'm sure I'm speaking for all of us when I say nobody can replace Stafford. But I'm sure they've chosen you as the person who'll come nearest to it. We've all a great respect for you—but nobody will ever be another Stafford."

Wilson thanked him. Then, referring to the senior official, he said:

"I want you to arrange to move Mr. So-and-so to another department."

Woods looked surprised. "Is this wise?" he asked. "I think you should not be too hasty. He may not be impressive in some ways, but he's a great deal better than he may seem at the morning meetings."

"I'm sure he must be," replied Wilson scathingly, adding: "I've nothing against him personally, and I'm sure he would fit well into many Civil Service departments—perhaps the Home Office? But for a department judged at the end of the day by the rate of exports delivered, or by the number of yards of cotton produced, he doesn't have the kind of executive mind required. He's too much in the old style, and he won't do."

Woods argued in his favour, and asked again: "Is your mind quite made up?"

"Yes," Wilson replied decisively.

"Right," said Woods, "I've done my duty and stuck up for

him." He paused, then added: "Can I now say to you—I think you're absolutely right."

A satisfactory transfer was arranged.

Shortly afterwards Attlee sent for the new President.

"Just a word about who's going to be your successor as Secretary for Overseas Trade," he said. "Have you any views who you'd like?"

"I don't know him very well," replied Wilson, "but Arthur Bottomley seems very good."

"Glad you feel that way," said Attlee, "because that's who you're getting!"

The problem of moving house had now become a personal priority. Much as they loved Oxford, it was obviously going to be impossible to keep their home there any longer. And with a salary jump to £5,000 a year, Mary and he could contemplate a house in London. The press reported this item of family interest, and among those to read a gossip-column item about it was the Vicar of St. Jude's Church in Hampstead Garden Suburb. He happened to know that a local resident was about to sell a house like the one the Wilsons were said to be seeking (three bedrooms, nice garden) and suggested to another local resident—Patrick Gordon Walker, a Labour M.P. and a Parliamentary Under-Secretary of State—that the new President might be interested to hear more about it.

The new President was. He offered to buy the house, leasehold, from its owner Gurney Braithwaite, Conservative M.P. The sum agreed was £5,100 and the Wilsons considered it a fair price. The only problem was how to pay for it. Although now earning a substantial salary, he had never previously earned enough to be able to save much.

Herbert came to the rescue. Ever since the move to Cheshire in 1932 he had rented his Milnsbridge house. Recently he had sold it, and had some capital to spare. He loaned £800 to Harold— more than enough to cover the deposit—and the balance was raised through a mortgage. Harold began to repay his father's loan at the rate of £20 a month and continued the arrangement for years after the original loan had been more than repaid.

Mary soon felt at home in their new surroundings. They joined the local Free Church, which embraced the non-conformist denominations, and where Harold has preached on several occasions. Opposite the house was a pleasant school, mainly for girls, but with a mixed nursery school department. It seemed just right for Robin, now aged four, and he went there each morning.

A few months after the move a second son, Giles, was born. The new baby's godparents were Mr. and Mrs. Attlee. The family was now complete.

\* \* \*

Wilson undertook his new responsibilities with characteristic vigour and application. As he became engrossed in his work, his initial feelings of inadequacy dispersed. He was determined from the start to be completely in charge of the running of the department, although ready to delegate specific responsibilities, wherever possible, to Arthur Bottomley and to John Belcher, his Parliamentary Secretary.

He soon asserted his authority. Besides the Permanent Secretary, his senior staff comprised three Second Secretaries, nineteen Under-Secretaries and eighty-three Assistant Secretaries—of whom only one was concerned with cotton, one with films, and one with trade with Russia, each a big and important subject. If he came home for an evening he would often have two or three red boxes awaiting his attention. Sometimes he sat up half the night studying Cabinet papers. At week-ends, if he was not away on business, red boxes would start arriving at home at about 5 p.m. on the Saturday. He would work through them all Saturday evening and all through Sunday.

He found membership of the Cabinet much less exciting than he had imagined. Everyone was friendly, however, and there was never any condescension from colleagues mostly old enough to be his father. Usually he sat between Chuter Ede, the Home Secretary, and A. V. Alexander, Minister of Defence at the time. Alexander had by now heard from Wilmut all about his former schoolboy admirer from Royds Hall, and went out of his way to welcome him.

If Bevan seemed the most imaginative and congenial of his Cabinet colleagues, there was no question that Attlee was the most authoritative. He presided with inflexible toughness and was punctilious in his expectations. Anyone arriving even slightly late, for example, was instantly made aware of his misdemeanour. Worse still—anyone submitting an ill-considered paper was subjected to a devastating cross-examination. Even hardened veterans like Bevan and Shinwell could wilt if they happened to be the target.

Wilson deeply respected Attlee's efficient command, his detachment, and his sense of fairness. He privately resolved never to submit any paper, or raise any issue, without first having briefed himself on every vestige of every facet. Meanwhile, he took very little part in discussing colleagues' work. He was a "new boy," and in any case quite preoccupied enough in fulfilling his own complex responsibilities. If anything went wrong over his wide field, a major political crisis would result. A wrong decision on clothes rationing, for example, could have disastrous results for the Government. His main concern was to ensure that Board of Trade affairs ran smoothly under him.

In December 1947, some two months after becoming President, he decided to look again at the question of trade with Russia. Timber supplies were a mounting problem, and the need for grain for feeding stuffs was becoming desperate. Tom Williams was more worried than ever. Wilson knew the Russians had their own shortages, and were anxious to purchase from us timber-cutting machinery, light rails for transporting timber, agricultural machinery, locomotives, and other products.

He conferred with Cripps, who suggested sending a team to Moscow, under Makins, Assistant Under-Secretary of State at the Foreign Office (and later, as Sir Roger Makins, British Ambassador to the United States). Wilson said he proposed to take charge of it himself; he knew the whole situation from his previous visits, could pick up where he had left off, and felt confident he could succeed.

All his officials advised against it. They pointed out that if he failed as President it would amount to a much more serious rebuff. To this Wilson retorted that if he went, and did fail after an honest attempt, at least there would be an irrefutable answer to left-wing critics in the House and elsewhere, who always spoke as if trade with Russia could be secured merely for the asking.

He cabled a message to Mikoyan, saying he proposed to come for three days, and that if he was unable to secure the outline of an agreement in that time, he would immediately break off and return home. A week later Mikoyan cabled in reply, saying he wanted to avoid any further disappointment; could he now have an assurance that the 50% civil supplies' payment would be suitably modified? To this Wilson replied sharply, saying he would negotiate round the table and not by telegram. "You have now lost a week," he added. "I propose to arrive next Wednesday."

Wilson set off with only a small team of experts—all the commodity supplies arrangements had been finally worked out at the summer negotiations, with the important exception of wheat prices. These would have to be considered entirely afresh. A recent wheat crisis had sent prices rocketing in the world markets.

In those days the journey took almost two days by air. To complicate matters, the plane was grounded for a day in Berlin owing to weather conditions. Wilson sent a telegram to the British Ambassador in Moscow, Sir Maurice Peterson, explaining the delay and saying they now looked like arriving on a Russian national holiday—Stalin Constitution Day. He was anxious not to lose one of his three negotiating days: and asked the Ambassador to invite Mikoyan to dine at his hotel immediately after arrival.

The weather was so bad that the team very nearly failed to reach Moscow at all. After the five-hour flight, the pilot said he would go down to one thousand feet and if he failed to see the ground he would turn back. He went down to eight hundred feet, saw the ground, and landed safely. The Ambassador was there to meet them. He had received the telegram, and said he had invited Mikoyan to the Embassy for dinner—it would have been improper, he said, to suggest him going to a hotel.

Wilson was annoyed that his wishes had not been carried out. He felt sure Mikoyan would not come to the Embassy. To his surprise—Mikoyan accepted. This, he concluded must indicate a strong wish to do business.

They met and talked informally—partly about trade, but also about political affairs: the cold war was beginning to be very serious and the Council of Foreign Ministers' meeting in London was running into deadlock.

The official negotiations started next day and the attitude on both sides was tough from the start. Wilson, however, had been authorised by the Cabinet to give way on the 50% issue—provided everything else turned out satisfactorily.

Two huge obstacles existed. These concerned guaranteed deliveries and prices. Since all Russian trading was state trading, Mikoyan could give a complete guarantee on both prices and deliveries. Wilson was quite unable to do either: to have given such guarantees for locomotives and the like would have required unprecedented interference with private enterprise industry in Britain, and perhaps involved giving priority to Russian orders over those from America and the Commonwealth. Yet Mikoyan was insisting on both. It was impossible, repeated Wilson. Complete deadlock seemed inevitable.

The following day meetings took place with Mikoyan's deputy, a legal draftsman. No progress was made. Wilson said he would prefer to resume with Mikoyan, and this was arranged.

The next day was the third—and last. It had an inauspicious start: telegrams from the Cabinet were imposing impossible conditions. They were emphatic, of course, on the guarantees question. Under pressure from Canada, with whom we had a long-term wheat agreement, they were also insisting on the wheat price being no higher than with Canada. Also, the offer price of $130 for coarse grain must not be exceeded. In addition Bevin, angered by the difficulties of the Council of Foreign Ministers, was emphasising the importance of making no concession which could be interpreted diplomatically as weakness.

Wilson sent a quick reply. In view of everything, he would cease negotiating for wheat and go for coarse grain only. Mikoyan might have an exclusive "package deal" in mind and might therefore not agree, but he would gamble on the fact that the

Russians were relatively short of wheat compared with grain. He would negotiate in his own way and in his own time, he said, but would not go beyond $130.

Another message came from Bevin: while it was essential to show no weakness, it was equally important diplomatically not to break off negotiations altogether: if agreement was not reached, one or two officials should remain behind under the nominal chairmanship of the Ambassador, so as to continue discussions.

Wilson astutely arranged a lunch at the British Embassy for the Czechoslovak trading representatives. They had just reached a wheat agreement with the Russians, and over lunch they compared notes on the Russian trading methods—but not their prices.

He then held a "crisis" meeting with his team, to discuss the best method of bargaining for the grain. One official advised him to force the issue by offering the final price of $130 right away—a take-it-or-leave-it technique. If the Russians declined, the offer could be left on the table and form the basis for discussion with the officials remaining after Wilson's departure, thus meeting Bevin's wishes to postpone a complete break.

Wilson, however, wanted to get the grain. But he completed a provisional memorandum with the final price of $130, and tucked it into his pocket ready to produce only as a final gesture if total deadlock were reached.

The official negotiations with Mikoyan resumed at 5 p.m. Wilson began by announcing he was prepared to give the 50% write-off on the civil supplies debt. Mikoyan was visibly pleased.

Next, he unfolded a formula of his own invention to try to overcome the guarantees problem.

"I appreciate the reason for your insistence on these," he told Mikoyan, "and you must appreciate my inability to provide them, owing to the basic difference in our respective systems of manufacturing and trading. I have, however, a proposal to make. We shall give you a 'break' clause. If, say, after five months you have not secured your orders for the commodities you want, or an agreed proportion of them, at prices you consider reasonable, you can break off. You will meanwhile have been supplying us with 100,000 tons of grain each month."

127

Mikoyan reflected deeply, then said he was prepared to accept the principle of the formula.

Wilson next told him: "We are no longer in the market for wheat. We now want only coarse grains."

Mikoyan was very surprised, but accepted it. "All right," he replied. "We have only 750,000 tons of coarse grain for you—and we could have let you have some wheat."

"I know," replied Wilson. "But we could never have agreed on the price. Now the only outstanding problem is the price for grains."

"You know our price," replied Mikoyan. "It is 91% of the wheat price."

"I don't accept your wheat price—I don't accept your 91% formula," said Wilson. "Let's talk in terms of pounds or roubles or dollars."

Mikoyan replied: "I can only offer you 91% of the wheat price. You were going to negotiate over wheat, now you've withdrawn. I'll have to have it worked out, and let you know the figure."

"Oh no," replied Wilson quickly. "You know what price you've charged the Czechs."

This rejoinder came as a severe jolt to Mikoyan. He had heard about the lunch for the Czechs; he could not be sure whether Wilson knew the price they had paid. His embarrassment was aggravated by the fact that the figure was not at hand, and he did not want to rely on his memory. He was temporarily at a loss, and called an adviser to produce the figure.

From where he was sitting, Wilson caught a glimpse of the document, and of the price the Czechs had paid for barley: $123 —well below his "break" figure of $130.

Mikoyan was obviously keen to reach a settlement. He did not realise Wilson had spotted the Czech price of $123. Turning to him he said: "Our price for barley is $115."

Wilson tenderly fingered the draft memo in his pocket with its offer price of $130, and smiled inwardly. He was anxious to strike a good bargain, as well as to get the actual grains.

"Your figure is quite unacceptable," he told Mikoyan. "I offer you $96."

Mikoyan was taken aback. "I cannot regard that as a serious bid," he said simply. Neither did Wilson.

They argued and haggled for a short while. Then Wilson proposed a short adjournment to enable their legal advisers to draft the "break" agreement on deliveries and prices. It was agreed they should meet again in two hours. They began to disperse.

Wilson's plane had been standing by throughout the three days. Once or twice he had instructed the pilot to start up the engine. Now he ostentatiously instructed the pilot to warm up the engine again. "We shall be setting off on our return any time from now on," he explained.

Mikoyan came up to him. "I really want an agreement you know," he said sincerely.

"So do I," replied Wilson, with equal conviction.

When they resumed, he recognised there was an obligation on him to make a fresh bid. He started by making a straight offer of $108: this was well below the $130 limit, but getting nearer to the $115 proposed by Mikoyan. A good deal of haggling ensued over this—also various drafting points which kept cropping up. Suddenly a new complication arose. Mikoyan had heard that Britain had meanwhile bought some barley from Australia. By another day he would know the price. It therefore became essential, he reckoned, to delay Wilson's return for a day. He knew the British leader would not be likely to agree to this as a straight request, so he kept on and on with arguments about drafting points —and prices.

In fact, the price paid to the Australians was much higher than the $115 offered by Mikoyan. This alone would have hardened Wilson's intention not to extend his stay. But in any case, he had made the three days his limit, and it would be most impolitic to yield to any pressure to depart from this decision.

Mikoyan, however, was never to be found lacking in guile. At midnight he suddenly looked up and beamed to Wilson, "I have great pleasure in telling you of a special honour it falls to me to convey to you," he said. "You are invited to have dinner with Stalin in the Kremlin tomorrow night."

This ought to have been the ace of trumps. An opportunity of such a kind rarely came the way of an individual Western politician. It would be an occasion of exceptional personal interest—and could, conceivably, have provided a valuable chance for a frank and useful discussion on the mounting East-West political difficulties.

For a second Wilson hesitated. "I am terribly sorry," he said, "that I cannot accept this kind invitation. The fact is that I must be back in London for another dinner engagement. My Prime Minister is giving a dinner party at Downing Street for our King and Queen, and I am due to be present."

The legal arguing and financial haggling dragged on. Mikoyan was still trying to calculate how he could delay Wilson's return. At 1.30 a.m. he suddenly produced another trump. "I am sorry to have to tell you," he said, "that my deputy who, as you know, is also my legal adviser, has become ill and has gone home."

"I am sorry," said Wilson. "I hope he will soon recover. I am pleased to assure you, however," he added with a smile, "that *my* legal adviser will now act for both of us."

The unexpected response trapped Mikoyan. He could hardly accept the suggestion—yet to reject it would be offensive. He was obviously having difficulty in deciding his next move.

Wilson thought it might help him if the pilot again slipped out and warmed up the engine.

Mikoyan looked up. "My deputy will continue," he announced solemnly.

The discussing and arguing ranged on until, at long last, agreement was reached.

The time was 6 a.m.: the price agreed—$111. The two leaders arose and firmly shook hands. They both still looked remarkably fresh. Several of their respective advisers were already fast asleep —including Mikoyan's legal adviser.

Besides the valuable consequences for their respective countries, the negotiations had pleasant personal results: they formed the basis of an enduring friendship between the two men. The more they had argued and bargained, the more they had come to respect and like each other. Wilson never returned to Russia as President. But years later—in 1953—he was the first senior Western politician to visit the country after the cold war—thanks to his old friend, who bore him no personal grudge over the partial embargo he had imposed on goods for Russia at the time of the Berlin airlift.

He has visited Russia many times since. Very cordial talks with Mikoyan, including abundant reminiscences over the tough bargaining in 1947, have been a pleasant feature on each occasion. Twice the necessary visa has been held up because, as Soviet officials later explained to him: "When you first applied, your friend was not in Moscow. He wanted to be sure to be there to greet you when you came, so we had to oblige you to wait until he had returned."

During Wilson's visit to Russia early in 1963 Mikoyan was not in Moscow—he was ill at his house in the country. Wilson visited him there. Months later, at the funeral of President Kennedy in Washington, Mikoyan represented his country. Suddenly, among the many hundreds of leading political figures from all over the world, he spotted Wilson. He went straight up to him and greeted him warmly.

The relentless negotiations of 1947 had culminated in a lengthy telegram from Wilson to Cripps: "After seventeen-hour session complete agreement reached," it began—and proceeded to elaborate the seven main points, showing how on each one the British interests had prevailed.

Cripps read the telegram with deep satisfaction. He knew the whole Cabinet would be equally pleased. But he thought there was one especially distraught colleague who ought to be told the excellent news instantly—Tom Williams. He sent for him and handed him the telegram.

The Minister of Agriculture read it and burst into tears.


CHAPTER EIGHTEEN

In the summer of 1948 the country was startled to learn, from a number of newspapers, that the President of the Board of Trade had had to go barefoot to school: he had stated it publicly, so there could be no doubt about it. An even greater shock was to follow: former teachers and other authorities completely repudiated the suggestion. Somebody, apparently, was lying. As disclaimer followed disclaimer, it seemed clear that it must be the President himself.

At the time, and for years afterwards, some old friends were bewildered and wounded—and many political enemies were pleased—by the impression that a man in high office, who had always prided himself on his truthfulness, had on this occasion been exposed as no better than anybody else, and perhaps rather worse than most, when it came to honesty for political purposes. But the private files on this episode reveal quite a different picture and I believe it should now be presented in its true perspective.

The background to this unpredictable event was simple enough. At the beginning of July, the President had had to answer several questions in the House about the shortage of good shoes for children. A few days later he was speaking in Birmingham, and decided to elaborate his Parliamentary answers. He said that the shortage was due partly to the increased birth rate and partly to the post-war shortage of machinery for producing good quality shoes. He also pointed out that rationing had led to a greater demand for the best quality; people did not want to spend money, and waste coupons, on poor quality products which would wear out quickly—especially for their children.

He went on to relate this to a wider social change, as he saw it, and to altering fashions. Compared with the pre-war years, he said, there was far less unemployment, and far more money: many more people could now afford to buy good shoes, and this increased the shortage meanwhile. In his elementary schooldays, he said, "half the children in my class never had boots or shoes to their feet. They wore clogs, because they lasted longer than shoes of a comparable price."

He continued: "I have been up there again. The children of my old school are now running about with decent pairs of shoes because their fathers are in safe jobs and have got the social security which we promised our people."

The speech was reported, in an abbreviated form, in a large number of newspapers. His reference to clogs was omitted. Soon he was widely being reported as having claimed that half his schoolmates had had to go barefoot to school and that he himself had had to do likewise.

Old teachers who were interviewed, including one from Royds Hall—not the Milnsbridge Council School in question—denied the claim when they were interviewed by press reporters. "I was very fond of Harold Wilson," said one, "he was a brilliant boy and I am proud to have had a hand in his education, but I was surprised to read his remarks today. I simply cannot imagine his statement to be true."

Even more damaging was a repudiation from the Mayor of Huddersfield, Alderman Oliver Smith, himself a Socialist. One paper headed his denial: "Mayor Rebukes Wilson." Another paper, a national daily of high repute, quoted the Mayor as saying: "I was a teacher at the time Mr. Wilson went to school and I cannot recall ever seeing a single child walking the streets without boots or shoes . . . It is possible that some children ran about in bad shoes with their toes sticking out, but frankly I do not remember seeing even that. Naturally one occasionally saw a child wearing poor shoes. I do not want to oppose Mr. Wilson, but one must speak the truth. When I read his remarks, I thought he had overstepped the mark."

The Mayor was not one of the President's former teachers; in fact, they had never met. Two days later the following private letter reached the President's office:

> Mayor's Parlour,
> Town Hall,
> Huddersfield.
> 6th July 1948

Dear Mr. Wilson,

I was both astonished and annoyed to read in yesterday's press a very garbled version of a comment I was alleged to have

133

made on a recent speech of yours regarding footwear for children.

I want to assure you that what appeared in the paper was a complete travesty of what I actually said. One would gather from the press reports that I contested the truth of your statement, whereas I merely contented myself with saying to the paper's representative when he called on me that I did not live at Milnsbridge and that I personally and as a teacher, had never come across a case of a child being shoeless, but I did say that I had come across many cases where the shoes worn by children were only shoes in name.

I feel constrained to write a strong letter of protest to the Editor that his representative's report is quite inaccurate but I recognise that if I do so, it might merely result in a prolongation of the press articles on the matter. That might be contrary to your wishes and before writing, therefore, I should like to know what your wishes are.

Yours faithfully,
Oliver Smith,
Mayor.

The President sent the following private reply:

9th July 1948

My dear Mr. Mayor,

Thank you very much indeed for your letter of 6th July. It was very kind of you to write to me and I can well appreciate that your remarks had not been quoted correctly. I should be grateful if you would write a letter to the Editor, even if it does prolong the matter, but as you will have seen from many newspaper reports I have more or less been called a liar and I feel that anything you could say would be of great assistance.

Once again with many thanks.

Harold Wilson.

The Mayor thereupon sent the following letter to the Editor.

Mayor's Parlour,
Town Hall,
Huddersfield.
10th July 1948

Dear Sir,

On Sunday the 4th July I was intreviewed by a representative of your paper with regard to a recent alleged statement by the President of the Board of Trade on the subject of footwear for children.

The report in the issue of your paper on the 5th July gives an entirely wrong impression and contains two definite inaccuracies. I did not say "It is possible that some children ran about in bad shoes with their toes sticking out, but frankly I do not remember seeing even that. Naturally, one occasionally saw a child wearing poor shoes" nor did I say "I do not want to oppose Mr. Wilson, but one must speak the truth. When I read his remarks I thought he had overstepped the mark." What I was careful to say was that while I as a teacher had never seen a child at school entirely shoeless, I had seen children come to school wearing footwear which was in such a dilapidated state as to be shoes in name only and that I can well remember, some 25 years ago, seeing many children distressingly ill shod.

I protest strongly at the inaccuracy of your representative's report and would also offer the comment that the heading to this article is very tendentious.

Yours faithfully,
Oliver Smith
Mayor of Huddersfield.

In reply the Mayor received a letter from the paper in question in which it denied that "you were reported as having said anything to which strong exception ought to be taken."

Meanwhile, the President had himself issued a public denial of press reports: "I never suggested that my school friends had to go to school barefoot, as was the case in many more depressed areas. Such a suggestion would have been quite incorrect. There were before the war, however, thousands of children who actually went barefoot before the war . . . in the slums of Liverpool and other big cities which I can certainly confirm from my own experience . . . in Liverpool, Manchester and Birmingham."

Despite the (ungrammatical) repetition of the phrase "before the war," this denial was widely reported in the press with the phrase "*during* the war" substituted, thus making the assertion entirely different. Not surprisingly, angry denials and protests flowed from various officials in the three cities mentioned.

The web of misunderstanding and distortion was now widespread and tangled. Years later the "barefoot" legend was still a favourite sneer in some sections of the press and a convenient way of implying unreliability. In 1956, the former President opened a new school in the West Riding. The Headmaster had been one of his former teachers at New Street Council School in Milnsbridge. Looking towards the reporters present, Wilson said: "I am now going to repeat verbatim my notorious Birmingham speech of July, 1948."

He did so. Afterwards he turned to the Headmaster and said:

"Can you, from your own knowledge and experience, confirm the accuracy of these observations?"

The Headmaster said he could certainly do so.

"I hope," added the former President, "that the press representatives present have taken full notes of this occasion."

If they had, their editors evidently considered them of no interest to their readers. In the following years, the distortion repeatedly reappeared, and in March of 1963 appeared to be gaining new strength. A series of letters in the *Daily Telegraph* ended with the following:

Sir,

The remarks attributed to Mr. Harold Wilson about boots in the 1930's should not be dismissed as propaganda.

I lived and worked in the West Riding of Yorkshire from

1920 to 1946, and it was a part of my duties to inspect hundreds of schools each year. I well remember the poverty-stricken miners and textile workers when unemployment was rife.

As Vicar of Dewsbury I received and distributed boots and shoes through the Personal Service League, and our collections at Christmas services were given to the Boots for the Bairns Fund.

I knew Mr. Wilson's school, and although Huddersfield was not one of the worst hit areas there were many children and adults in the West Riding who had to rely upon welfare efforts, in those grim days, to provide footgear.

Yours faithfully,
W. J. Brown

Formerly Canon of Wakefield Cathedral and
Vicar and Rural Dean of Dewsbury,
Clacton-on-Sea, Essex.

Also in the summer of 1948 another issue, potentially involving much more than his personal repute, threatened to engulf the President. Nothing less than the integrity of Government conduct was at stake.

The origins of the scandal were within the Board of Trade. Wilson told me how the first intimation reached him on his return from a development area tour of Cumberland. The Permanent Secretary came to see him about a "very serious matter." He reminded him of a current case in which the Board of Trade might be prosecuting a football pools firm for alleged breach of the paper control orders. The firm in question had now informed the department that a certain individual had said he could get the prosecution called off if they paid him £5,000. Unpleasant insinuations had arisen in connection with the name of John Belcher, the Parliamentary Secretary and the alleged activities of a certain Mr. Sidney Stanley.

The President had never heard of Sidney Stanley, but, like the Permanent Secretary, he took an extremely serious view of the matter, and authorised all the papers to be referred instantly to the police, with the assurance of their complete freeedom to examine everything and everyone in the department. He also went immediately that evening to report the matter to Attlee, who said he would refer it to the Lord Chancellor. The police report would go to the Lord Chancellor, who would also interrogate Belcher. He did so, and Belcher submitted a document, which gave rise to a slight doubt about the propriety of his associations with Stanley.

The police conducted their enquiries rigorously. They questioned Belcher himself at length, and Belcher's Secretary, who had been very badly disabled in the war, was closely interrogated for eight hours.

The Lord Chancellor recommended the setting up of a Tribunal of Enquiry—a serious measure to deal with a serious situation. Attlee did not hesitate: the Tribunal was set up under Mr. Justice Lynskey, and given the widest possible powers to investigate all the ugly rumours of bribery and corruption in various Government and civil service circles.

Nobody had ever impugned the integrity of the President himself. Nevertheless, the source of the trouble was the Board of Trade, and he was the Minister responsible for everything in his department. If corruption on a serious scale were to be unearthed—enough, for example, to destroy the Government—he would technically be to blame. It was an unenviable position. The possible repercussions caused the Cabinet serious anxiety for several months. But Attlee's action in setting up the Tribunal was wholly endorsed: the truth, however unpleasant, must be discovered and revealed.

It was impossible to foresee the outcome. Police enquiries were extremely far-reaching—not a single rumour was overlooked, no matter how august its victim. There were ugly whispers against Dalton, for example—that he had favoured certain industrialists with financial concessions. Special Branch police were at work for many weeks in his constituency; they confirmed that he *had* given help to certain firms—but only in the entirely honourable fulfilment of the Government's policy on development areas.

The Government and Civil Service emerged with their probity

intact—with the distressing exception of John Belcher. He, too, was cleared of every charge of corruption, but was criticised for indiscretion on five issues—each of them directly or indirectly involving social contacts. He immediately resigned with what all observers described as dignity and honour.

Wilson told me that he himself thought privately that if the Tribunal could have been more familiar with the complexities and pressures of a vast department like the Board of Trade, where each day scores of quick decisions might have to be reached on such vital matters as controls or dispensations or special allocations, the findings on Belcher might have been less critical. He also regretted losing a most efficient Parliamentary Secretary. But there could be no question about the need for Belcher to resign. He had chosen some of his social contacts unwisely, his indiscretion could have affected his work—he could no longer enjoy full public confidence. The highest personal standards in public life must be upheld: to the President, as to all the Cabinet, there was only one thing for Belcher to do. And he did it.

* * *

Nobody at the Board of Trade was ever in any doubt about who was in charge during Harold Wilson's Presidency. He was in complete command and never at a loss either for action or for words. His authority, in fact, was almost a weakness: it depended partly on such a total mastery of every branch of the work that he often tended to become too absorbed in detail. He also found it difficult to refuse any of the multitude of invitations to business lunches and annual dinners of various Trade Associations and the like.

He believed in the importance of direct personal contact with all bodies of this kind, but several such functions each week, with a detailed speech at each—always composed by himself—demanded too much of his time and thought. Cripps had warned him of this risk, but he paid too little attention to the advice.

There were, of course, clear advantages too in his countless meetings with industrial representatives in all parts of the country: he could see for himself exactly what the difficulties and problems were. He was certainly tireless in his travels. The city of Dundee, for example, over 450 miles from Westminster, had several visits from him as President. Years later he returned there—in 1962—to attend an informal gathering of businessmen and others to discuss plans for industrial development.

"We're planning to send a deputation to the President of the Board of Trade," they told him.

"Don't do that," he replied, "it's a waste of time. The President will be meeting one deputation after another, and you will probably make little impact. What you should do is to get the President to come here. If he sees for himself what the situation is, it will give him a much more vivid impression of your needs."

The suggestion seemed to surprise the gathering. It turned out that he had been the last President to visit the city. During the eleven years since he had ceased to hold office, not one of his successors had found time to come.

As President, he was impatient of any departmental incompetence. This, and his inflexible command, made him unpopular with some. On the whole, however, he was liked. Most of his staff found him an excellent mixer. There was no "side" to him and he easily established friendly relations with all ranks. His relentless devotion to work never obliterated a capacity for gaiety. Even on occasions demanding solemn deliberation, a schoolboy exuberance could suddenly explode into a string of sparkling witticism. He quickly spotted an absurdity in any situation and enjoyed exposing it to incisive ridicule.

The personal qualities his staff found most admirable were his exceptional intellectual capacity, his tenacious determination and the sense of dedication he brought to his task—with a missionary conviction of the rightness of his policy for the country. They noted, too, that no matter how urgently he might be engaged in Governmental affairs, he always found time for family matters—and old friends.

Sometimes his senior staff speculated about his ultimate future. They never doubted that he was likely to go ahead. The Chancellorship seemed a likely office eventually, though his increasing

140

intcrest in the overseas features of his work led some to picture him as a future Foreign Secretary. Several, recalling that he was still only in his early thirties, could just imagine him ultimately as a Prime Minister. They felt, however, that he would first have to develop more rounded political sensibilities: he still seemed more like a kind of Ministerial Permanent Secretary than a statesman.

They also believed that his Parliamentary performances at this stage did little to promote his prospects. His determination to be comprehensive made his speeches too long, too crammed with every fact and figure, and spoken at breakneck speed. Every word was prepared in advance and this led to a stilted and monotonous delivery. His repetitive preoccupation with the need for increasing exports, in particular, produced some turgid results for those Members present. Worst of all, his speeches were humourless, and gave no suggestion of the wit he could display in less formal surroundings. He had, however, one saving grace: he knew how dull he was. If, by now, he was able to speak in the House without strain, at least he recognised that the task of his listeners was more arduous.

Sometimes his staff were irritated by his meticulous concern with detail, and by what they regarded as his almost obsessively cautious method of reaching an important decision. The issues involved were, of course, highly complex: at a time of acute national shortages, with recurring financial crises, any decision affecting controls and rationing, for example, incurred grave risks. He would hold conference after conference with senior officials, going over the same points again and again before reaching his decision.

"That *bloody* man," said one exasperated official on emerging from an unusually protracted session. "He's taken exactly twice as long as Stafford would have done in reaching his decision."

"Yes," said another. "But he's at least three times as likely to be right."

From late 1948 to early 1949 he engaged in what some called, "an orgy of de-controls."

He had no doctrinaire socialist views about the continuing existence of what were, after all, war-time rationing schemes. They were geared to provide fair shares for all in a time of insuperable national shortages, but in his view there was no good doctrinal reason for perpetuating arrangements for manufacturers, exporters and importers to have quotas based on percentages of their pre-war averages, for example. The result, he believed, was simply to penalise the enterprising firm and feather-bed the unenterprising one. He therefore introduced a new departmental principle: henceforth, the onus of proof for continuing a control was to be on the official responsible for operating it, instead of the other way round.

Often more work was involved in lifting a control than in maintaining it. Despite all the after-dinner speeches—and all the clamour in the press—demanding a speedy return to full private enterprise, traders often came to him appealing for controls to remain. Hardwood merchants, for example, appealed for the control not to be lifted. If it were, they said, they would devise a market-sharing scheme whereby each member would receive a pre-arranged percentage of the total supplies. The President reminded them of the arguments in favour of unfettered competition which had featured at timber trade dinners. "When I lift this control," he said, "you are going to compete. That's the whole idea."

"But—new people will come into the trade," they protested.

"Isn't that what you want?" he asked.

"Not really," they said. "We might get some spivs coming into the trade."

"How do I know some of *you* aren't spivs?" asked the President. "You're putting a fence round yourselves: everyone inside it is all right—is an honest, good and efficient trader. But what about the newcomers—ex-servicemen, for example—who want to come into the trade?"

"Well," they replied, "we might make special arrangements to give jobs to men out of the forces."

The President was unimpressed. "Ex-servicemen might want to set up in business themselves," he said. "Why shouldn't they be free to do so? No—I am going to de-control, and you must compete."

With a number of other industries the same arguments arose—
the cosmetics industry, for example, who opposed de-control for
fear of newcomers "who wouldn't have the same standards."

"Or who might break into your market, you mean?" said the
President—and lifted the control.

Some of his Government colleagues felt uneasy over the speed
of his de-controlling policy; not everyone shared his view that
there was no political principle involved. This did not deter him.
He was in charge of the Board of Trade, and it was up to him to
decide. Even on some major policy matters, he reached his decisions without always seeking Cabinet approval. On derationing of
clothing, for example, he conferred only with Attlee.

Towards the end of 1949 he was still essentially an administrator, pre-occupied almost exclusively with his own extensive
bureaucracy. He felt relatively uninformed on other Cabinet
affairs—and largely unaware of the various shades of doctrinal
opinion developing among many of his Parliamentary colleagues.

A dramatic enlightenment lay ahead.

# PART FIVE

*Opposition*

෨෨෨

## CHAPTER NINETEEN

The ferment of disagreement which was to sweep the Parliamentary Labour Party into disruption first touched Wilson in late 1949. The truth behind his subsequent rôle differs sharply from the traditional version of events.

Earlier that year he had gone on an extensive trade tour of Canada and returned convinced that Britain would have to devalue the pound: he found British prices right out of line with current trends. Later, Cripps became ill, and during his absence Wilson was put in ministerial charge of the Treasury. It became his responsibility to sign all the chits for the sale of British gold reserves.

"It's like watching yourself bleed to death," he told his friends.

Douglas Jay, Economic Secretary to the Treasury, and Gaitskell, who was becoming increasingly concerned with economic affairs, took the initiative in proposing devaluation. Attlee consulted Wilson, who agreed. He was shortly due to have a continental holiday with Marjorie, and arranged to call privately at the Swiss clinic where Cripps was receiving treatment to tell him of the latest developments.

The large expenditure on armaments was beginning to alarm a growing number of Labour M.P.s, especially in the light of the seriously deteriorating economic situation. Hints about the imminent need to curtail the social services added to their anxiety. A sign of the coming trend was a reduction in the housing programme from 200,000 to 175,000. Contrary to Wilson's advice, Bevan agreed to this cut as the only way to save the health services from the economy axe. Wilson regarded this as undue manoeuvring, though he endorsed the motive behind the tactics. In fact, the reduction was never made: at the first sign of easing Bevan successfully applied for the Treasury's approval to reinstate the programme.

The General Election in February of 1950 reduced the very substantial Labour majority of 186 to an actual working majority of 6. This, of course, delayed the coming storm: many Labour M.P.s, reluctant to imperil a Government based on such a slender majority, restrained their criticisms and sometimes even voted against their consciences.

Tensions were not confined to the back benches. They were beginning to develop equally strongly within the Government. Cripps, who had by now succeeded Dalton as Chancellor of the Exchequer, was convinced his 1950 Budget must provide for health service charges. Gaitskell, who became Minister of State for Economic Affairs, was urging him to curtail the constantly rising cost of these and other social services. To a substantial section of the Labour movement, however, the National Health Service was an integral and sacrosanct part of the Welfare State. The principle of essential medical services being freely available to all, irrespective of the total cost, was regarded by them as inviolate. A first-class row was thus inevitable.

Cripps was known by his colleagues to be intending to introduce some health charges in his coming Budget and his fiercest opponent was the Minister himself, Aneurin Bevan. Wilson was very close to Bevan in his thinking, and was also on terms of close friendship with him. At the same time, he was equally friendly towards Cripps. For a while he found himself mediating between the two. He constantly urged Bevan not to press Cripps too hard, pointing out that the latter was now a sick man. To Cripps he kept stressing that Bevan was in earnest in his threats to resign.

In the event, although the Budget did provide for health charges, none was introduced. This placated Bevan and Wilson and those who shared their view, but it angered some others—including, especially, Gaitskell. Expenditure on the health services was steadily and sharply rising and continuous discussions on their financial implications were held under the Prime Minister's chairmanship. At these Gaitskell continued to press strongly for the introduction of health charges, as he did also at the Thursday evening meetings, presided over by Cripps, and attended by all Ministers directly concerned with the country's economy, including Bevan.

The purpose of these meetings, which were held over dinner, was partly to exchange information and partly to reach as much agreement as possible without having to refer matters to the Cabinet. In July Bevan ceased to attend: Gaitskell's attitude angered him, and he said he was not going to sit and have dinner with a man who was out to destroy the one thing he most believed in.

The split was widened by the consequences of the Korean war. American stockpiling created a serious shortage of raw materials and a sharp rise in prices. The cost of living was soaring. American pressure led to a big increase in the British armaments programme to £3,600 million over three years. This was accepted by the Cabinet with varying degree of reluctance, and with extreme foreboding by Wilson. He knew from his war-time administrative experience of programming and progressing that the country was poorly equipped for an effort of such magnitude.

In October Cripps retired through ill-health, and Gaitskell, as Minister of State for Economic Affairs, was his natural successor as Chancellor.

In December renewed American pressure for a further big expansion in armaments led Gaitskell to propose an increase to £4,700 million over three years—a figure, Wilson believed, which was quite unrealistic. He recalled his experiences at the Ministry of Supply in 1940, when maximum programmes for everything had been introduced. One hundred per cent achievement had been reached with motor vehicles, for example, which were easy: with tanks, which were difficult, only a five per cent achievement had been reached. Within certain tolerances, the lower the target, the higher the result. In terms of real resources, he concluded, the latest armaments programme was physically impossible for the country—however necessary it might seem in principle.

He also disapproved of Gaitskell's conception of the Chancellor's rôle. He thought he seemed too ready to yield to pressure.

Wilson also felt uneasy about the pressure for China to be branded an aggressor. Bevin's health was now steadily declining and he had much less grip on his conduct of foreign affairs.

The raw materials shortage was now becoming more desperate owing to the cornering of supplies by America. The sulphur shortage was especially menacing. Sulphur was essential over a large range of industries, including steel. Without adequate supplies large sections of industry would grind to a halt, there would be widespread unemployment—and the armaments programme itself would be nullified on those grounds alone.

In January of 1951 the new provisional £4,700 million armaments programme was introduced—provisional as a result of pressure from Bevan and Wilson: if the programme were to prove impossible because of the raw materials situation, or for any other reason, it could be cut back.

As preparations for the coming Budget began, it became obvious that a head-on clash was inescapable. Gaitskell argued that a cut in expenditure on the social services was going to be essential, and stated his intention to budget accordingly. Bevan and Wilson remained implacably opposed to this. By now Bevan, who had ceased to be Minister of Health and had become Minister of Labour, was discussing his future tactics with a number of backbench members of the party, including Barbara Castle, Richard Crossman, Hugh Delargy and Ian Mikardo.

Meetings of this informal group were also attended by John Freeman, Parliamentary Secretary, Ministry of Supply (who later became Editor of the *New Statesman*, and the celebrated interviewer in the television "Face to Face" series). Sometimes other Ministers, including John Strachey, Secretary of State for War, were also present. The general trend of Government policy was kept under anxious scrutiny, and there developed a bond of understanding between members of the group in relation to possible resignations—a moral commitment that if Bevan felt it necessary to resign, those associated with the group would be prepared to stand by him.

As the time for the Budget drew near, Attlee became ill with serious internal trouble and had to enter hospital. It was clear he

148

would be away for some time and Morrison became Acting Prime Minister.

A few days before the Budget, Bevan made an important speech in the East End of London. He said he would never remain a member of any Government which introduced health charges. The speech was reported in the press, but some of his colleagues regarded it as mere bluster—and bluff. Dalton was one: Wilson assured him he was mistaken: "Nye means business —he can't climb down after committing himself in public like that," he emphasised, adding: "What's more—if Nye does resign, he'll take over the leadership of the Left throughout the country."

Dalton seemed aghast at the prospect, and said he would see Gaitskell and counsel great caution. But nobody seemed able to do anything to heal the bitter split in the Cabinet. Ernest Bevin, who had by now become Lord Privy Seal, was asked to look into the whole matter. He interviewed Bevan and Wilson and appeared to sympathise with their views. He subsequently tried to persuade Gaitskell to modify his plans. But Bevin was seriously ailing. He failed in his efforts, and several days later he died.

On the day before the Budget Gaitskell reported to Cabinet colleagues that health charges were to be introduced, and it was reported that argument raged in an atmosphere of prolonged consternation. That evening Bevan and Wilson went to see Attlee in hospital and expressed their total opposition to the proposal. Attlee was very disconcerted, and afterwards sent for Gaitskell, strongly advising him to exercise caution. Gaitskell was unyielding, however, and stated unequivocally that he must be free to proceed with the proposal—or he would resign.

By Budget day the Cabinet disagreements had become common knowledge and the possibility of Bevan's resignation was the subject of much press comment. On the following day a meeting of the Parliamentary Labour party produced anxious appeals for no resignations. Bevan declared his loyalty to the party—and his anxiety, for the party's sake, not to resign. Granted equivalent forbearance "from the other side," he said, he would gladly stay.

There emerged a feeling that the ultimate disruption was somehow going to be averted. The immediate bone of contention—fifty percent payment for spectacles and dentures—would require a new Bill. Despite the provisions of the Budget, it looked as if this measure might not now be used.

Throughout this crisis, Wilson's outward calm never cracked. His closest advisers at the Board of Trade were quite aware of the Government disagreements, and realised that they might lose their President as a result. He appeared, however, to be following his usual diligent routine in his usual unruffled manner. Clearly, they thought, he must be facing the situation with no great personal distress.

Mary knew differently. She could guess something of the agony he was suffering. He told her of each development in the evolving crisis, and of his own mounting disquiet. For the first time in their married life he found it difficult to sleep. He lay awake, sometimes for hours, before finally dozing off for a few hours.

She recognised he was facing a major issue of conscience. She had always regarded Bevan with tremendous admiration and felt instinctively that Harold, in identifying himself with Bevan's position, must be in the right. She supported his steadfast adherence to his principles and his readiness to resign if necessary.

Herbert was also anxiously following every act in the unfolding drama. He heard confidentially from his son more about the particular arguments and personal alignments; and he needed no briefing on the vast issues at stake. He kept emphasising the serious consequences certain to follow from resignation—knowing all the while that his son would make his own judgment, however damaging the personal repercussions might be.

Wilson felt himself caught in a cruel dilemma. If he remained in office, he would be committed to a policy with which he fundamentally disagreed. This, he believed, would be unfair both to his colleagues and to himself. What was involved was one of the basic assumptions of the entire economic policy and the whole Government should be united in agreement on it. As a Minister directly responsible for part of this economic policy, he would be in a totally false position. (He had seriously considered resigning in February over the raw materials shortage, but had been dissuaded by Bevan.)

Yet to desert the Government, with its tiny majority, would strike a blow against the party which alone could create the kind of society he believed in. His action would be condemned as treachery. His political career, so rich in promise and early fulfillment, would certainly be hurtled into reverse—if not altogether wrecked.

His family would suffer materially, too. His ministerial salary of £5,000 a year would drop immediately to an ordinary M.P.'s salary of £1,000—and this at a time when the boys' education was beginning to cost more, the house mortgage was heavy, and Mary's widowed mother was dependent on continuing financial help from them. Herbert was nearing retirement, and he and Ethel would certainly need increased help in their old age.

He was facing a situation not uncommon in politics, when the ultimate decision is bound to be wrong, although the alternatives are probably even worse. He believed in the importance of strong and effective armed defence, but he had always argued that the latest armaments programme was physically beyond the country's capacity. The proposed interference with the original principles of the health service was, he believed, irrefutable evidence of this—besides being unacceptable in terms of Socialist morality. In his view, the Government's actions on this must become the acid test of their whole policy—and of his own willingness to remain in office. He devoutly hoped that a compromise might still somehow be reached, and he kept urging the impulsive Bevan to make no hasty decision.

Ten days after the Budget, Wilson was in Norfolk to address a Friday meeting of the Yarmouth Chamber of Commerce. He was called urgently to the telephone. The Minister of Labour was at the other end.

"I'm resigning," said Bevan, simply. "They've introduced the Bill."

Wilson returned to the meeting. His subsequent speech gave no hint of the momentous storm about to break on the Government, and his usual placid demeanour revealed nothing of his personal strain.

He now had no doubt about what he must do, and in some measure this alleviated his distress. He played a round of golf at Yarmouth next morning before returning to London. When he arrived home a 'phone call came from Freeman. There had been a meeting of the informal Parliamentary "Bevanite" group: it was felt by them all, including Bevan, that there should be no further resignations—it would be too great a blow for the Government.

"I entirely disagree," said Wilson. "Since I share Nye's views, this would put me in an impossible position."

Wilson and Freeman decided to go to see Bevan the following day—Sunday, 22nd April. By the time they arrived, Bevan's formal resignation was already a day old. But he seemed to be feeling shaken and almost guilty over the enormity of what he had done. He kept dwelling on the consequences, as if to expose his conscience to their scrutiny, evidently hoping to secure moral reassurance. It had been a devastating decision with a grave impact on the party, he emphasised—and it was important to have no more resignations.

Wilson was unshaken. "Look," he said, "ninety-eight per cent of the blow has already come from your resignation. John and I are only the small remaining balance."

Bevan repeated that he felt strongly that quite enough had already been done to shake the Government and pleaded with Wilson and Freeman not to resign.

Wilson was quite adamant. "You're asking me to do the impossible," he said. "Since I share your views on the health service, and since I also regard the armaments programme as economically impracticable, I must in honour join you in resignation."

Freeman was surprised by Wilson's unyielding authority in taking his stand. He had never had close dealings with him, and had felt no special reason to be impressed by him. Now he began to see him in a new light. Noting the unbending resolve, he wondered whether he was witnessing a future party leader in action.

Wilson and Freeman were in complete accord about the area of disagreement. They went with Bevan in deploring the health

9. *Wilson and Kennedy after conferring in Washington in April 1963.*

10. *June 15, 1963. Khrushchev interrupts conference with Wilson to announce a new space flight, that of Lt. Col. Velery Bykovsky.*

11. *Wilson leaves his Hampstead home to attend a House of Commons debate on the Profumo scandal in 1963.*

12. *Prime Minister with foreign secretary Patrick Gordon-Walker.*

13. *Mr. Wilson discusses bulb growing during holiday in St. Mary's, largest of the Scilly Isles.*

14. *In August 1963 Mr. and Mrs. Wilson with their sons (Robin, 19 and Giles, 15) on holiday in the Scilly Isles.*

15. *At the Labour Party Convention, 1964.*

charges, but their essential case had all along rested on the physical impracticability of the armaments programme. They now urged Bevan to stress this much wider area. It would be absurd, they said, to have resigned simply on the "teeth and spectacles" issue. He would make himself look ridiculous—and many would believe that he was prompted by pique.

Bevan was persuaded. The following day his resignation speech to the Commons went far beyond the original objection to charges for spectacles and dentures. Bevan, in fact, had become a Wilsonite—a reversal of the rôles constantly ascribed wrongly to them. Bevan's evolving policy owed much more to Wilson's intellectual inspiration than was ever recognised.

Up to now, Freeman had felt far from sure what action he himself should take. The official facts made public at the time—and since—suggest little of the crude events which actually decided him. They are worth disclosing now as an integral part of the background picture.

While Freeman fully shared Wilson's views and admired his resoluteness in deciding to resign, he was also impressed by Bevan's ardent plea to avoid further resignations. Others too were urging him to stay—Dalton, for example, privately saw him twice and advised him strongly not to be influenced by Bevan and Wilson; they were completely mistaken, he said, and in any case Freeman could be sure of a big political future if he remained in office.

Suddenly the Chief Whip summoned Freeman. Lest he might be thinking of following Bevan's example, said the Chief Whip, he would like to tell him privately that the Prime Minister very much hoped he would stay. Only the other week, he said, the P.M. had been talking of Freeman as a likely future Financial Secretary to the Treasury.

Freeman was shocked by this form of pressure. "I am not interested," he said simply, and walked away.

The Chief Whip misinterpreted the reaction, and later sent for him again. There were, he assured him, even more tempting jobs in the offing than Financial Secretary to the Treasury. It now seemed, for example, that the Board of Trade was to become vacant, and Freeman would undoubtedly be a strong candidate for that. In any case, continuing loyalty would be rewarded with a much more important job than his present one, and—whatever it might be—a seat in the Cabinet was almost certain.

Freeman was incensed by the crude implication that his allegiance might be subject to barter. However much he might have preferred to remain in office, to do so now would irreparably impair the integrity of his outlook. The Chief Whip had achieved the reverse of his intentions; he had swept away all Freeman's remaining doubts about resigning.

When Bevan delivered his resignation speech to the Commons on Monday, 23rd April, 1951, Wilson had already been to see Attlee in hospital. It was a painful encounter for both men. Wilson's regard for Attlee was exceedingly high, and his personal relations with him had always been excellent. It was especially unpleasant to have to inflict a blow on a leader he liked and respected at a time of illness and when any further weakening of the Government's position must make his action seem like a major defection.

The interview was typically short and sharp. Attlee knew, of course, of Wilson's longstanding disquiet over the increased armaments commitments, but by now he had been ill and out of direct touch for some time; reports from Morrison and others could never make up for his recent lack of first-hand, personal observation. So the resignation came as a shock. He thought very highly of Wilson's abilities, and regarded him as a man of maturing stature. He much regretted losing him and—like so many others—assumed that Bevan's dynamic personality had proved too much for Wilson's relatively inexperienced youthfulness.

Since Wilson would not have resigned if Bevan had felt able to remain in office, it was in one sense right to credit Bevan with having influenced him. In other respects, however, the view underestimated Wilson's single-hearted resolution and detachment. In fact, all Bevan's formidable powers of persuasion had been employed to try to induce Wilson *not* to resign.

Attlee believed that had it not been for his own illness, all three resignations could have been avoided. Although this must always remain a matter for speculation, it is worth recording that this belief was shared by Bevan, Wilson and Freeman themselves.

They felt that the Government's disarray owed as much to Gaitskell's threat to resign as to their own actual resignations, and that if Attlee had been in command throughout the crisis he could have prevented the Chancellor from committing himself so uncompromisingly.

Compared with the headlined sensation of Bevan's resignation, Wilson's departure was greeted with much less drama. The Parliamentary Correspondent of *The Times* commented:

> Mr. Wilson's action has the appearance of making the rift in the Cabinet more serious, but this second resignation appears to be treated by the Government and the Labour Party as a matter of no great consequence. The President of the Board of Trade—who was the youngest member of the Cabinet—has been in Parliament only since 1945, and he lacks the political or trade union background and affiliations which are common to most Labour Ministers.

Under the front page headline: "A Prodigy Returns to the Wilderness," another Parliamentary commentator wrote:

> Mr. Harold Wilson's resignation today means a step from the sunlit path of a former Whitehall prodigy to the bitter winds that blow in a political wilderness. And it has taken him only six years in which he first appeared on the Parliamentary scene to make the move . . . The chubby economist, "baby" of the Government, the one-time council school scholarship boy . . . from his election at Ormskirk had a short route to becoming the Government's Young White Hope and he moved up the political escalator at a tremendous pace . . . He seemed, at 35 last month, to be near the top of a very high ladder with perhaps glittering prizes still to come. Now it looks at first glance as though the upper rungs have been taken out.

Most initial press comment was highly unfavourable, and some was scathingly contemptuous.

An exception was an article in a trade union fortnightly journal with a limited circulation. After summarising his career, it continued:

And now the prodigy has moved to a seat on the back benches —a seat he might well have never known. He has deliberately evacuated a position of power in the orthodox hierarchy to enunciate a policy dictated by conscience . . . Harold Wilson, at an age when most men are only beginning to make their way in the world has turned his broad back on a career that many twice his age would be proud to have to their credit. But it should be remembered that at his age the door of opportunity is still wide open: ambition remains a cogent force. Who can doubt that in the hurly-burly of contemporary politics, the talent and ambition of Harold Wilson, plus his native common sense, will lead him once more through that door?

Wilson had hoped to avoid making a statement in the House, but felt he ought to do so after the cool reception given to Bevan's performance. Bevan had been diffuse, rambling and bitter, and even his supporters had found it difficult to show enthusiasm. It was important, Wilson thought, that the criticism of Government policy should be precisely stated and clearly understood.

He took Mary with him to the House. She had listened to some of his major speeches as a Minister. Now, as he waited to make his personal statement from the lowliest position he had ever occupied since entering Parliament, she watched him with a mixture of pride and sadness.

"Thirty minutes on the Argentine agreement kept him fidgeting with his notes," wrote one reporter, "but he got off coolly enough. For one so suddenly removed from the convenience of the despatch box he made a dexterous job of his neatly-strung notes. It was a total contrast to Mr. Bevan's performance. Mr. Bevan had ended with his boats ablaze. Mr. Wilson's boats carried fire-fighting equipment."

Press comment on his statement was generally favourable. The *Manchester Guardian* described it as "a lesson in how to resign," and *The Times* reported:

Inevitably the personal explanation which Mr. Harold Wilson made in the House of Commons today of his resignation from office compelled comparison with that offered by Mr. Bevan from the same place in the Chamber yesterday. It was a sober, modest and restrained performance, with no oratorical flourishes and no attempt at personal recrimination. Moreover, it breathed a sense of loyalty to his own party which commanded much acclamation from his own side of the crowded House when he ended.

Mr. Wilson made his points simply and concisely, speaking—more slowly than usual—from notes. He at once declared his strong support for an effective defence programme, but equally firmly he asserted that the Budget was based on a series of estimates including a rearmament programme which he did not believe to be physically practicable with the raw materials available to us. The effect was to disrupt the basis of our economy and endanger our standard of living—including the social services. We had not had our rightful share of the materials available as members of the Atlantic community.

There was a burst of cheering from the bench below him—in which Mr. Bevan's voice emerged sharply—when Mr. Wilson declared bluntly that the American Government and people must choose between their partners' defence programme, on the one hand, and their own stockpile and the level of their unrestricted civil consumption on the other. Until the right choice was made, our defence programme remained an illusion.

He ended with a sentence which drew the warmest and widest Labour tribute—promising that although he had found it necessary to leave the Government, he intended inside and outside the House to do everything in his power to support the party and the Government in the difficult times which lay ahead.

Mary's feeling of pride and sadness were heightened as she afterwards walked by Harold's side along the corridors of the House. She was also upset by the personal reactions of some party members; as they walked along, they passed some of the people who had been close colleagues of Harold's until the day before. Now one or two passed by looking sourly angry, while others drew aside in embarrassment. Whatever they felt, they all walked by in silence. So too did Winston Churchill, Leader of the Opposition. Mary had once been introduced briefly to him and now he bowed majestically to her as she glanced in his direction.

Mary went home on her own. Whatever the future might hold, Robin and Giles still had to have their tea and be put to bed.

As each hour passed, a mounting feeling of melancholy overcame her. She kept thinking of the sour looks she had noticed—and of the venom sure to be directed against Harold. By now, she feared, it must have started.

She went upstairs, but was too unhappy to sleep. At last, at 3 a.m. Harold returned. He seemed surprisingly buoyant, and told her he had received some friendly comments on his speech, even from several members of the party who disagreed with him. He had also had some bitter reproaches, and more than one former Government colleague had angrily assured him his career was irretrievably in ruins:

"And now," he went on, "I have an important personal message for you. Brendan Bracken came up to me in the smoke room and said Winston had asked him to deliver a message—to ask Harold Wilson to tell his wife that it was a big step for a young man to give up the fruits of office; he knew, because he had done it himself. But she musn't worry, because if he felt he was doing the right thing, that was all that mattered, and in any case her husband wouldn't have to face the same degree of obloquy that he himself had suffered when he was out of sympathy with his own party before the war. Brendan told me," added Harold, "that the old man asked him to get this message to you, and said to be sure you should know how much he felt for you."

The sympathetic warmth of the message flooded over Mary. For a moment she forgot the strain and burst into tears. Next morning she asked Harold to be sure to thank Churchill for his comforting words.

Wilson had often confronted Churchill in the House, but had

seldom previously had direct dealings with him on a personal level. He sought him out and told him how much his wife had appreciated his kind message.

"It moved her very much," said Wilson, noting that Churchill, always quickly moved, was himself in tears.

Later that day Wilson said to a friend: "Until forty-eight hours ago I had a full-time job. Now it seems my only job is to act as a messenger between my wife and Churchill, each of whom is moved to tears by a message from the other."

The characteristic friendliness of Churchill's private message contrasted sharply with some of the savage public utterances as the week went by. The Socialist peer, Lord Quibell, said: "I think the main trouble with Mr. Wilson is that he was given an important post and it went to his head."

Sir Hartley Shawcross, who became the new President of the Board of Trade, was presumed to be referring to his predecessor when he spoke of "some highbrows educated beyond their capacity," and Dalton referred to Wilson as "Nye's little dog."

Attlee greatly deprecated such utterances. He himself never questioned Wilson's sincerity. He regarded him as mistaken and as unduly influenced by Bevan, but he felt no personal rancour towards him.

The Wilson family expected anger, but felt wounded by the vilification. Mary, Herbert and Ethel believed Harold's action showed courage and sincerity and they deeply resented any addition to the private suffering they knew he had already undergone.

They grieved unnecessarily. The one person quite unmoved by the abuse was Wilson himself. No personal attacks could be as painful as the dilemma itself had been. He had made his decision and acted on it; attacks, however bitter or unwarranted, must simply be shrugged off. This meant no loss of inner personal sensitivity, but reflected a strengthening of outer professional purpose. The steel had been tempered, and now the short restless nights of fitful sleep were over. Harold Wilson, super-bureaucratic President of the Board of Trade, had died.

Harold Wilson, politician, was born.

# PART SIX

## *Party Leader*

### CHAPTER TWENTY

Within hours of his resignation, Wilson received a variety of impressive offers of jobs. Some of them were rather vague and mentioned no specific remuneration. Others, however, had a precise sum attached to the offer, and together these amounted to £22,000 a year. One was the chairmanship of a big public company; another was an executive job in the film industry at a starting salary of £13,000 a year. His handling of the important films deal, as President, with America, had impressed a number of key people in the industry, and in some respects he had enjoyed this particular transaction more than most.

Some of the offers would have required him either to reduce drastically the time he could give to politics, or even to abandon a Parliamentary career altogether. This was out of the question. In any case, he was in principle opposed to accepting a business directorship. He therefore declined all the invitations.

Shortly afterwards, however, he accepted the position of part-time economic adviser to the timber firm of Montague L. Meyer. Besides giving him a salary, the firm took on his secretary and provided him with an office. The arrangement was ideal in every respect. It enabled him to maintain his income not too far below the same level as for the previous five years, and gave him valuable inside knowledge of the workings of industry. It was in the interests of the firm that he should undertake a good deal of travel abroad; this enabled him to strengthen his knowledge of foreign affairs, and develop an increasing number of fruitful contacts in other countries.

He took his business responsibilities seriously. Before the war, the firm had been mainly importers. During the war, they had had to specialise in home-grown timber production. After the war, they developed their interests in countries overseas, including Sarawak, Corsica, and elsewhere. This involved their new economic adviser in a detailed study of local foreign taxation, exchange rates and foreign laws.

His part-time job with Montague Meyer continued until 1959. By that time the firm had altered the direction of some of its chief interests, and Wilson felt his usefulness would be reduced. He was also anxious to concentrate more fully on political affairs, and his chairmanship of the Public Accounts Committee—one of the most important Select Committees of the House of Commons—was going to require an exceptional share of his time. Although he felt the loss of the substantial part-time salary, he was able to supplement his income by consultancy fees from several other firms, and by fees for articles in the press.

Not the least satisfactory aspect of his association with Montague Meyer was his freedom, right from the start, to pursue all his main political interests. Several weeks after his resignation as President in 1951 he wrote to a friend:

Looking back on it, I have no regrets at all either politically or personally. Politically we felt we had to make a stand somewhere and already the effects of these resignations have been seen both in America and in domestic politics. Personally, after six years in office—and at the finish working sixteen hours a day, including Sundays—I was getting pretty near the end of my tether, and most people who know me say I now look ten years younger than when I resigned. I certainly feel it and although I am working pretty hard, I am now doing only the things that interest me and not all the things that I had to. I am doing a fair amount of writing, one or two books, a series of articles for *Reynolds News* (which has the great advantage of being read by most people in the Labour movement), one or two pamphlets and so on. It is wonderful to feel free after six years of the other life, and indeed, to take a closer interest in Parliamentary duties and in my constituency.

In fact, his constituency required a great deal of attention. His majority in the 1950 General Election had been only 834. Although his local party backed him loyally and enthusiastically in his resignation, popular opinion in the country was going steadily against Labour, and his Conservative opponent was conducting a vigorous campaign. The seat was clearly in great danger.

To add to the difficulties, the Conservative candidate looked like benefiting from the local religious situation. The Roman Catholic Bishop of Leeds had publicly deplored the actions of "crypto-Communists" in the Labour Party. This was being interpreted nationally as a reference to the "Bevanites," and could have been interpreted locally as a reference to Wilson. It was certainly clear that the Conservatives in the constituency were intending to treat it as such, and several Catholic supporters resigned from the local Labour party. With a large number of Catholic votes at stake, the outlook became serious.

Wilson acted promptly. With the encouragement of a good friend in the constituency who was a priest, he communicated privately with the Archbishop of Liverpool, who advised him to write directly to the Bishop of Leeds: he assured him he would receive a denial.

The subsequent repudiation was unequivocal, and its publication was very helpful. Wilson, said the Bishop of Leeds, had done excellent work for the Catholic schools in the area, and was in no way in his mind when he had made his criticisms of certain elements in the Labour party.

When the General Election of 1951 came to be fought, the struggle in Wilson's constituency was especially fierce. Despite a national swing against Labour which converted their Parliamentary majority into an overall Conservative majority of 17, Wilson increased his majority from 834 to 1193.

Wilson's assiduous efforts to retain his seat—and his diligent study of the timber trade—never deflected him from his wider political interests. After his resignation most of his time and energies were absorbed by the "War on Want" movement. The object of this was to campaign for a policy of assistance to the underdeveloped countries. He created the title for the movement and wrote the inaugural pamphlet. Its aims accorded wholly with his personal ideals and economic principles—and coincided with his F.A.O. experience. In association with his fellow-M.P.s Sir Richard Acland and Leslie Hale, and with Victor Gollancz, he threw himself zealously into the campaign, and addressed "War on Want" meetings throughout the country. For two years this campaign remained his greatest interest.

He was also finding himself in increasing demand elsewhere on a variety of issues—but chiefly the highly controversial proposals for German rearmament, the British armaments programme, and the health charges. At one stage in 1951 he made twenty speeches in as many days, at distances as far apart as Newcastle from Taunton on successive days. He was also a member of the Tribune Brains Trusts—a group of speakers generally associated with the so-called "Bevanite" movement.

The members of the Bevanite group had welcomed Wilson as something of a hero after his resignation. The strength of the movement, and of the kindred "Keep-Left" group, had at first taken him by surprise. Although he agreed with many of the views being formulated by them, and at times worked closely with them, he never entirely identified himself with them. He disagreed strongly with the extremist views of some of the members, and he heartily disapproved of the disruptive tactics some of them were prone to employ.

He believed in party unity, and was very unhappy about the bitter kind of attack made on the party leadership in the Tribune publication *Going our Way*. This appeared at the opening of the General Election of 1951. He had seen no advance copy of it, and its publication was a great embarrassment to him.

A substantial number of Labour M.P.s and a large number of constituency parties looked to Aneurin Bevan as the spiritual force behind much of the new thinking which was taking place. It was true that in the House he had the unwavering support of various factions discontented with the official leadership. But sometimes the very mixed nature of his following embarrassed and exasperated him. "Thank God I'm not a Bevanite," he once declared to a gathering of admirers.

Wilson's personal relations with Bevan were close, and he held him in high esteem. He admired his dynamism, and although he was often irked by Bevan's stubborn refusal at times to master the details of an argument, he valued his instinct for the essentials. Sometimes he was anxious about the effects of Bevan's tempestuous personality, and he regarded his judgment as erratic; but he felt his eloquence provided a spur to everyone involved in shaping policy.

In common with 56 other Labour M.P.s he defied the official party decision and voted against the Conservative Government's armaments programme in the spring of 1952. The official Labour policy was to abstain. The "rebels" were in some danger of having the Whip withdrawn, but the large number involved ruled out any such drastic measure. Later that year, Wilson and the increasing number who thought like him had the satisfaction of witnessing the Conservative Government reducing the armaments programme to a level well below the one which had been introduced by the Labour Government, and which had led Wilson and Freeman to resign. They thought it ironical that the policy of their political opponents appeared to vindicate their action.

In May of 1952 another equally significant "vindication" took place. In arguing against the Government's health charges for prescriptions, the Labour leadership stated that the health charges they had introduced were related to the three-year rearmament programme, and now pledged the party to remove all health charges.

Meanwhile Wilson's standing was increasing in the party as a whole. In 1951 he had stood for election to the National Executive Committee, but had just failed to win enough votes. The following year at the party conference at Morecambe he fared better. The voting uprooted two veteran stalwarts. Morrison was unseated by Richard Crossman, and Dalton was unseated by Wilson. On the day of the results, Wilson observed to a friend:

"Nye's little dog has turned round and bitten Dalton where it hurts."

*     *     *

With these advances, Wilson's anxiety to achieve party unity gained strength from its apparent practicability. To his delight, Bevan was elected to the Parliamentary Committee—the "Shadow Cabinet"—and was thus to all intents and purposes firmly back in the fold as part of the official leadership. Wilson himself had also stood for election, but had just failed. He came thirteenth in the voting, and was thus in the "line of succession."

There was now one outstanding policy issue which deeply divided the party: the question of German rearmament. The arguments about this raged fiercely throughout 1953, and came to a peak in 1954. Several of the Shadow Cabinet, including Bevan and Dalton, were firmly opposed to it. So was Wilson. He introduced a motion opposing German rearmament at the Parliamentary Labour Party. After a powerful debate it was defeated by 111-109 votes.

By now Wilson, although not a member of the Shadow Cabinet, was again a Front Bench spokesman for the party, and had led two vigorous all-night sessions of the Finance Bill. With Attlee's goodwill, he now spoke from the back benches on behalf of the substantial minority of the party opposed to German rearmament. He said the conception of Russian military strength and German industrial strength constituting the chief permanent dangers could well prove ill-founded; in the years ahead, the rôles might all too easily be interchanged.

Despite the sharp disagreements about German rearmament, there seemed a more positive trend now towards party unity than for several years. Suddenly this hopeful movement was drastically reversed.

It happened after the Shadow Cabinet had been discussing American policy in South-East Asia, and the formation of S.E.A.T.O., a military alignment which Bevan strongly opposed. Later in the House he figured in an unruly scene. He appeared to brush Atlee impatiently aside in order to take it upon himself to denounce angrily, on behalf of the party, American foreign policy.

His conduct was subsequently sharply criticised by other members of the Shadow Cabinet. He lost his temper, walked out and announced his resignation from the Shadow Cabinet owing to disagreement with their policy.

Wilson received the news with dismay. This was a serious setback for party unity. It also placed him in an extremely awkward personal position. As the unsuccessful candidate with the highest vote, he would now have to decide whether or not to accept the membership of the Shadow Cabinet to which he was automatically entitled.

His first reaction was to decline. He agreed with Bevan's general views on S.E.A.T.O. and it seemed logical and honourable for him to associate himself with his friend's gesture.

On further reflection, however, the right course of action began to look different. Closer consideration of Bevan's action led him to believe it was due not so much to policy disagreement as to anger over the criticisms made of his behaviour. The constitutional position, too, turned out to be different. According to the party's standing orders, his succession to the vacant seat on the Shadow Cabinet was automatic: it was not a question of declining membership—he was already a member, and must either stay or resign. Two resignations, he believed, would be very bad for the party—and in any case, would indelibly stamp him in the public mind as a mere satellite of Bevan.

For six hours he discussed the situation with Bevan himself. There was no doubt in Bevan's mind about what Wilson should do—this time he really *should* join him in resignation. Otherwise, Bevan warned him, he would lose a great deal of popularity in the party, and would forfeit his seat on the National Executive. But Wilson had decided otherwise. He was going to remain in the Shadow Cabinet.

He next went to see Attlee, and told him of his decision. He told him he would take his membership seriously and always accept majority decisions, at the same time reserving the right to try to alter some decisions, especially the one on German rearmament.

In the formal letter of acceptance to the Secretary of the Parliamentary Labour Party he said: ". . . what matters in the last resort is the unity and strength of the party."

At the subsequent Party Conference, Bevan, by standing unsuccessfully against Gaitskell as Party Treasurer, lost his seat on the National Executive. Wilson, far from forfeiting his, apparently reaped the reward of his independent position and his constant plea for unity: he came triumphantly at the top of the poll with the largest number of votes.

\* \* \*

Before the year was out, another "rebel" vote took place in the Commons with Bevan—but not Wilson—among those defying the party line on defence. There was another row, with threats of disciplinary action, but no lasting damage was done.

The following March a serious crisis arose over Bevan's conduct in an extraordinary episode in a Parliamentary debate. Waving his hand, apparently in the direction of his own Front Bench, he exclaimed:

"If *they* don't give a lead, *we* shall."

Some argued that the "they" referred to the Government, but most observers regarded it as an indictment of his own party's leadership—and as a threat of insurrection on the part of himself and his supporters. There was immediately talk of suspending him from the Parliamentary Party. Wilson thought the withdrawal of the Whip would be a stupid blunder. He discussed it in these terms with Attlee and with Jim Griffiths. Both agreed.

Others, however, took a different view, as did a large majority of the Shadow Cabinet. The decision to recommend to the Parliamentary party the suspension of Bevan was carried by an overwhelming majority—with Wilson strongly opposed. He wondered whether to resign, but decided not to. He asserted his right, however, to abstain when the matter came before the Parliamentary Party.

In the event, the Party considered the proposal in the form of a vote of confidence in Attlee's leadership. Despite this, the recommendation was endorsed by a majority of only sixteen.

Wilson was dismayed by the divisive implications for the party as a whole, and was even more alarmed to discover that there was a plan to secure Bevan's expulsion from the whole Party at the forthcoming meeting of the National Executive. Party rules on collective responsibility precluded him from speaking against the decision already taken—the withdrawal of the Whip. They did not preclude him from trying to prevent in advance the even more drastic punishment now being planned. With calculated forethought he made a Saturday morning statement in his constituency, carefully timing it to secure the maximum week-end publicity. Referring to rumours of the next move, he said:

"Speaking for myself, I would say surely enough harm has been done in the past few weeks without wantonly indulging in action which would have disastrous consequences for the party throughout the country . . . Up to about a year ago every effort was made, on contentious issues, to work out policies which would command the widest possible measure of agreement. Over the past year, too often policies have been forced through by the narrowest of majorities, and the resultant decisions made binding on reluctant and large minorities."

When the issue came before the National Executive, Morrison, Gaitskell and others pressed vigorously for Bevan's expulsion. Mrs. Jean Mann, who generally favoured this, nevertheless thought it best that justice should be seen to be done. She proposed an amendment to the effect that Bevan should be summoned for questioning. This was carried by 14 votes to 13. The delay saved Bevan. By the time he appeared before the Executive, tempers had cooled—and pressure from the constituencies had revealed the catastrophic split which his expulsion would cause.

The whole episode was regarded by Wilson as a calamity. He believed that Eden, who had just succeeded Churchill as Prime Minister, was influenced by this at least as much as by fears of the forthcoming economic crisis in holding an early General Election. The Conservatives were returned to office in 1955 with a big increase in their overall majority—from 17 to 59. In Wilson's view they owed their victory mainly to the apathy created in Labour's rank and file by the public dissensions.

\* \* \*

After the Conservative victory of 1955, it was generally assumed that Attlee would shortly retire. He was now aged seventy-two, and had obviously lost his final chance to return to Downing Street.

It had usually been taken for granted that Herbert Morrison

would succeed him, but there were many, including Wilson, who regarded the prospect with the reverse of enthusiasm, and who would on almost every score have preferred the vigour and vision of Bevan. Others regarded Bevan as intolerable on both political and personal grounds, but felt Morrison at the age of sixty-seven was too old. Some were beginning to think seriously of Gaitskell as a possible successor to Attlee. Gaitskell was one of them.

At the annual Labour Party Conference in the autumn of 1955, most commentators were nevertheless still confidently predicting a smooth succession for Morrison whenever Attlee might choose to retire. Wilson, however, had decided differently. Despite his close friendship with Bevan, he was convinced that Gaitskell was now the only possible choice for the new leader.

He did a joint broadcast with Gaitskell immediately after the conference. Afterwards they sat in Gaitskell's car and had an important private talk. Wilson spoke frankly to him:

"As you know, I've disagreed with a lot of things you've done. And I'm not going to withdraw anything—I think you were seriously wrong on a number of issues. But I now think you're the only possible leader. I say this with some regret, because I'd have preferred Nye. But the last few months have made this impossible. I don't think you're ideal, Hugh, but I'll back you for it wholeheartedly—so long as you stop trying to force every issue, by always trying to get a majority decision on everything that crops up. If you'll really try to work with the *whole* party, take a unifying not a divisive view of your responsibilities, you can count on my complete support when Attlee goes—and on my continuing loyalty."

Gaitskell was very pleased. He respected the frankness, welcomed the backing, and they both agreed to work together.

The partnership was quickly put into practice. The Government introduced an autumn Budget. In considering who should be the chief spokesmen for the Opposition, the Shadow Cabinet agreed it should be Gaitskell and Wilson. It was also agreed that after the few days of the Budget debate, the Opposition should put down a motion censuring he Government for alleged duplicity and pre-election manoeuvring with rash financial promises. This was timed for the following Monday, and it was decided Gaitskell should be the chief spokesman.

"And Harold," suggested Gaitskell.

Wilson unexpectedly demurred.

"I think Herbert should do it," he said.

In the event Morrison's speech, as Wilson had foreseen, was something of a disaster. It was coldly received and caused even some of his closest supporters to doubt whether they could honestly back him for the succession.

In the following days Gaitskell and Wilson collaborated effectively on the Finance Bill, culminating in an all-night sitting which ended after uproar with Wilson—at 8 a.m.—moving the Chairman of Ways and Means out of the Chair, and carrying it with the support of the Government, who wanted to end the Debate. The Finance Bill was killed after the kind of Parliamentary debating triumph that had seldom been witnessed before.

There was great excitement in the Parliamentary party. The Chief Whip enthusiastically told Wilson: "You know what they're all saying—*this* is the party we want now: Gaitskell as Leader, and you as Deputy Leader. Forget Nye, forget Herbert, this is the new shape of things."

Attlee, too, was delighted with the success of the debate, and congratulated Wilson. It has often been suggested that Attlee remained in office long enough to prevent Morrison from succeeding him. Whatever the truth of this, there is no doubt that he timed his departure at least partly in relation to the working partnership now amicably formed between Gaitskell and Wilson. He told them both that because of this he now felt free to go, safely leaving a more united party in good hands.

As expected, Morrison, Bevan and Gaitskell were the candidates for the Leadership. Informed observers now expected the chief contest to be between Gaitskell and Bevan.

A few days before the election, it was reported that an approach had been made to Gaitskell to stand down. If he agreed, Bevan would do likewise, thus giving Morrison an unopposed run. This was widely interpreted as a naked manoeuvre designed by Bevan and his supporters merely to prevent Gaitskell from gaining the Leadership. Morrison, it was suggested, would be too old in another few years to remain in office; by that time, Bevan would have redeemed himself fully with the whole party, and would have gained enough support to succeed automatically to the leadership.

Wilson was shocked and affronted by what he considered immoral tactics. Three years earlier Bevan had been privately approached by some leading trade unionists. Attlee, they said, was becoming too feeble to go on much longer; Gaitskell was too controversially right-wing for many members' tastes, and Bevan himself was a disruptive influence, with his strong left-wing following. They would be prepared to ditch Gaitskell and back Morrison if Bevan would agree to work with him and become Deputy Leader.

This could have proved a guaranteed pathway to power for Bevan, but he repudiated the proposal outright. The idea of working in such close relationship with Morrison outraged him. "I'd sooner be dead," he said.

Now it seemed he *was* prepared to do a deal with Morrison, primarily to keep Gaitskell out. To Wilson this looked like an unworthy manoeuvre and quite out of character for Bevan.

Wilson was not alone in feeling offended by Bevan's manoeuvre. In the polling, Gaitskell received 157 votes, Bevan 70, and Morrison 40.


## CHAPTER TWENTY-ONE

The result of the voting came as a shock to Morrison. He had spent nearly fifty years in political life, and had given exceptional service to the Labour movement in a variety of distinguished offices. To be denied the highest office of all was in itself a bitter disappointment; to be denied it so overwhelmingly was a cruel blow. However strongly most of them felt he was no longer suitable to be their prospective Leader, all Labour M.P.s now shared regret over the humiliation inevitably inflicted on an honoured veteran.

He was urged to remain as Deputy Leader under Gaitskell. Having had years of service in this rôle under Attlee, he understandably declined, and Jim Griffiths was elected to the office.

Gaitskell soon demonstrated his anxiety to unite the party at every level. But of all the decisions he made, the most significant was the appointment of Bevan as Shadow Foreign Secretary. This crucial step was widely interpreted as indicating a unifying wish to restore Bevan to the higher ranks of the party. From Bevan's point of view, the arrangement was excellent. For years he had been passionately interested in foreign policy, and in a future Labour Government would have made a strong bid for the Foreign Secretaryship.

Bevan's aspirations were usually misunderstood. It was generally assumed that his unremitting and overriding ambition was to secure full power, and there were certainly times when his behaviour justified such a view. In fact, it was an over-simplification. Sometimes he did feel the urge to be completely "in charge," but more often his full-blooded impulsive response to a particular situation made his basic wishes seem larger than they were. He had many interests outside politics, especially in literature and the arts, and there were periods when his interest in political affairs waned to the point where he lacked the sustained application necessary for eventual leadership. This wavering interest sometimes dismayed his own supporters.

Bevan sometimes used to say he would find certain functions of party leadership, and of the Premiership, extremely irksome. He had a dread of pageantry and ceremonial occasions, especially religious ones, where the presence of the party Leaders is virtually an obligation of office. His interest in philosophical and religious thinking never altered his own agnosticism, and the Cenotaph Remembrance Service was an occasion he often cited as an illustration of the kind of function he would find a severe strain. Yet he felt a missionary zeal for his political faith, and certainly wanted enough power to put his principles into practice. "Power —not place: that's what I want," he would often say. Now, as Shadow Foreign Secretary, he felt he had some of the "Power" he needed, without too much of the "place" to embarrass him. He worked closely and on fairly good personal terms with Gaitskell.

So did Wilson, who succeeded Gaitskell as Shadow Chancellor. Wilson's standing in the party as a whole was becoming very high. Not only was he consistently at the top, or near the top, of the voting for membership of the National Executive; equally significantly, by 1956 he was at the head of the poll for the Shadow Cabinet by the surprisingly large number of 36 votes. This event was described by the *Manchester Guardian* as "a resounding triumph for Mr. Harold Wilson."

Wilson was by now widely respected rather than liked: apart from his transient fringe flirtations with the Bevanite movement, he had steered clear of all factions. This political independence was the essential counterpart of the deep personal reticence which made it so hard to know him well. But it reinforced his constant plea for unity. He had been elected chairman of the important organisation sub-committee of the party, and from this key position was working hard on ways and means to readjust the party's machinery after the recent General Election defeat.

It was as Shadow Chancellor, however, that he made most public impact. His Parliamentary debating prowess became radically transformed. In charge of the Opposition's attack on the Government's financial policy, yet himself freed of ministerial responsibility, he was steadily escaping from the shackles of exhaustive facts and figures which had cramped many of his previous speeches.

He still worked hard on his speeches beforehand, but no longer devoted the intense preparation to a complete, verbatim script; he was beginning to be a true debater. This more relaxed approach in turn led to another improvement: he began to be humorous. If he still mistrusted and despised personal flamboyance, he began to appreciate the value of some degree of political showmanship, and to spice his attacks with skilful displays of wit.

In the course of his speech in the 1956 Budget Debate, he said:

"As far as I can see, the Government today are in a state of complete schizophrenia about the wage-price problem. First,

174

we have the flat earth school, obviously working towards an attempt to persuade prices to remain stationary for long enough to enable the Prime Minister (Sir Anthony Eden) to appeal to the unions for wage stabilisation. The Prime Minister started on these lines until rebuked recently by the Chancellor of the Exchequer. Now, of course, we have the Minister of Transport saying that fares and charges must be pegged despite a rise in costs. That is one school.

"Then we have the intellectuals. There is the Postmaster-General (Charles Hill) who just cannot wait, on hearing of a wage award, before he rushes to put up his prices. Also, we have the Economic Secretary (Sir Edward Boyle), the Rasputin of the Treasury, a mystic of little power but enormous influence, sufficient to persuade two Chancellors of the Exchequer of widely different views, even if he could not persuade anybody else, that the way to lower the cost of living is to raise prices so as to mop up some of the increased wages . . . Government policy is cynical opportunism in place of leadership, an appeal to cupidity rather than to the moral purpose of the nation. The Government offers a scramble and free-for-all in place of a common effort . . ."

The sharpness of the attack did not prevent the Chancellor, Harold Macmillan, from privately congratulating Wilson on his speech. Wilson had carefully studied Macmillan for some time. He greatly respected him as a shrewd politician and a brilliant debater, and at the same time regarded him as a potential figure of fun. Wilson never lost an opportunity to concentrate on Macmillan, who seldom resented the attacks, however penetrating they might be, and who laughed as much as everyone else when, as sometimes happened, the attack was delivered in the form of a rollicking burlesque. When Macmillan ceased to be Chancellor, Wilson felt sadly bereft. He found debating with Peter Thorneycroft much less stimulating, so he continued to concentrate on Macmillan.

With Macmillan as Prime Minister, and Wilson eventually Opposition Leader, the House was often fascinated by the brilliant debates between the two, both highly expert in political tactics, and each quietly respecting the skill of the other. It was Wilson who had christened his opponent "Mac the Knife," and Wilson who called the Tory Cabinet a "row of antimacassars." And commenting on Party strife, Wilson said: "Talk about splits in the Labour Party? Every time Mr. Macmillan comes back from abroad, Mr. Butler goes to the airport and grips him warmly by the throat."

Macmillan and Wilson respected the polished professionalism they found in each other, and seldom marred their mutual respect by introducing personal acrimony. Although no actual friendship developed between them, it was a great personal regret to Wilson when Macmillan had to retire from the Premiership because of illness. For months the political scene had been dominated by the seemingly endless repercussions of the Profumo affair. When the final Debate on the subject took place towards the end of 1963, Macmillan made one of his last appearances in the House.

He had not long been out of hospital after his operation. As he sat now, an ordinary back bench M.P., Wilson noted sadly how frail and aged his former chief target looked. Originally he had planned to deliver a devastating indictment of the ineptness and dilatoriness allegedly shown by Macmillan; now, he felt, the sordid affair was nearly at an end, and the time for recriminations was over. The rebuke he did deliver was milder than most expected, and deliberately muted out of respect for the situation.

After the Debate Wilson went up to Macmillan in the Chamber and asked after his health. They had a short friendly chat, and the House was moved to witness the former Prime Minister walking slowly from the Chamber, leaning on the arm of the Leader of the Opposition. After eight years of critical confrontation the last round was over. The gesture marked the close of the long and keenly-fought contest, and Wilson was sorry the duel was at an end.

Apart from Macmillan's illness, Wilson had not expected him to have to relinquish the Premiership. The political scene had changed rapidly on both sides: only a year earlier, Macmillan could not have foretold that Wilson himself was so soon to become his chief political opponent. Gaitskell was still almost as firmly in the saddle as he had been at the time of the 1959 General Election.

* * *

When that General Election drew near, Gaitskell was in complete command as the Labour Leader, with Bevan and Wilson loyally consolidating his position. The only reservation in Wilson's mind about the quality of Gaitskell's leadership was caused by the existence of the so-called "Frognal Set"—a group of Gaitskell's closest political friends and advisers, most of whom were reputed to be right-wing, and who often met at Gaitskell's Hampstead home in Frognal Gardens. This, thought Wilson, laid Gaitskell open to the charge of seeming not quite independent in his judgments, and liable to show favouritism. Apart from this, however, there was a much greater measure of co-operation and trust between the top ranks of the Labour party in 1959 than there had been for a decade.

This was due primarily to the effective relationship now formed between Gaitskell and Bevan—despite some moments of peril—for example, in the preparation of the pre-election policy statement on nationalisation called *Industry and Society*. Both men, however, had a strong wish to preserve the peace—and the final statement was worded so vaguely that it could be taken to provide for as much—or as little—nationalisation as the individual reader might choose to believe.

The statement suffered from the weaknesses of most similar efforts to reconcile conflicting viewpoints, and its all too obvious defects invited exploitation by the Conservatives, who made the most of its vagueness—and who won their third successive General Election, again substantially increasing their over-all Parliamentary majority.

## CHAPTER TWENTY-TWO

Gaitskell was greatly shaken by the results of the October 1959 Election. He had felt confident of victory for the Labour Party, and was immeasurably dismayed when it eluded him. He was also exhausted. He had not spared himself at all in the campaign, and some of his friends—and critics—thought he badly needed a rest. But he took none. Instead, he held a number of meetings with his closest friends and advisers, and anxiously began to look for ways and means of improving the party "image."

He had always been much concerned to secure the floating vote, and several of his right-wing friends now began to suggest several reasons why he might recently have failed.

One big reason, it seemed, was Wilson. Unlike Gaitskell, who was publicly accepted as sincere and dynamic, Wilson, they said, seemed at best coldly doctrinaire and at worst equivocal. Wilson's public image was bad, they said. Wilson, in short, should no longer hold senior office.

Several inspired political articles appeared in the national press. Through them, and through private information, Wilson quickly learned that attempts were being instigated to move him out of the Chairmanship of the organisation sub-committee, and to demote him from the Shadow Chancellorship.

Even bigger moves were afoot. The whole concept of nationalisation was also apparently at fault. At the Blackpool "postmortem" conference in November 1959, Gaitskell quite suddenly threw into the melting pot the sacred Clause 4 of the party constitution—the commitment to "common ownership of the means of production, distribution, and exchange." This created uproar and turmoil. The move had been made without any advance reference to the National Executive or to the Shadow Cabinet, and resistance to any tampering with this basic socialist principle was angrily expressed by many at the Conference, including some leading trade unionists.

Angriest of all was Aneurin Bevan. His immediate urge was to oppose Gaitskell publicly. Wilson begged him not to—and prevailed. In public, Bevan "threw his mantle of protection round the beleaguered Gaitskell," as several commentators put it. In private, however, he was determined to fight Gaitskell tooth and nail; he told several friends he was intending to oust Gaitskell from the leadership and take it over himself. Bevan told Wilson he now intended to resign from the Shadow Cabinet and fight it out with Gaitskell in the country.

Wilson, who was dismayed by the disunity suddenly sweeping right through the party, and splitting it into fragments, urged Bevan not to resign again. Only a few weeks earlier a remarkable degree of unity had been achieved. Now it was smashed, and this, Wilson believed, was due to Gaitskell's misguided tactics. He neither doubted the sincerity nor the courage of Gaitskell's leadership. But he entirely disapproved of his interpretation of his rôle. Instead of seeking issues to maintain the unity of the party, Wilson was convinced he had reverted to his former technique: seeking to assert his authority by singling out a divisive issue, and "resolving" it by securing a majority vote for his own point of view.

Wilson recalled the private pledge he had given Gaitskell after the 1955 Margate Conference of his continuing support so long as his leadership was geared to uniting, and not to dividing. He now considered that Gaitskell had abandoned this concept.

He told Bevan how he was thinking, but emphasised that he would take part in no intrigues to oust Gaitskell—or make statements calculated to embarrass him. The political controversies must be fought out on proper constitutional grounds.

This reticence led to a great deal of criticism. Because Wilson had avoided commenting on the Clause 4 controversy, he was repeatedly accused of "sitting on the fence." Challenging articles appeared in the press: "Where does Wilson stand? Is he in favour of outright nationalisation—or opposed to it? Is he for Gaitskell—or against him?" To Wilson, the extreme question seemed wrongly posed. To answer it one way, he observed to a friend, would be like telling the Salvation Army, after forty years of marching, that there was no salvation and no sin.

Eventually Wilson broke his silence: in February of 1960 he spoke to the Parliamentary Press Gallery, and enunciated a reconciling policy, adding the claim that in ten minutes he could produce the outline of a practical programme on nationalisation which would unite at least 90% of the party.

The argument shortly fizzled out. An official compromise statement was produced which added little to the party's policy, but which allowed tempers to cool. And Wilson remained the Shadow Chancellor.

Gaitskell, however, seemed anxious to find another issue upon which to assert his authority, and defence policy soon provided one. So far, the Labour party had in general supported the Government's defence programme, but with the cancellation of Blue Streak, George Brown argued in the Commons on behalf of the party that the case for the independent nuclear deterrent had now collapsed. Wilson, dealing with the economic aspects, endorsed this departure from the party policy.

At the time, Gaitskell was attending the Socialist International at Tel-Aviv. On his return, he publicly supported the new party line; privately, he expressed great anger at what had happened, implying he had been "stabbed in the back."

There was some confusion about where the Labour party now stood on defence policy. At a Leeds May Day Rally, Gaitskell made a bitter attack on unilateralism and the C.N.D. movement. He appeared to regard the latter as a dangerous communist-influenced conspiracy attempting to seize control of the Labour Party.

Wilson thought this an unwise move. He rejected unilateralism just as strongly as Gaitskell, but he believed that any British nuclear strength should now be part of N.A.T.O. Gaitskell, he believed, should have stressed a positive policy of this kind, rather than attack a minority movement.

Meanwhile, there was a good deal of radical thinking taking place in some of the unions about the independent deterrent. From union conference decisions, it looked as if a unilateralist policy might well win the day at the forthcoming Labour Party conference in the autumn of 1960.

In July of 1960 Aneurin Bevan died. The whole nation seemed to mourn the passing of a man who had once been reviled by a substantial section of it.

To Wilson the loss was acute. The two had usually shared an identity of view on policy, and Bevan's death made him feel especially solitary at a time when he was already isolated. He also sorely felt the loss on personal grounds. He had disliked some of Bevan's tactics, but had always held him in great affection—although he was sometimes irked by Bevan's impatience over details.

Some months before he died, Bevan had asked him what career his elder son Robin planned to follow.

"He looks like becoming a mathematician," replied Wilson.

"Ah," grunted Bevan, a broad smile spreading over his face. "Just like his father, I suppose—all bloody facts, no bloody vision!"

Wilson faced the coming party conference at Scarborough with much foreboding. Attempts had been made to secure a widely agreed defence policy with some of the leading trade unionists. At one stage a heated argument broke out between Gaitskell and Frank Cousins, General Secretary of the Transport and General Workers' Union, and himself a C.N.D. supporter. Gaitskell's neighbour whispered to him: "Don't press Cousins too far—he's agreed with the document so far."

"That," replied Gaitskell, "is the one thing I'm afraid of."

The whispered retort was overheard, and renewed the speculation about Gaitskell's real intentions. It seemed to some that he was not genuinely seeking a unifying policy, but was determined exclusively to secure a better "image" in the country, and felt he would fail if party defence policy had the support of people like Frank Cousins. He had apparently been persuaded that prominent Left-wing leaders like Cousins suffered from such a disreputable image among middle-class sections of the electorate that it was necessary virtually to disown them if there were ever to be any hope of winning the "floating" voter.

As expected, the vote at the Labour party conference was decidedly unilateralist in complexion. Gaitskell refused to accept it, and publicly gave his famous assurance that he would "fight, fight—and fight again" to have it reversed in the future. This reaction was variously interpreted as extreme stubbornness—or as courage of a high order.

Wilson himself regarded the unilateralist policy decision of conference as illogical and unacceptable, but felt that Gaitskell's repudiation of it was a deplorable breach of his constitutional and moral responsibilities as Leader.

In Wilson's view the right course of action would have been to try to devise a fresh policy statement, taking cognisance of conference's views, instead of renouncing them outright, but making clear Labour's support of the Western Alliance.

Wilson felt that Gaitskell had driven into the unilateralist camp a large and ill-assorted number of people who could have been won over to the National Executive point of view—including Cousins. In Wilson's view the test should be neutralism, rather than the misleading description unilateralism: in one sense Gaitskell and the National Executive had themselves adopted a "unilateralist" position through their statement that—

". . . we must accept the truth that a country of our size cannot remain in any real sense of the word an 'independent nuclear power.' We believe that in future our British contribution to the Western armoury will be in conventional terms, leaving to the Americans the provision of the Western strategic deterrent."

The real issue to Wilson was continuing membership of the Western alliance—and whether the Western alliance should have nuclear weapons so long as Russia did.

Wilson's "middle-of-the-road" position had its obvious attractions to large sections of the party, and was hailed by some as a welcome threat to Gaitskell's controversial position. Personal relations between Gaitskell and Wilson had been poor ever since the Clause 4 debate, but were now at their worst. Gaitskell was intensely suspicious of Wilson's motives and intentions, and aware of Wilson's view that his leadership was proving disastrous. Gaitskell's closest political friends and advisers regarded Wilson as a menace, and antipathy to him had become fierce and blatant. There was another move to get him out of the Shadow Cabinet.

After the conference, which ended on a discordant note, Wilson was approached by a number of fellow-M.P.s, including Bevan's widow, Jennie Lee, and urged to stand against Gaitskell in the forthcoming annual election for the Leader: ordinarily, Gaitskell could have expected an unopposed return.

Wilson felt strongly disinclined to place himself before the

Parliamentary party as a direct rival to Gaitskell. Although he knew he would secure the support of all the unilateralists and neutralists in the party, this in itself could be an embarrassment, because he disagreed with this position as much as he disagreed with Gaitskell's. In any case, he would be bound to lose; loyalty to the established leader would assert itself and he, as the unsuccessful challenger, would be accused of disloyalty as well as disruption—a harmful incongruity for someone always loudly advocating the virtue of unity—and could ruin for ever his chances of eventually becoming the natural Leader, a development he now regarded as highly desirable and, in the ordinary course of events, as inevitable.

Yet *not* to stand could be taken by Gaitskell as an endorsement of his position. True, Anthony Greenwood, a convinced unilateralist, had announced that he would stand. Wilson felt it would be unfortunate and misleading if it appeared that the only opposition to Gaitskell's view was the unilateralist case: Gaitskell, if opposed at all, should be faced with a challenge as serious and widely based as possible.

Wilson began to feel trapped in the same kind of dilemma as had ensnared him before his resignation as President of the Board of Trade, when he felt confronted by a choice of evils. Now, as before, whichever alternative he chose was bound to be seriously wrong from one point of view.

He also began to suffer the same kind of private agonies. He went badly off his sleep, and in his daily dealings with associates showed an unprecedented short temper. When he finally made his choice—to oppose Gaitskell—his torment increased. He was actively cold-shouldered, and even some of his supporters were afraid of being seen talking to him; on occasion he was left to sit alone in the House of Commons canteen. The ostracism hurt him deeply.

In the published statement about his decision to stand, he had said:

During and since Scarborough I have been under strong pressure from many colleagues, centre, left, and right—particularly

183

centre—to accept nomination for the leadership of the Parliamentary party.

To all inquiries I returned the answer that I did not consider myself a candidate, and still hoped that the Scarborough mood of fighting and fighting again within the party would give way to a more conciliatory spirit, and that any fighting there was to be done should be directed against the Tories . . .

It is a tragedy that this 60-year-old party, united as we saw at Scarborough on all other issues, should be torn apart by differences on defence policy, which, by the very nature of things, changes from year to year and even from month to month . . .

But the issue facing us today is not defence. It is the unity, indeed the survival, of this party. I want to see party unity given a much higher priority than it has enjoyed in the past year . . .

Twice within the past twelve months—at Blackpool over Clause Four, at Scarborough with the call for defiance and reversal of conference decisions—we have been plunged into deep and bitter controversy, and some of us, despite our disagreement with these actions, have done everything possible to secure a compromise and maintain unity . . .

It is being said that if Hugh Gaitskell is returned unopposed as leader of the party this will be taken as a mandate from his parliamentary colleagues to defy Conference, to ignore the National Executive Committee, and to plunge the movement into still worse conflict.

I cannot allow this approach to go unchallenged . . . as conscious as any other Labour M.P. of the great qualities and sincerity of Hugh Gaitskell, with the greatest possible regret and with the fullest appreciation of all that is involved for the party and for myself, I have, with reluctance, decided that I have no alternative to accepting nomination for the leadership of the Parliamentary Labour Party.

Press comment was fairly hostile. One widely-read commentator wrote:

By coming out against the leader Mr. Wilson has brought down on himself the eternal judgment of politics: That the man who wields the dagger can never proceed to pick up the crown.

Greenwood withdrew his candidature. It became a straight contest between Gaitskell and Wilson. Gaitskell received 166 votes, and Wilson 81.


## CHAPTER TWENTY-THREE

Despite the acrimonious atmosphere of the whole period, which was exacerbated by Wilson's candidature for the leadership, Wilson was re-elected to the Shadow Cabinet, although—to his annoyance—he dropped to ninth place. But Gaitskell seemed anxious to restore the amity they had previously enjoyed, and Wilson was similarly disposed.

New political issues were looming on the horizon, and these speeded the healing process. The Common Market negotiations, and the whole Western economic position, began to supersede defence as the big issue, and Gaitskell and Wilson found themselves largely in agreement about the right policy for the British economy.

As the months passed, it became clear that Gaitskell's continuing determination to reverse the unilateralist decision of 1960 was going to succeed. This proved to be so at the 1961 Labour Party conference. Gaitskell reacted to his triumph magnanimously, and seemed anxious now to concentrate on new issues. All the while Wilson and he were moving closer together in their thinking.

There were still some reservations on personal grounds, however, and these were aggravated, as far as Wilson was concerned, when he learned of a move to terminate his Shadow Chancellorship and appoint him Shadow Foreign Secretary. He suspected it might be a trap: the move, he believed, could be prompted by the view that he would "flop" in foreign affairs, thus being shown up as inadequate for the all-round requirements of future leadership.

He discussed it with his father. Herbert also suspected a trap, but encouraged him to take it on.

The more he reflected on it, the more favourably Wilson felt inclined to accept the challenge. He believed himself well qualified in foreign affairs, and certainly interested enough, to make a success of the new position. And if he *did* fail—well, it would show that his abilities were indeed not comprehensive enough to justify his eventual aspirations. In that case, the assurance he had given his teacher thirty years earlier would be proved right: "Number eleven will do me quite well."

Another point in favour of his acceptance was his increasing boredom with economic affairs. He had now been Shadow Chancellor for eight years, and had specialised for so long in economic affairs that he was beginning to find the whole field almost unbearably tedious; a change to foreign affairs would be refreshing and stimulating.

The Chief Whip and Gaitskell in turn sounded him out on the prospective change. He readily concurred, and at the end of November in 1961 became Shadow Foreign Secretary. He retained the chairmanship of the Public Accounts Committee and of the Home Policy Committee of the Labour Party. He was also Chairman of the Labour Party for that year, so altogether was directly involved in every major sphere of Parliamentary and party activities.

He spent a lot of time consolidating his political contacts in Europe and the United States. In January of 1962 he went to Washington and met the main American political leaders. He also spent a lot of time, as party Chairman, travelling and speaking in Britain.

He enjoyed the Shadow Foreign Secretaryship. With the Common Market as the big issue, he was able to combine his economic expertise with his increasing interest in international affairs; and his personal and political relations with Gaitskell were steadily improving all the time.

In November of 1962 he decided to stand against George Brown for the Deputy Leadership of the party. Various reasons lay behind this controversial step. Wilson thought the Gaits-

186

kell/Brown leadership of the party from the Right was part of a "post-Scarborough" situation which no longer prevailed. Also, there was some criticism of Brown's interpretation of his rôle, and a number of fellow-M.P.s were urging Wilson to stand. In deciding to do so, Wilson had his eye on the future as much as the present. He was ten years younger than Gaitskell, and believed himself a natural eventual successor, so long as he were now seen as still a prominent member of the leadership team. He also thought he might beat Brown. In the event, Brown won by thirty votes.

Many members of the Parliamentary party, including Gaitskell, regretted Wilson's candidature as a divisive act, but apparently no lasting damage was done. Wilson was subsequently re-elected to the Shadow Cabinet, and his personal relations with Gaitskell and Brown seemed unharmed. Indeed, the frank and friendly basis of the dealings he now had with Gaitskell completely restored the harmony they had once achieved and afterwards lost.

In December Wilson went on a visit to Israel. On his return he attended to an important family matter—his father's eightieth birthday. Herbert, a widower now for several years, was living with Marjorie in her bungalow in Cornwall. Harold took him a bottle of wine from Nazareth and a cactus plant from Jerusalem.

Early in 1963 he went on a lecture tour to America. Gaitskell had been ill and was not progressing well—and the news of his condition was disturbing. Reports were reaching Wilson in Chicago of mounting anxiety; by the time he reached Missouri, two days later, they were still more serious. He wondered whether he should curtail his tour and return to London. Transport House, anxious to protect Mrs. Gaitskell from the additional distress implied by such a move, advised him against doing so. But the news became even more serious. He was now in touch with London by telephone every two hours, and eventually was advised to return immediately.

He reached London some hours after Gaitskell's death. The whole country was grieving over the premature death of a man who had won universal respect for his courage and sincerity; the

Labour party was mourning the loss of a Leader who, despite all the earlier bitterness and controversy, had finally forged unity throughout the party and had commanded the allegiance of all sections; Wilson was mourning the loss of a colleague he had come to admire and like more and more, and under whose eventual Premiership he had keenly looked forward to serving.

Mary and his secretary, Marcia Williams, came to meet him at the airport. So did a host of press reporters and photographers: speculation about his future intentions was already intense, but he confined his comments to the only matter on his mind: his sorrow over the death of Hugh Gaitskell.

In the car from the airport the silence was eventually broken.

"I suppose you're going to stand for the Leadership?" asked his secretary.

"Yes, I expect so," Wilson replied, adding: "And if I'm elected, the first thing I'll do is to recommend Dora Gaitskell for a life peerage."

\* \* \*

The Parliamentary Labour party, responsible for electing Gaitskell's successor, was faced with a choice of 3 candidates—Wilson, Brown and James Callaghan.

In the first ballot, Wilson received 115 votes, Brown 88, and Callaghan 41. The result eliminated Callaghan from the running, but left Wilson short by only eight votes of the absolute majority necessary to succeed outright. There must, therefore, be a further vote to decide between Brown and Wilson.

Some members of the Parliamentary party regarded this as a choice between two evils. Others, especially some of the trade union members, felt that Brown—tempestuous and temperamental as he might be—was the sounder man, and personally preferable to Wilson, whom they regarded as cold as well as politically untrustworthy. His previous opposition to Gaitskell for the leadership had created a legacy of intense partisan dislike in an influential section of the party; in addition, ardent supporters of the Common Market preferred Brown to Wilson.

The choice, however, was for the likely next Prime Minister.

In the final ballot Brown increased his support to 103 votes. Wilson was victorious with a total of 144.

The widespread misgivings about his capacity for leadership began to evaporate speedily. He made it clear from the start that he would associate with no cliques, and would have no favourites: everyone in the party was to be on an equal footing, and he would be available to all at any time for consultation.

He asserted his authority immediately, and by word and action took full responsibility for everything to do with the party. At the same time, he proceeded to delegate specific tasks to members and groups within the party; he quickly made good his promise of impartiality by appointing to key positions several able members who had previously been his bitter opponents.

He once jokingly likened the Labour party to an old stage coach: if you rattle along at a great speed, he said, everybody inside is either too exhilarated or too seasick to cause any trouble. But if you stop, everybody gets out and argues about where to go next. Now he drove the stage coach fast: he stepped up the attacks on the Conservatives, and fully mobilised all sections of the party for the coming General Election campaign. Everybody seemed to feel exhilarated. Nobody complained of seasickness.

The speed with which he established full command astonished even his greatest admirers. Not a single major issue escaped his scrutiny—the Profumo affair, arms for South Africa, the steel strike in Wales, the threatened rail strike . . . he seemed bold and authoritative in his pronouncements, and faultless in his tactics.

Many potential bones of contention disappeared. The party policy on immigration, for example, imminently a source of awkward dissension, was quickly resolved; and the five "rebel" M.P.s, including Michael Foot, were brought back into the party fold.

Several months after Wilson's succession, it began to look strange that there had ever been any doubt that he would be the right man for the job. The annual conference in Scarborough in October 1963 was his first as the new Leader. From all over the country constituency and trade union representatives hailed Wilson's leadership with an enthusiasm far exceeding anything based simply on the kind of traditional loyalty to be expected with a General Election inevitable in the near future.

His keynote speech on science and the future made an immense impact. As one Right-wing paper reported:

> Mr. Harold Wilson, in what will rank as the most courageous and inspiring speech of his life, yesterday blazoned Labour's concept of life in Britain in the golden age of science and delegates cheered him to the echo. Never, not even Hugh Gaitskell in his Common Market speech at Brighton last year, has a Labour leader so clearly established his authority over every section of his party . . .

Reported another Right-wing paper:

> At Scarborough he gave the party a new direction in modern language; and they cheered rapturously his revelation of how Labour was to embrace the new race of scientists, technologists and technicians in an exciting future. He is the only leader who could have erected the new signposts without a trace of rancour or dissension. In four major speeches in four days he established his leadership on such a scale that even his most uncompromising critics admitted that in the leadership struggle after Mr. Gaitskell's death, their mistake was not that they had overrated George Brown (who clearly increased his stature among *his* critics by a notably able speech), but that they had underrated Harold Wilson.

As Wilson developed his theme of the supreme need for more universities, more scientists, and more drive to expand and modernise industry, one of his listeners noted every word with special pride. Herbert, thinking back over his long years as a works chemist, and his struggle for proper professional recognition and status; his years of unemployment—could it be, he wondered, that his own experience of difficulty and rebuff had inspired Harold that day?

As Herbert listened on, and noted the immense enthusiasm

greeting his son's speech, he recalled vividly his own father's remark when Harold recovered from typhoid:

"Herbert—that lad's been spared for something."

Herbert himself had been "spared." His presence at the Conference was something of a miracle. A few months earlier he had been seriously ill with pneumonia. At the time his son had just become the new Leader of the Opposition, and was excessively immersed in grappling with his new duties. But pneumonia in a man of eighty is a very dangerous illness. Marjorie and the doctor advised him to go and see him.

He dropped everything, cancelled important engagements, bought a carefully-chosen gift, and caught the overnight train to Cornwall.

When he arrived, his father was indeed in a critical condition, and was receiving emergency oxygen. Harold entered the bedroom quietly, smiled, and handed over his gift—a book, he explained, his father simply must read, since it concerned his son's future interests.

Herbert glanced at the title: *No. 10 Downing Street* by R. J. Minney.

He proceeded to recover rapidly.

# PART SEVEN

## On the Threshold

❧

*After completing the foregoing chapters, I
thought there were still important questions to
be answered about the outlook and personality
of the man who, although only forty-eight,
had reached the threshold of Downing Street.
In less than three years he had risen from the
depths of cold political rejection to being
the most enthusiastically acclaimed Leader the
Labour Party has ever had. To complete the
portrait, I went to his home one week-end
for a final long interview and for further talks
with his wife.*

## CHAPTER TWENTY-FOUR

However adversely their husbands may be regarded, the wives of
leading politicians are usually written up favourably, with their
main feminine virtues singled out for kindly—if patronising—
mention. Mary Wilson is no exception. But, being the retiring
kind of person she is, she has so far proved more elusive than
most to the gossip columnists.

She is, in fact, an exceptionally shy and sensitive person, who
feels ill-at-ease in the high-pressure atmosphere of public affairs.
Her home and family's welfare are everything to her, and she
brings to them qualities of infinite care and gentleness. She is
incapable of affectation or pretension, and dislikes these qualities
in others as much as she distrusts materialist motives. Each time I
have met her I have been impressed above all by her genuineness—the natural charm, the religious compassion which keeps

obtruding, and the independence of outlook on people and politics. It is impossible to imagine anyone disliking her. She has a sharp insight into human behaviour, and can be disarmingly frank about people—and about herself.

This candour has always been present when I have discussed Harold's career with her, especially after he became Leader of the Opposition.

"Well, it's certainly not thanks to me," Mary assured me. "The only way I've ever tried to influence Harold's career is by urging him, at every critical point, to leave politics and go back to Oxford. I've given it up now, of course! In any case, I realise that politicians never get tired of politics. But that's the only direction I've ever tried to push him. You can see how I failed! I really believe Harold would have got exactly where he is today if I'd never existed."

I knew what she meant. Granted his intellectual capacity, his inner sense of destiny, and his driving professional ambition with its practical quality of thrustfulness—this formidable combination, favoured at last by the accidents of fate, has carried Harold Wilson to his pinnacle of eminence without any positive help from a wife whose interests lie elsewhere. Yet she is mistaken in her view. He is much too self-reliant to welcome or want the kind of support a politically active wife might have been tempted to provide: he might have felt his essential independence threatened, and his strength for the political fray would have been sapped by the inevitable domestic disharmony.

There are more positive reasons, too, why Harold Wilson's career owes more to his wife than she can easily recognise. Just because of his absorption in the political game, he could have become obsessed with it. He could have been tempted to stay up all night, every night, arguing politics and rigorously excluding all other interests from his life—a poor foundation for the rounded outlook and mature background an aspiring politician should have. Perhaps he is innately too shrewd to have allowed this to happen; but as it is, Mary has ruled out the mere possibility. I put this to her:

"Yes, I suppose you're right," she said. "Of course, when the

House is sitting it's usually very late when he gets home—11 o'clock or after, and I rush to get him a meal, because I know how exhausted he feels. If he comes home with a big worry on his mind he tells me about it, and of course I listen for a while before telling him the family news. But usually he has to hear first from me about Robin and Giles and home matters, and he often says it's such a relief to have a wife who isn't in politics, because he does get a complete change when he comes home. He says it must be difficult for couples who are both in politics and talk about nothing else."

His daily routine varies little when the House is sitting. He wakes at 7.30, has a cup of tea in bed and reads the papers, dresses, runs Giles to school, returns home for breakfast or another cup of tea, and leaves for the House at 10 o'clock. At weekends, if he is not away on political business, he gets up later—about 8.30—brings Mary a light breakfast of tea and toast in bed, sits in his dressing-gown reading the papers, and afterwards does some local shopping or, occasionally, plays a round of golf. Mary looks after all the household affairs and maintains the garden, though Harold sometimes cuts the grass. Mary even mends the fuses, though if a plug has to be changed, she leaves it for Harold.

Wilson's home life, with all the privacy he deliberately insists should surround it, provides him with an essential release. In family affairs, as in sleep, he can completely cut himself off from politics. Unlike Mary, he is sleepy in the morning and very alert in the evening. Once in bed, he sometimes spends a few minutes recapturing the main events of the day, but usually he turns over on his side and is asleep within seconds. He needs no alarm to waken him in the morning.

Besides his family interests, he has two favourite relaxations: golf and reading. He enjoys the fresh air and exercise golf provides, but he values even more the concentration it requires. "The trouble with bridge and chess," he told me, "was that I got so involved that I was still playing the game in my sleep. But with golf it's different. Three hours completely away from thinking about work, and afterwards—back to politics."

He told me he used to have trouble making sure he took any

195

time to read books—now a favourite relaxation whenever possible. "I used to think it was a crime to sit and read when there was work to be done. But then, of course, I realised I'd do my work better if I did sometimes read a book, so I convinced myself that it would be purposive—that Russian literature and history, for example, would help me to understand the Russians better. Ditto with the Americans."

Recently one of his old teachers asked him what he most enjoyed reading, and his reply is a fair summary of his approach:

"My reading? I get very little time apart from documents and diplomatic stuff and endless periodicals, and usually save my reading for holidays, and occasionally for train journeys, if—unusually—I haven't a full bag of accumulated work. History mainly, and as far as possible from the present. Collingwood's *Roman Britain* twice in the last two summers: Dead Sea Scrolls. various: Mattingley's *Armada* this Christmas and Gibbon, which I have never previously read through. I am reading for pleasure and history. I do like Dorothy Sayers. I've read all of hers a number of times. They no longer mystify but I like to re-read them. *The Nine Tailors* I prefer to all other detective fiction. I've re-read *Gaudy Night* this week. Motley, Mahon, Holland Rose —I've read them all at various times. Apart from that most of my serious historical reading has been in Russian history—pre-revolution."

His interest in the arts generally is average, and in painting almost non-existent. He enjoys comedy films and light music, especially as a background to working at home. "But under Robin's influence I'm being educated in more serious music."

Robin, a serious-minded young man with a quiet charm, regards music as the most important thing in life. He had a brilliant career at school, and at eighteen won an open State Scholarship to Oxford. His professional aim is to be a teacher of mathematics, preferably a university don. But music is even more important to him than mathematics. He became secretary of the Balliol Musical Society, the main one of its kind in Oxford, and each evening attends the College chapel service, largely on account of the church music.

196

Giles, four years younger, is fascinated by everything to do with model and real aircraft. He hopes, after leaving school, to become a pilot. Less shy than Robin, he quickly gets on friendly terms with people. Both boys were protected from politics in their childhood. "I've seen some politicians' children so nauseatingly knowledgeable about it all," Mary explained to me. "I don't know whether we did the right thing, but we leaned over backwards not to have ours like that. It got to the stage when Robin, aged about fifteen, would come home from school quoting the other boys' remarks about his father. So we had to start telling them more about politics. They began to read the papers, of course, and now they both know a lot about it. They're used to it all now, of course, and take their father's position for granted. Robin has joined the Labour Club in Oxford, but I don't think either of them is going to be very active politically."

The "taking-it-all-for-granted" approach was well illustrated on the night of Wilson's election as Leader of the Opposition. Very much the man of the moment, he was being rushed from studio to studio for radio and television interviews. Giles, aged fifteen at the time, accompanied him on the tour, apparently oblivious of any notion of personal involvement in his father's fame. At one stage a producer asked him if he was enjoying himself. "I've just spotted Brian Connell," he answered, and darted off in his direction. A few moments later he reappeared, beaming with delight. "I've got his signature in my autograph book," he said proudly, adding that he was looking forward to showing the autograph of a celebrity to his schoolmates next day.

The happiest family gatherings in recent years have taken place in Scilly, where the Wilsons acquired a small holiday bungalow on a mortgage some years ago. If ordinary home life, reading and occasional golf provide Wilson with essential but brief releases, Scilly at Christmas, Easter, and in the summer affords the prolonged refreshment all the family want—and the total escape he needs. They no longer regard themselves as holidaymakers there, but as part of the local community, and are accepted as such. They delight in Scilly's remoteness from the affairs of the mainland, and value the natural friendships they have with the permanent residents. Boating, swimming, walking, reading—local island affairs and gossip: they love them all, and the feeling of isolation from London occupations.

Even on Scilly Wilson never likes to be without the daily papers, which he always studies minutely, and it always takes him a few days to "unwind" on holdiay, but after that he becomes absorbed in the picnics and other family expeditions they all enjoy. "Though mind you," he told me, "I do sometimes find my mind straying on to politics if I'm on a ramble. Then suddenly I come across the remains of an old Roman burial chamber, and I'm back on the island again. I couldn't do without Scilly every summer, and I never get long enough. I'm not like Mary, though—she'd be happy to stay there for ever."

To Mary, Scilly, with its peace and remoteness, is bliss. She longs to return when she is away from it, and dreads leaving it when she is there. Solitude is one of her mainstays. "I love being on my own," she once told me. "What I like about domestic life is that I can spend so much time of each day on my own. It sounds an awful thing to say, but it's true. If I had to be with other people *all* the time I'd go mad. I love to go for long walks by myself, and think my own thoughts. I'm trying to put all this into a poem."

At the time the poem was unfinished, but she completed it in honour of this book:

## THE HOUSE AT THE EDGE OF THE WOOD

*Sometimes, as I struggle through crowded rooms*
*Thick with tobacco and whisky fumes*
*And vapid voices shrilling high*
*In one continuous parrot cry—*

*Suddenly, I can see it there!*
*I can see the bluebells, can smell the air,*
*And the dusty sunlight slants in lines*
*Across my house at the edge of the pines.*

*And a heavenly, healing silence falls*
*Upon my soul, and the caging walls*
*Melt, and the clanging voices die,*
*And we are alone, my house and I.*

*Somehow, someday, I shall be free*
*To go to the place where it waits for me.*
*For ever and ever my house has stood,*
*And all its windows face the wood.*

Herbert and Marjorie often join the family for a few days in the Scilly bungalow, and it is on holidays especially that Wilson indulges in something he always keeps hidden from the public—a bubbling sense of merriment. The boys tease him constantly. As Mary put it to me: "He's a very indulgent father, really. He takes an awful lot from the boys. At home he's always terribly interested in their progress, and helps them whenever he can. I've seen even him break off work on an important speech to help Giles with his homework. But on holiday they certainly take the mickey out of him."

Within the family circle Wilson is completely relaxed and often jovial. The devastating wit so often displayed in Parliament is something quite different—the public and professional aspect of a sense of humour which has a much lighter side. The comic side of human (and animal) behaviour delights him, and it is quite usual for him to burst into laughter at the sight of some unexpected natural slapstick.

This exuberance and glee is a part of his personality seen only by those very close to him. On public occasions, dignity is often tempered by wit—but never by anything which might look like facetiousness or, worse still, triviality. But joking is an integral part of his personality—part of the boyish gusto inspiring him. He gets a boyish delight, for example, when each Christmas Marjorie gives him the same present he has always had from her since childhood—a box of "selection" chocolates. She kept the practice up throughout wartime sweet rationing, and he always looks forward to getting it. The same procedure is invariably followed:

once unwrapped, the box is placed on the floor. Crouched on all fours, Harold carefully ponders the contents, picks out the ones he likes least, distributes them round the family, and starts eating the remainder himself.

Harold and Mary Wilson are a remarkably complementary couple who both value their independence of character, interest, and outlook. Mary's interest in politics, for example, is highly personal. She follows Harold's progress closely, and reads most of the press comment about him. She is always upset by any unkind comments, even when she may not entirely agree with his policy.

"I try very hard not to become involved in political squabbles," she told me. "I know all about them, but I don't enter into them. I am influenced more by my friendships. I just can't be political about everything, especially family matters."

She holds strong views about nuclear weapons. "I'm probably not logical about them—I just feel we shouldn't have anything to do with the horrid things. I don't work out the implications of it, but I do feel strongly about it." Strongly enough to have written a striking poem:

### AFTER THE BOMB

*After the Bomb has fallen,*
*After the last sad cry,*
*When the earth was a burnt-out cinder*
*Drifting across the sky,*

*Came Lucifer, Son of the Morning,*
*With his fallen-angel band,*
*Silent and swift as a vulture,*
*On a mountain-top to stand.*

*And he looked, as he stood on the mountain*
*With his scarlet wings unfurled,*
*At the charnel-house of London*
*And the cities of the world,*

*And he laughed . . .*

*And as that mocking laughter*
*Across the heavens ran,*
*He cried "Look" to the fallen angels*
"This *is the work of* MAN

WHO WAS MADE IN THE IMAGE OF GOD!*"*


# CHAPTER TWENTY-FIVE

Wilson's qualities of patience and tolerance are valued by his closest working associates—I use that word deliberately, rather than "staff." One secretary said: "He never speaks of me as somebody working *for* him. He always speaks of me as someone working *with* him." Another said: "He's a very happy person—extremely happy. He's so friendly that anyone can say anything they like to him. I've never known him lose his temper, or even get angry—though once or twice I've known him appear to get angry, but it always struck me that it was completely under control, a kind of pose which he thought necessary at the time."

There is one unfailing exception to the unruffled calm. If anything is done or said to upset Mary, or any other member of his family, Wilson is incensed. He goes to great lengths to make amends, and to hit out at the culprit. And there is nothing feigned about the anger on such occasions. Sometimes the hurt can come through an anonymous letter. When Giles was a toddler, for example, Mary received a letter one day sharply criticising her for letting him eat ice cream in his push-chair—a messy thing for a child to do in public, said the writer, and something never done in respectable circles. Mary was greatly upset by the letter, and Wilson was enraged. Instead of tearing it up, which was the usual fate of hostile letters, he set about trying to identify the sender—and succeeded. She turned out to be a local resident and she got in return what must have been the angriest personal letter anybody ever received from any President of the Board of Trade.

This is no isolated episode. Any upset caused by any outsider to any member of the family immediately evokes vigorous action as well as wrath from Wilson—whether the offender is a press reporter unfairly pestering his father in Cornwall, a party member troubling his sister, or an amateur photographer trying to snap Mary at home without previous permission. "I always feel very sorry for Mary over things like this," he told me. "After all, she didn't choose this kind of life, and I always try to protect her from things she suffers just because she married me. I've always felt a slight guilt complex about not being a normal husband and father, in the sense of not being at home much to help with the boys and so on. Therefore anything I *can* do I tend to overdo, and that includes anything to protect them from my being a public figure."

All this is true, but the explanation for the inconsistency of this extreme reaction lies deeper than he realises. Wilson himself is capable of suffering deep personal hurt, but he never under any circumstances exposes the wound. The intensely self-contained child, who always sorted out his own anxieties and troubles as a boy, is unaltered. But his family are projections of himself: if they are hurt, so is he. To react vigorously on their behalf is one thing, but to do so on his own behalf might seem soft and expose weakness. So he suffers his own hurts privately and passively, and compensates by lashing out whenever Mary or anybody else in his family is made to suffer.

The same applies to his staff. He protects them with fierce devotion from outside criticism. "I expect them to be loyal to me, and I'm loyal to them," is his attitude. But again a much deeper process than this is involved. His staff, like his family, are part of him, to be defended—however much his own injuries are to be hidden. And hidden they are. Direct political criticism or attack never hurts him—rather the reverse—but unfair personal abuse always does, and he wilts under it.

When I was interviewing him for the earlier sections of this book, covering his days as a Scout, he told me how a journalist had recently advised him to drop in future any reference to "all this Boy Scout nonsense." He was annoyed by the insinuation that there was anything artificial in his Scouting interests, and said so. But the sheer injustice of the aspersion on an integral part of his background and beliefs caused him actual hurt—but the journalist never knew.

I asked him how aware he was of his sensitivity: "Well, now that I look back I can see that I've always been fairly thin-skinned," he admitted. "I was very sensitive to the fear of derision at Oxford—and terribly sensitive about social things with Beveridge and Lady Beveridge—what to do at sherry parties and that sort of thing. I always tried to avoid a position where I was personally criticised or, worse still, where I would have to criticise anybody else. I did the same with the Civil Service, and I suppose I still very often use my brains and my footwork to avoid a situation where anything tough or unpleasant occurs. And I go to great lengths sometimes to avoid the Party being hurt. But I'm much tougher now than I was, in all sorts of ways. Mary used to feel sometimes I was weak. I can remember an occasion when we were waiting to get on a train at Chester. It was crowded and a lot of tough types rushed past us and grabbed all the seats and I made no effort to fight my way in. She thought I should have been more assertive and used my elbows a bit. Well, I do use them much more nowadays. And of course in political debates I'm far tougher than I was.

"But I still have this perennial dislike of hurting people's feelings. And if you've got power you must use it gently. And I don't believe in using unfair arguments with people. As you know, my father brought me up to believe that all snobbery is bad, but the worst of all is intellectual snobbery. If I'm having an argument, I never want to win by flaunting my academic studies —by saying: 'Look I've studied this, and I really know about it. You don't . . . !' I am prepared to hurt someone if I *have* to, but I hate having to do it."

This claim reminded me of an experience I had with Wilson during the preparation of this book, when I invited him to scrutinise the draft manuscript to verify the accuracy of all the biographical facts in it. He asked me to delete four points—they were quite accurate, he assured me. I knew they were not actionable, could cause no political trouble, and were in his favour. "I think So-and-So would be hurt by them," he explained.

If Mary deplored his earlier passive attitude in some directions, she certainly marvelled over his strength in others. "When we used to discuss his political aspirations, I often said to him—'How could you bear the responsibility, it must be trrible?' he always said: 'I'd far rather be there taking the decisions than seeing somebody else make mistakes about it.' I think he's much more relaxed since he's become the Leader than he ever was before because now it's in his own hands. I don't want to make him sound arrogant—it's just that he has complete self-assurance because he knows his brilliance. It may sound funny to say so, but I've only come across this in recent years. It's been there all the time, possibly, but he's always just been the man I married. I never thought of him in any other capacity. People have always talked of him as a clever and astute politician, but this is an aspect I never used to notice. Anyway, these aren't the qualities that attract me—I've always fought shy of successful men. It's something to do with my own dislike of publicity—the more I come into the public eye, the more I want to go in the opposite direction—and live in my house on the edge of the wood. But Harold can't bear to be frustrated—he'd rather be overworked or anything than frustrated. The more authority and responsibility he has the better."

If Wilson has become tougher, I asked him how far he thought this was due to the fortitude required by particular political crises: "Well, I really went through it during my resignation as President—and my stand against Gaitskell for the leadership. I really went through the flames on those two and they toughened me enormously. I can take an awful lot more now; I don't mind, as I used to, if a lot of people hate my guts just because I'm the Socialist leader. They don't know me personally, and I recognise that of thirty million voters some millions will vote Tory when it comes to the day, so I must expect them not to like me. But I get annoyed if some of our people in the country refer to Tory leaders in immoderate personal terms. These attitudes arise in politics, of course, and I can face that kind of criticism against myself now. But I'm still more sensitive to political criticism than I appear, especially when it's personal. When people call me a cold, calculating careerist, for example, that still needles a bit."

Nobody could study Wilson's political career without noting immense powers of calculation meticulously applied to every level of activity—the trade negotiations with Mikoyan, for example, could never have succeeded without the subtle calculation he used to outwit his Russian opposite number so brilliantly. And there is no doubt that his powers of calculation have at times been deployed to defend and advance his own position. They have more often been deployed for the benefit of his party. As Prime Minister they will be deployed for the benefit of his country: his dealings with Mikoyan in 1947 were bulldog Britain at its most tenacious as well as its most subtle. I asked him what he thought about comments that he is all head and no heart: "With family matters, of course, my heart is constantly ruling my head. But in politics it's different, of course—so many others are depending on you. But I very often allow my *instinct* to rule my head. I very often get a strong hunch—maybe about public reaction to a proposal, or about what the press will say. There can be calculation here too, of course, but often I get a strong intuitive hunch and follow it without knowing why. Afterwards, I usually rationalise it. But I think the most accurate phrase about me is that I fly the political plane by the seat of my pants and not by instruments. There's an awful lot of flair and instinct in my judgments."

Wilson has no grounds for taking offence over his powers of calculation being recognised—they are a valuable part of his political equipment. The offence occurs when the suggestion of careerism is implicit—the suggestion that his decisions and judgements have been determined by self-interest. "A careerist," Lord Attlee told me, "is a fellow who puts his career before anything else. Harold has never done that." But Mary Wilson is right—the more authority and responsibility he has, the better. This has been so ever since he first became a Patrol Leader. There has always been a missionary zeal about his search for power, not for its own sake, but to put into practice policies which he is convinced are right, and which he believes that he, and he alone, can satisfactorily carry through.

Ever since he became Leader of his party, and began to possess power on a wider scale than ever before, he has revealed an almost ludicrous disregard for the personal importance of his position. The inescapable details of celebrity were still taking him by surprise over a year after taking office—the fascinated stares of passers-by in London, the curiosity of sightseers in Scilly, or the sudden request for autographs from strangers on trains: they all almost puzzled him, although he derived a boyish pleasure from them.

On the evening of President Kennedy's assassination he was speaking at a meeting in North Wales when the news came through, with an urgent request from the BBC to go to the nearest studios in Manchester. He set off in a fast car with a police escort of two cars in front and two behind, and covered the distance of 46 miles in 51 minutes, including a stop en route. The stop was to buy something to eat: he had had nothing since lunch, and was feeling the strain of the occasion. At his request, the whole convoy screeched to a halt outside the first fish-and-chip shop they came to, in Altrincham. He leapt into the shop and hurriedly gave his order to the man behind the counter. He was soon involved in an argument. On returning to the car with his supper, he said to the driver with surprise: "The man in that shop recognised me—and wouldn't let me pay."

At one stage I asked Wilson for his collection of personal press cuttings, and he immediately assured me he would gladly let me have them all. So I awaited the arrival of the crate which I felt sure would be necessary to contain the scores of thousands of articles about him. When they arrived, they were all containted within the slimmest folder from his filing cabinet—a few about his resignation as President, several articles he had written himself about his visit to Russia in 1953, and one with a photograph of Robin and himself when he opened the annual stamp exhibition in 1958—about a dozen in all, quite useless to me except as an indication of a lack of what is usually meant by vanity.

Wilson, of course, needs no collection of press cuttings. He reads most of them at the time—and remembers them all. He can often quote exactly who said or wrote what, and on what dates. His extraordinary memory sometimes infuriates people—it has so often been used to prove himself right and others wrong. It can even annoy a secretary, who may have spent hours searching in vain for some reference, only to discover that he recalls it verbatim, with dates and times, and in any case can tell her precisely where to find it in his office. Memory is an indispensable part of his equipment and he often uses it to test out his own agility. It can also be a devastating political weapon against others, as many opponents inside and outside his party have discovered.

Wilson is proud of his memory. He is proud of his achievements, of his family, his home, and his position. He is also proud of his country. His patriotism runs deep, and he gives some passages in his speeches a Churchillian ring. Speaking in Scarborough in 1963 he said:

"Labour rejects the carping and jibing of those abroad, friends or enemies, who say that Britain has lost her way in the world, that our flame if burning low, that we have nothing to offer except the memories and nostalgia of a faded imperial grandeur.

"The mistake they make is to confuse the image of the Britain we have presented under the Conservatives, with the Britain we really are, the Britain we are going to be.

"We are not a flag-waving party. But we are a deeply patriotic party, because we truly represent the British people. And it is because of this that we are angered by the sight of this country lagging behind our industrial rivals as we do three years in every four, until the approach of the election brings on our accustomed quadrennial spasm . . . I believe we are on the eve of a new greatness for Britain, a greatness based not on military oppression or the ability to mount a colonial expedition, not on economic imperialism or colonialism, but on a contribution we have it in our unique power to make to the peace and happiness of mankind. A contribution based not on separatism, but on leadership in an interdependent world . . . If Britain is to count in the world, as it should, we have to call into active endeavour the full energies of our people: all our people. We have reserves of skill, and craftsmanship, of science and technology, design and creative ability, of organisation and salesmanship, which, if given full scope will make Britain what we should be, the pilot-plant, the tool-room of the world . . ."

If anyone attacks Britain the Wilson jaw suddenly juts pugnaciously. "It gets under my skin if anyone calls me unpatriotic—hence my resentment of Home's jibe about 'economic Jonah' and 'merchant of despair.' I'm terribly proud of being British, and terribly angry when I see us sliding behind through economic frivolity."

I reminded him that he has been accused of being a Little Englander, and disliking foreigners.

"Don't imagine I regard foreigners as inferior—they fascinate me, and I enormously enjoy international conferences. They always interest me. I like to see how the same problem looks from the other side of the hill. I don't take the view that foreigners are difficult to get on with. Perhaps I'm a little insular in how I feel about the way they run their Parliaments and Governments."

Wilson could never be anything but British—his whole attitude and make-up are characteristic of his country—the reserve, the stiff-upper-lip, the tenacity—and even the excessive sentimental affection for animals: he can never resist a cat or dog, and delights in their antics. He can sit happily for hours with one on his lap, talking nonsense as he fondly strokes it.

He loves historical ceremony, and says he would have liked to wear the colourful clothing of men in centuries past. "I've great respect for tradition," he told me, "especially in the House of Commons. I still think it's right to slam the door in the face of Black Rod because of what Charles I did. And I like the real ceremonies of the monarchy—the opening of Parliament, the Coronation—all that. And of course the opening of the new House of Commons Chamber in Westminster Hall when all the Speakers from the Commonwealth were present. The lying-in-state of the King, too, was impressive, though rather sombre. But I've got a tremendous sense of history. Now and again you can feel you're a small part of it. With the Finance Bill, for example, or the Public Accounts Committee, it's all part of House of Commons tradition, and you can identify yourself with the tides of history and Gladstone and everything you've read. Mind you, like Nye I'm interested in power, not place. But if one were Prime Minister, one would feel part of a long historical line—Peel, Disraeli, Gladstone, and so on."

One of the British traditions he most values is devotion to sport, and to fair play. When the Earl of Home had abandoned his title and was standing as an M.P. to take up his Premiership in the Commons, various unofficial attempts were made to suggest that, if successful, he might still be debarred from entering the Commons on constitutional grounds. I was with Wilson in his room in the House one evening when these attempts were at their height. A party official kept coming in to report news of the latest developments, which Wilson heard in silence. After the fourth such interruption, he suddenly became impatient, "Look," he said, "I don't want to hear any more of this. Let him be elected and take his place in the Commons. I've no wish to see the Captain of the other side disqualified on a technicality before he's had a chance to lead his team, let alone come on to the field."

Even his prejudices are peculiarly British, with heavy non-conformist and Yorkshire overtones. "I was brought up with the view that it's wrong to get something for nothing. I've a terrific prejudice against waste—especially waste of time. By the way, that's really why I hate cocktail parties. I *hate* them—they're such a waste of time. I never go if I can possibly avoid them. It bores me stiff to have to engage in small talk. It's not that I'm always wanting to discuss politics—I'm very happy to chat about history, or railway development, say, or even golf, but I'm useless when it comes to talk just for the sake of talk.

"I've no prejudice at all against big business or industry. Industry produces things. I am in favour of investment—but not speculation. I like to think of people earning their money. When I read press accounts of rich young people gambling away thousands, or living it up in cars they haven't bought for themselves, I remember how I bought my first car for £11 and I really had to earn those £11. I'd hate to see Robin or Giles with a car they hadn't bought with money they'd earned themselves. I'd feel they'd missed something important in life."

After all the rationalisation, a puritan streak remains as an integral part of the idealism. This sometimes emerges in Parliamentary debate. In his speech to the House on 11th July, 1960, he said: "A financial speculator can clear £1 million overnight on a property deal, buying and selling a block of flats with someone else's money. That is smart business. But if we pay a decent wage to an engine driver, with the lives of hundreds of people in his hands, that is raging inflation. The banks can lend tons of millions of pounds more, as they have, to Stock Exchange speculators; that is in the national interest. But local authorities trying to cope with their heritage of slums or with chronic overcrowding are forced into costly borrowing operations at penal rates of interest.

"The Chancellor can knock £5 million off the tax on port, but he cannot find an equal sum for removing the individual prescription charge for chronic sick people. Private enterprise can use able-bodied men in their thousands to go touting round, putting coupons or advertising literature through letter boxes, or inflating the cost of the Health Service by pressing new-branded drugs on hard-worked doctors. Yet we cannot afford a few more factory inspectors. We can titillate the consumer with striped toothpaste, or all the other luxuries of an Americanised Society, but our beaches and rivers are a disgrace. This is the society that we are creating under the right hon. Gentleman."

Wilson never claims too much for his idealism, but I believe that without it he might not have chosen a political career. Of the various other careers open to him, I asked him which had most appeal. "Don't forget," he said to me, "that I'm a political animal. I was born with it in my blood. And why does a duck go into the water? Because that's its natural habitat. Well, to me political conflict—the whole political game—is enjoyable."

"Yes," Mary Wilson told me on another occasion, "although Harold gets great happiness in family affairs, there's no doubt that what excites him most is politics. It's after a successful by-election that I ask for any extras I need. But in time of real difficulty the family always takes absolute precedence over his work. In the household he always expects me to carry on in the usual way and deal with all crises that arise, but if there's anything really major I ring him up at once. For example, I had to go into hospital some months ago. I rang him up and told him I'd have to have an operation. He rushed straight out and made a point of putting everything on one side. At times of crisis he's always there—and that's the important thing, I think."

Throughout the hot summer of 1959 there was a prolonged crisis: Mary's mother was dying. Wilson kept every Saturday and Sunday afternoon free to drive over to Wembley to be with her, sometimes with Mary, but often on his own, just to sit and talk with her. The year before he had suffered the greatest sadness of his life with his own mother's death.

"He feels these things very deeply," said Mary. "He went about his ordinary work, he had his meals, slept as usual, people couldn't have guessed how much he was grieving. But he was up and down to Cornwall ever so many times, rushing back here and down again to Cornwall just to see her. And this is what he's like."

In her last weeks Ethel was lying gravely ill in the bungalow at Cornwall. Herbert was there, and towards the end was joined by Harold, whose grief was equalled only by his concern for his father. Ethel and Herbert had been married for over fifty years, and Herbert's sorrow was intense. Harold arranged for him to go to Plymouth to buy mourning clothes on the day the coffin was taken to the Chapel of Rest. On the day of the funeral he was afraid that his car, with Herbert beside him, might get stuck behind the hearse on the narrow roads to Truro and the cemetery. He privately contacted the local police to solicit their help in avoiding this strain for his father, and he arranged to have "engine trouble" for a few minutes if necessary

The effect on Wilson of his mother's death was considerable. His religious faith, always strong, was reinforced. Knowing and loving his mother as he did, he could not accept that death was the end. In an interview some years later he said: "I found I couldn't believe—and I reckon I'm a pretty rational kind of man —that death was the end of my mother. I simply cannot believe that there is NOT some kind of an after life. And if there is an after life then the idea of God, and then of Christ, is relatively easy to accept."

It is difficult to persuade Wilson to talk about his religion. Occasionally he is drawn into argument about it: "Somebody said to me: 'I don't believe in God.' I said: 'I wonder if God believes in you?' A bit arrogant, but I thought it a fair reply.

"Biblical phrases keep cropping up when I'm preparing

speeches—I suppose that's my background—but I usually cut them out in case they affront people who'd think I'm using the Bible for political purposes."

I asked him whether he regarded himself as a practising Christian: "One Christian's job may be to help redeem an individual, another to be a prison visitor, maybe. I'm not doing as much personally as the dedicated Christian who goes to relieve poverty or loneliness among old people. There has to be a division of labour and I'd use my abilities to improve old-age pensions to help two million people. I think everybody has a job to do, and it is a Christian duty to try to do it well.

"I get upset and worried if there's nothing I can do. I remember a woman in my constituency who became widowed and was desperately short of money. She asked me to get her post-war credits released. But she wasn't entitled to them, according to the law. I raised it with Amory, who was Chancellor at the time. He wanted to change the law in favour of this woman and others similarly placed. But this would give rise to anomalies and he was afraid the Opposition would take advantage. The moment I gave him an undertaking that we wouldn't, he made the necessary change, and put it in the Budget. I was really pleased to be able to write to her and tell her she'd helped to get the law changed."

Wilson's response to individual need is instant and total. I put to him my deduction that although his initial mainspring is compassion, the individual in question quickly becomes a challenge to his ingenuity and ability rather than a human in need.

"Yes," he agreed, after reflection, "I meet the human problems in Liverpool. By the time I'm in London I'm trying to find the administrative answer. I see them either as the victim of a muddled system—and it's up to me to clear up the muddle for them—or else the victim of a bad law which needs changing, and I must try to have it changed."

Wilson's concern with individual human suffering extends far beyond his constituency. He is often waylaid by strangers with a problem about pensions or housing, and he finds it impossible to be indifferent to their anxiety. When he arrived at London Airport for his trip to America early in 1964 to meet President

Johnson, Mary and Giles were already there. They had come from home in a hire-car, and Mary told Harold she had discovered that the driver had a serious housing problem he needed help with. The plane was to take off in a few minutes, and a battery of press and broadcasting interviewers were waiting to question Wilson about his plans for his important trip. Wilson immediately said the interviews must wait, and privately arranged for the driver to meet him in the lounge. He took full particulars of his problem and instructed party officials to take the matter up. Only then did he meet the reporters, who had no idea why they had been kept waiting, or why they had even less time to put their questions than they had expected.

Proud as Wilson is of his achievements and record, he thinks he has made some serious mistakes. "My worst, undoubtedly, was in connection with the Bank Rate Tribunal. I used an unprepared choice of words when I referred to Oliver Poole as having vast city interests. I was after the Chancellor, not Poole. I thought it indiscreet of the Chancellor, immediately on the eve of the biggest-ever bank rate increase, to discuss the economic situation at all with party officials and Poole; Conservatives interpreted my words as an allegation against Poole which wasn't in my mind. I'd certainly have used different words if I'd realised beforehand how they would be misinterpreted."

I asked him whether it might not have been better to withdraw the phrase altogether.

"No," he replied, "because I stuck to my interpretation of what I meant."

The final debate on the Tribunal, which officially cleared the Government, produced a situation of extreme difficulty for Wilson. The Conservatives had never regarded anyone with such hatred. He was suffering from the after-effects of inoculation for a Far Eastern tour, and had returned overnight from a by-election meeting. But he delivered the most pugnacious speech of his life. It took twenty-five minutes to get a hearing at all, and then he proceeded to dominate the House. He sat down after nearly an hour and a half, with a temperature of 102°.

"And of course there was my candidature for the leadership

against Gaitskell in 1960. I still don't know whether I was right or wrong to oppose him. I believe I had no alternative, but it was perhaps a mistake."

Mistake or no, it was a decision which certainly made many bitter enemies. Their numbers have since sharply decreased—partly through a wish for unity and a resolve to forget old scores, but in many cases out of a genuine newfound respect for Wilson's ability and integrity and his own readiness to bury the hatchet.

He does not harbour enmity. I pointed out that in the election for party Leader a majority of his Shadow Cabinet had not supported him. He said: "That ended as far as I was concerned when the votes were counted—as it would have if the result had gone the other way. You can't go on looking backwards and you certainly can't lead a united team if some members are regarded in your own mind as less acceptable than others. I'm sometimes told I've got a good memory. Much more important in human relations is to have a good 'forgettery.' Anyway, life's too short.

"It's the same with people who've attacked you in the past—very often people who've never met you have accepted some Fleet Street legend or other. So if a journalist has for years been writing vicious stuff about me, it gives me great satisfaction if he finds he has to start writing pleasantly about me.

"You can't harbour resentment because of some slight—or imagined slight—in the past.

"It's the future that matters."

# In Power

꠸

The Future, at least for the next few years, was due to be settled on Thursday, October 15th, 1964. On that day the nation was to decide whether the next Prime Minister was to be Harold Wilson as head of a Labour Government, or whether Sir Alec Douglas-Home was to continue in office, thus giving the Conservatives the all-time record of winning four successive General Elections.

Six months earlier the outcome had seemed certain. All the by-election results and opinion poll findings combined to suggest a substantial Labour victory. After thirteen years in office the Conservatives apparently presented on balance an uninspiring image to an electorate disillusioned by the blatant public bickering over the succession to Macmillan's leadership the previous autumn, when Home had emerged none too decisively from the naked rivalry between Butler, Hogg (formerly Lord Hailsham), Maudling, Heath and Macleod. The country seemed all set for a change.

Constitutionally, it was the Prime Minister's responsibility to decide exactly when to appeal to the country, but he was obliged to hold the General Election before the legal expiry of his Government's mandate in early November. Everyone confidently expected he would choose some time in late spring or early summer. After that many people would be on holiday until the end of September. The only other possibility would be October, but this, it was felt, was most unlikely: it was too near the last possible moment. Besides, the American Presidential campaign would be under way, and it might be inadvisable for the two great democracies to be electioneering simultaneously. So, by process of elimination, it was widely predicted that the day of decision would fall sometime in May or early June.

With the tide of public favor running strongly against them, Conservatives faced this likelihood with bleak misgiving. Some members of the Government, as well as many backbenchers, depended on slender majorities likely to vanish altogether in an election. If by-election results and opinion polls were reliable guides, a Labour landslide could be the only outcome; pressure on the Prime Minister to avert such a catastrophe mounted. Eventually Sir Alec Douglas-Home was persuaded: there would be no election until October. The five extra months might work wonders in restoring confidence all 'round.

The decision was greeted angrily by Labour, who argued in vain that since all the evidence suggested a loss of confidence in the Government, the only proper course was to go to the country without delay and settle the issue. The postponement seriously threatened Labour's expectations. All their plans and hopes had been geared to the earlier date, and their resources were not large enough to sustain their expensive publicity campaign throughout the summer. Besides, the electorate would become bored by incessant campaigning. The only thing to do now was to stop the race temporarily, and start up again with renewed vigor in the early autumn. But would Wilson, so far the unmistakable pace-setter, still be in the lead by then? And, if not, how could he recapture it?

The summer months passed quietly, with both the Prime Minister and Wilson taking their usual three weeks' August holiday—and with the public opinion polls showing the Labour lead steadily declining. By the beginning of September the outlook for the Conservatives seemed far from hopeless, and, as poll after poll showed Labour's lead still declining, a Conservative victory began to be predicted.

The campaign proper started in the last week of September, and the main basic issues between the parties were quickly evident. As Wilson had foreseen precisely many months before, the Conservatives based their appeal entirely on peace and prosperity. Peace, it was argued, could be maintained only by a strong Britain retaining her independent nuclear deterrent and thus holding her place among the leading nations. As for prosperity—

216

well, with full employment and a steadily rising standard of living all 'round, who could doubt its reality? Why should anyone risk their present affluences—allow the Socialists to destroy it with their madcap schemes for nationalization? Surely the benefits of free enterprise and initiative had proved much more successful and congenial than all the horrors of state planning and bureaucracy?

The Labour Party acknowledged the increased prosperity, but argued that compared with other expanding industrial countries Britain was lagging. In any case, affluence was not being universally experienced. Old-age pensioners and widows with young children were often suffering near-poverty. And there were pockets of serious unemployment in various areas. The taxation system spread unfair burdens and had too many loopholes for avoidance by certain business sections. Far more hospitals and schools were needed; much more had to be spent on the social services generally.

The housing situation was singled out as a special disgrace. Apart from the slums still existing in large cities, many thousands of families had inadequate accommodation: houses were scarce and expensive, largely because the price of land had risen astronomically owing to "profiteers" and "speculators." Labour would end this exploitation. Above all, Labour would "modernize" Britain and equip her for the scientific age, and would secure a faster rate of growth in her economy.

On these respective issues the campaign was fought, with few apparent blunders on either side. The Labour policy received a bonus from the publication of official trade figures, showing a serious gap between imports and exports. The Conservatives' campaign received an unexpected bonus from an unofficial strike among London Transport's Underground Workers. For three vital days before voting, tens of thousands of voters from key marginal constituencies in the London area were seriously inconvenienced on their way to and from work. Wilson denounced the men's action and urged a return to work—but Labour's image was bound to suffer.

Despite a vigorously conducted campaign, the electorate appeared to be unexcited. The Gallup Poll produced an analysis showing there was less interest in the election than in any of the four previous campaigns, and a National Opinion Poll survey revealed that more than 70 per cent believed the outcome would have little or no effect on them personally. Side by side with this apparent apathy came surveys showing a relatively favorable "rating" for Wilson as a prospective Prime Minister. Even so, Labour appeared to have no clear lead. The main polls were at variance over the likely outcome, and three days before voting Viscount Blakenham, chairman of the Conservative Party, was able to point out that a "poll addict" could choose anything between a Conservative majority of 90 and a Labour majority of 55.

By General Election day the chance of the main parties seemed evenly balanced. The National Opinion Poll showed a Labour lead of 3 per cent, and the Gallup Poll one of 3.5 per cent. Owing to the distributions of voting strength, the minimum lead needed by Labour for a Parliamentary majority was 3 per cent. The parties seemed poised for a dead heat. Not surprisingly, the *Daily Mail* front-page splash headline ran: "WE DON'T KNOW!"

With roughly 45 per cent of the electorate firmly inclined to Labour, and the same proportion to the Conservatives, both parties had directed much of their campaigns to the uncommitted voters. The Liberals, with 366 candidates in the field, were clearly not going to win enough support to form a government. They hoped to secure an impressive aggregate vote, and to increase their numbers in Parliament. But in over 260 constituencies no Liberal was standing. How local Liberals voted could decide the final outcome.

Wilson's leadership of the Labour campaign was masterly. His total command over his party and its strategy was plain for all to see, and his daily press conferences and frequent television appearances demonstrated an alert, if often solemn, authority. By contrast the Prime Minister seemed often ill-at-ease and, especially on economic matters, at best amateurish—and at worst feeble. Yet he came over as a smilingly human person.

Was it, perhaps, easier to identify with this man who, like most voters, sometimes hesitated and made mistakes than with the unerringly clever Wilson who instantly gave all the answers almost before the questions were put? Was there not something a little frightening about all this formidable brilliance conveyed with such polished professionalism?

In their campaigns both leaders were subjected to heckling which, in the Prime Minister's case, amounted at times to concerted hooliganism aimed at drowning his words. Wilson, who welcomed honest heckling, publicly deplored rowdyism of this kind. He suffered some himself on a smaller scale, but treated interruptions with a deft skill that quickly regained the attention of the audience. Once, when the silence was suddenly rudely broken by a yelling baby, he called out to the distraught mother, "Don't take it away. It's his future we're going to be voting about."

On another occasion, when he was about to address a mass meeting in Manchester, the police informed him an anonymous caller had phoned to say a bomb had been placed under the platform. "Probably as phoney as the British independent nuclear deterrent" quipped Wilson.

As the campaign mounted, Wilson's qualities as a speaker developed. The ever-present wit became sharper, and the flat tonelessness gave way to a more dynamic delivery, with an engaging resonance as its main new feature. There were even signs of true oratory, and his final broadcast appeal to the nation was his most immaculate ever:

". . . There's a basic difference between the philosophy and approach of the two parties to the kind of society that we want to create. As President Roosevelt once said: 'Better the occasional faults of a Government living in the spirit of compassion than the consistent omissions of a Government frozen in the ice of its own indifference.' And the Labour Party, which sprang from the people, is concerned about people—people as individuals, people as families: their health, their happiness, the opportunities they have to develop their talents and to live a full life. Our opponents approach the problem of government in a much more materialist way. For them the supreme test is how well business is doing, how high is the level of profit, how are stock-exchange prices doing—because they believe in the old Victorian idea that the profit and loss account is the sole criterion of the national welfare. And this is one reason why we've had in these recent years a decline in the values upon which our society is based— a feeling that the man who *makes* money, however he makes it, is more highly esteemed than the man who *earns* his money producing for his fellow-men, or providing the necessary services on which a civilized society depends. . . . So this is the choice that we face on Thursday: if you're content to settle comfortably into a standard of living which is rising—not rising as much as it ought to be rising; if you're content to see this country sink into a rut of cozy complacency; if you feel that we mustn't reach out to the heights that are within our grasp; if you feel that as things are, they must remain; if you think that Britain's role in the world depends upon our ancient monuments and nuclear posturings; if you're satisfied with the stop-go-stop seesaw which is the Tory substitute for real economic planning— then your choice is clear: you stick with the Tories. Lloyd George once said; and President Kennedy repeated it in his election four years ago—'A tired nation is a Tory nation.' But if you want to see Britain moving ahead and getting ahead—if you want to sweep away outmoded ideas, the 'old boy' network which has condemned so many of our ablest young men to frustration; if you want to see that at every level of our national life talent and ability are recognized and given their head—then you will feel with us the sense of challenge and of excitement and adventure. For if the past belongs to the Tories, the future belongs to us—all of us. Isn't the choice that we're making on Thursday just this: that we want the children for whom all of us are voting to look back and to say that these were the great days, this was the moment, when the people of Britain said: 'Enough is enough.' When they decide to take their future, and the future of our country, into their own hands. *This* is what we shall be voting about on Thursday."

The Parliamentary Correspondent of *The Times* was moved to

observe: "The whole effect was slightly reminiscent of Henry V before Agincourt, but none the worse for that. After all, it is the eve of Battle."

Besides directing the entire strategy of his party's nationwide campaign, Wilson had to attend to his own constituency of Huyton in Lancashire, where his majority in 1959 had been just under six thousand. His private ambition was to double this majority. Having traveled thousands of miles and given scores of speeches in all areas, Wilson spent the closing days of the campaign among his own constituents. Mary, also exhausted yet often strangely exhilarated, had accompanied him on his travels and now was constantly by his side as the climax approached. Herbert, nearly eighty-two but determined to be present as usual at the count, traveled from Cornwall to join his son. His hopes were high, and he was even tempted to invest 2/6d in a sweepstake on the party's victory at the polls. "Send the winnings to me care of Harold," he joked to the organizer. "But use a sealed envelope. He's a Yorkshireman, you know." Whatever the result, the occasion was bound to be a very important one for the whole family, and Marjorie arranged to have two days' leave of absence from her school in Cornwall to travel to Huyton, while Robin and Giles took time off from their respective studies to be present.

Weather conditions have been known to play a curiously effective part in British politics. Wilson was among those who feared that the exceptionally long spells of sunshine throughout the summer could have induced an unreal sense of contentment among prospective supporters. Powerfully aided by the pre-dominantly anti-Labour national press, a mood of complacency could all too easily spread. And when it came to polling day itself, bad weather could have disastrous results for Labour: with the majority of their supporters working fixed hours, and with fewer cars available to transport them to the polling booths, a heavy shower of rain in the crucial evening hours could be enough to lose a marginal seat to the Conservatives, with their larger fleet of cars and greater choice of voting time.

Not that Labour supporters were confined to the traditional working-class sections of the population. If this were so, no

Labour Government could ever achieve office. Significant support from middle-class professional sections of the population was indispensable; surveys revealed that approximately one-third of the working-class vote in recent elections had gone to the Conservatives. With rising prosperity, the old cloth-cap image of Labour was spurned by increasing numbers of workers anxious to "better" themselves socially as much as they had already done financially. If only four out of every hundred who had previously voted Conservative now voted Labour, there would be a new government in office under Wilson. But had the image of affluence and prestige associated with Conservatism attracted too many traditional Labour supporters for a swing of this order to take place? Why *should* people vote for a new and untried government whose last term in office, under the old management, was widely associated with the bleak post-war years of austerity and rigid controls?

It was bound to be touch-and-go. And just as the last votes had been cast on the night of October 15th, a startling news item flashed throughout the country: Mr. Khrushchev had been deposed. If the news had come only a few hours earlier it might have ensured a victory for the Conservative Government. Many uncommitted voters, and even some of those firmly intending to vote Labour, might have felt it would be safer to vote for the party already in office, with sudden new international strains looming up. Sir Alec Douglas-Home's constant insistence on the retention of the independent nuclear deterrent might suddenly have assumed a significance it had lacked throughout the campaign. But it was just too late. The last vote had been cast. The verdict was awaited.

*     *     *

The first results began to flood in. They all revealed a swing to Labour strong enough to defeat the Conservatives. Shortly the computers and statistical analysts were confidently predicting a Labour majority of nearly thirty. Wilson, awaiting the declaration of his own poll in Huyton, watched the ceaseless flow of news flashes on the television screen in his nearby Liverpool hotel.

Excited press and television interviewers rushed expectantly to secure his claim of victory. Puzzled, they had to content themselves with his one comment about feeling "moderately encouraged." Persistent attempts to elicit anything more positive failed. Characteristically, Wilson had noticed something which the computers and analytical experts had not yet interpreted—the swing to Labour was far from uniform, and several of the seats Labour had hoped to capture remained Conservative. With wide regional variations in the trend, a decisive Labour victory was far from certain.

But if the final national outcome was in doubt, his own constituency result far exceeded his private ambitions. With a majority of over 19,000, his previous figure was more than trebled.

At 4:30 Wilson went to bed. By that time the computers and experts had nearly caught up with him: a Labour victory still seemed certain, but the majority now predicted was approximately nineteen.

After little more than two hours' sleep, the Wilson family boarded the train for London. Well over a hundred results had still to be declared. Most of these were either safe Conservative or Labour seats where the result was a foregone conclusion. But the voting in a number of key marginal seats was still unknown, and these were enough to determine the outcome one way or the other. Already the voting had been so close in many of the marginals that recounts were under way. The final result was often perilously close: in one constituency where nearly 45,000 votes were registered, the Labour candidate was finally declared elected by a majority of seven—after seven recounts.

Back in London, Wilson and his family went straight to the Labour headquarters at Transport House and awaited developments. The trend in favor of Labour was continuing, but the results by now suggested an extremely marginal outcome. Sir Alec Douglas-Home, watching the results on television at Downing Street, had still made no move to tender his resignation. He realized that Labour seemed certain to win, but determined to delay his final move until his party's defeat was beyond doubt.

The moment came shortly after 3 o'clock. Labour had won

316 seats out of 630. An absolute majority, therefore, was assured. Sir Alec drove to Buckingham Palace and tendered his resignation to the Queen.

Wilson, meanwhile, was still watching the results at Transport House. Suddenly dramatic information reached him: the latest trade figures had just been released. They showed an alarming increase in the balance of payments deficit: the gap between imports and exports proved Britain had had one of the worst trading months ever. Throughout the campaign the Conservatives had repudiated Labour's suggestions of an economic "crisis." If these latest figures had been published a day earlier, Wilson now mused, Labour might have gained a decisive majority.

As things were, the majority was going to be infinitesimal. With only a few results still to be declared, the final figures could now be foreseen: the Labour Party would have 317 M.P.s, the Conservatives 303, and the Liberals 9. So here was a party not majestically swept into power by an enthusiastic electorate, but creeping in by a hair's breadth with an overall majority of only five. The aggregate Labour votes underlined the half-heartedness of the triumph. With just over 12 million to their credit, they had polled even less than 1959—evidently a very reluctant endorsement of Labour's policies and aspirations. Altogether over 27.5 million votes had been cast. Yet it would have needed, out of that total, only 301 Labour supporters in seven of the constituencies with the smallest margins to cast their votes differently to produce a fantastic situation: 10 Liberal M.P.s, and 310 each for Labour and Conservative. Complete stalemate had been averted by only a tiny handful of voters.

The Parliamentary outlook was bleak. Everyone had agreed— and Wilson had repeatedly emphasized—that the winning party should be given a good working majority. This meant an overall majority of at least twenty-five. How could a party, committed to fundamental changes based on a five-year program, ever hope to succeed on such a minute and perishable majority as five? Would not the Conservatives, triumphant in the narrowness of their defeat and anxious to demonstrate Labour's incapacities, immediately harry and quickly paralyze the new Administration?

Would they not force an early defeat and finally smash all the precious hopes, so methodically fostered and fondly cherished, of Labour's "New Britain?"

The prospect for Wilson personally was disheartening—and more daunting even than the burden suddenly thrust on his youthful shoulders seventeen years earlier, when Atlee had unexpectedly appointed him President of the Board of Trade. The doubts and dismay, the deep sense of inadequacy . . . but also the challenge. He had risen to it then—he had overcome all the misgivings in himself as well as in others. Just as, many years earlier still, he had overcome the grueling ordeal of singing a solo verse at the age of eleven in his piping little voice at Milnsbridge Baptist Church. He had gone back to Milnsbridge only a few days ago, snatching a brief respite from the campaign to look at the dark little terraced house in Warneford Road which was his birthplace. His father was with him, helping to provide what Wilson always values and sometimes needs—the refreshment and sustenance which can come only from his roots: his family, his boyhood friends, his old surroundings, the settings where he first declared: "I should like to be Prime Minister."

The wish of the twelve-year-old boy, solemnly proclaimed thirty-six years earlier to every interested enquiry about his ambitions, was about to be fulfilled in tantalizingly adverse circumstances. But in that very adversity lay the supreme challenge of his life. There could be no more than a fleeting moment's doubt— he would rise unhesitatingly to meet the challenge. He *must* rise to it.

The situation could, in any case, be seen in a much more positive light. Labour, after all, had increased the number of its M.P.s from 258 to 317. The Labour majority, although so small, had obliterated a massive Conservative majority of a hundred. Labour had increased its share of the total from 43.8 per cent to 44.1 per cent—slight, admittedly, but the Conservatives had dropped from 49.4 per cent to 43.4 per cent—the biggest percentages decline for any party since 1945. If Labour's victory seemed minimal, the vote of no confidence in the Conservatives was emphatic. Counting the three million votes for the Liberals and others, nearly 60 per cent of the voters had registered their clear wish for radical reform and change. Significantly, the swing to Labour had been especially marked in many of the seats being defended by Conservative Ministers, and no fewer than six of them had actually been defeated. And if the net results had been so narrowly yet vitally affected by a handful of voters in Labour marginal seats, the same could be said the other way 'round: taking the three Conservative seats won by the smallest margins, if only 20 voters altogether had cast their votes for Labour, the Parliamentary majority over the Conservatives would have been increased to the respectable total of nineteen.

None of this, of course, could affect what would be a drastically precarious Parliamentary situation. At any moment the Government could be endangered simply by illness among Labour members, or absence on essential business—not to mention the crippling effect produced by a Conservative Opposition possibly determined to impede some legislation, or even to over-throw the Government at an opportune stage. But if anyone could handle this kind of threat it was Wilson, recognized by all as Parliament's unrivaled debater and supreme tactician. And if the Conservatives *did* seek prematurely to defeat the Labour Government—what better issue to place before the country than that of a disruptive Tory Opposition obstructing a Government seeking to discharge its responsibilities? The electorate, already weary of party bickering, would surely respond negatively to an Opposition which irresponsibly plunged the country into another campaign just to try to regain power before the new Administra-tion had even had a chance to translate its policies into some kind of action.

Besides, the Conservatives were unlikely to want an early election. Their morale was low, their policies discredited, and their future leadership the subject of widespread questioning and speculation. They were going to need time to restore their ranks, revise their policies, and perhaps find a new and more dynamic leader. Labour, on the other hand, could be sure of total unity. The risks of splits, never far away in a party which had often demonstrated a lack of basic cohesion, had never been less. The "papered-over" cracks were now cemented. Wilson's leadership had accelerated the process, and the tiny majority had completed it. His command was absolute. No Labour leader had ever exercised such authority and strength.

When the call came from the Queen summoning Wilson to Buckingham Palace it found him ready and confident. The great moment had come, and it presented a climax not to be missed by his nearest and dearest. If others before had gone alone to the Palace to kiss hands, this was certainly going to be a family journey. On the short drive from Transport House the family pride was obvious: in Mary, Robin, Giles, Marjorie and, above all, Herbert. "Herbert, that lad's been spared for something." Grandpa Wilson's comment on the safe return home of the undernourished schoolboy after his critical typhoid illness was beginning to have its ultimate meaning. At various stages the prophesy could have had a kind of fulfillment—successful journalist, perhaps, or even more successful Head of an Oxford College, or a higly placed civil servant. But destiny had all along had a grander design, and Herbert had not doubted its eventual completion.

As the car swept through the Palace gates, a transistor radio among watching crowds broadcast the latest news: China had exploded a nuclear device. It should have been no surprise—the development had been predicted for some time. Yet, had this also come a day earlier, how easily the impact of its reality might have swayed an uncertain electorate in favor of the Conservatives' policy on the British deterrent.

The new Prime Minister lost no time in asserting his authority as the country's leader. The fever of the campaign was over. The time had come to gain the country's confidence by assertive leaderships, and to assure a watching world that Britain had a new Administration about to give decisive government. Less than four hours after leaving the Palace, and already fortified by a phone call with reassuring greetings and good wishes from President Johnson, Wilson broadcast briefly to the nation.

". . . I should like to take this first opportunity of pledging my colleagues and myself to do everything we can to the fullest extent of our abilities in the interests of this country and our people. We are facing at this time very great problems, but I feel there is nothing we cannot do all together."

Immediately afterwards came the news of the first key appointments in the new Cabinet. They include George Brown and James Callaghan, both of whom had strongly opposed Wilson for the leadership less than two years earlier. Most of the others had also been ardent opponents of Wilson in former times. Now they were united under his command, glad to serve under someone whose gifted leadership they had grown to acclaim.

There was a breathtaking speed and urgency about Wilson's first vigorous days in office. Besides forming his Government— one of the largest ever—he held emergency meetings to plan measures to deal with the whole economic situation, and started a major reorganization of the civil service. Whitehall was galvanized. "There's been nothing like it since Winston at the height of the war," commented one experienced veteran, wondering how many more weekends were to be so drastically disturbed.

Wilson's stature was beginning to win grudging regard even from his sharpest Tory critics. The image of a new-style Premier was already clearly emerging, and the pattern of Britain's political concepts was swiftly being transformed. Could anything ever be quite the same again, especially the concept of political leadership? The strategy of all parties must in future compete with the bold imagination, dynamic authority, and intellectual eminence displayed by the man who, in 1964, had set out to translate the party slogan of the "New Britain" into something approaching a national reality.

# INDEX

229

Edmonton, 89
Elland, 88

Fabian Society, 47, 87
Flanders, 75
Foot, Dingle, 48
Foot, Michael, 189
France, 78, 80
Franks, Oliver (later Lord), 99
Freeman, John, 148, 152–4, 165
Fulton, John, 79, 82

Gaitskell, Mrs. Hugh (later Lady),
   187–8
Gaitskell, Hugh, 81, 94–5, 102, 145–
   149, 155, 169–74, 177–88, 190,
   204, 214
Gallipoli, 5
Geneva, 107, 115–6, 118
Gladstone, William Ewart, 63, 208
Gledhill, Olga, 39
Gollancz, Victor, 164
Grayson, Victor, 32
Greene, Lord, 81–2
Greenwood, Anthony, 183, 185
Griffiths, James, 168, 173
Grimsby, 88–9

Hale, Leslie, 164
Hampstead Garden Suburb, 122
Harrow, 84
Heathcoat Amory, Derick (later
   Lord Amory), 23
Hill, Charles (later Lord), 175
Hitler, Adolf, 75
Holland, 22
Home (formerly Lord), see
   Douglas-Home, Sir Alec
Honley, 38, 41
Huddersfield, 1, 13–4, 17, 25, 46,
   48, 133, 135, 137
Hyndley, Lord, 95

Israel, 187

Jay, Douglas, 145
Jerusalem, 187
Johnson, President Lyndon, 212–3

Kalgoorlie, 17, 44–5
Kennedy, President John, 131, 206

Key, Charles, 106–7
King-Hall, Cdr. Stephen (later Sir),
   88, 90–1

Laski, Harold, 93
Lee, Jennie, 182
Leeds, 41, 180
Leeds, Bishop of, 163
Liverpool, 89, 136, 212
Liverpool, Bishop of, 163
Lloyd George, David (later Earl),
   6, 120
Lloyd George, Gwilym (later
   Lord Tenby), 82
Luton, 72
Lynskey, Lord Justice, 138

MacDonald, Ramsay, 46
Macmillan, Harold, 175–6
Makins, Sir Roger, 124
Mallalieu, E. L., 46–8
Manchester, 2, 5, 7–8, 16, 136, 206
Mann, Mrs. Jean, 169
Mann, Tom, 32
Mansfield, 46, 48
Margate, 179
Marquand, Hilary, 107
Marx, Karl, 63, 114
Maud, Sir John, 74, 77
Meltham, 41–2
Meyer, Montague, 105, 108, 161–2
Meyer, Tom, 105
Mikardo, Ian, 148
Mikoyan, Anastas, 109–15, 124–31
Milnsbridge, 2, 7, 12, 16–9, 26, 28–9,
   37, 40, 45, 122
Minney, R. J., 191
Missouri, 187
Morecambe, 165
Morrison, Herbert (later Lord), 88,
   119, 149, 169–73
Moscow, 108–9, 111, 119
Mullion Cove, 116–7, 120, 122–3, 126
Mundaring, 17
Munich, 73–4

Nazareth, 187
Northampton, 72

Old Byland, 3, 8
Openshaw, 5

# DATE DUE

| APR 5 '71 | | | |
|-----------|---|---|---|
| FEB 1 5 '72 | | | |
| FEB 2 1 '73 | | | |
| | | | |
| | | | |
| | | | |
| | | | |
| | | | |
| | | | |
| | | | |
| | | | |
| | | | |
| | | | |
| | | | |
| | | | |
| | | | |
| | | | |
| GAYLORD | | | PRINTED IN U.S.A. |